my revision notes

AQA A-level

COMPUTER SCIENCE

Bob Reeves

HODDER
EDUCATION
AN HACHETTE UK COMPANY

Acknowledgment

Many thanks to Oli Howson for his significant contributions to this book.

Photo credits

The Publisher would like to thank the following for permission to reproduce copyright material:

p.6 © chombosan - Fotolia.com; **p.166** © ra3rn - Fotolia.com; **p.118** © davemhuntphoto - Fotolia.com; **p.125** *l* © TheVectorminator - Fotolia.com, *r* © R+R - Fotolia.com; **p.146** *t* © Maksym Yemelyanov - Fotolia.com, *b* © finallast -Fotolia.com; **p.149** © KarSol - Fotolia.com; **p.164** https://commons.wikimedia.org/wiki/File:Embedded_World_2014_SSD.jpg/https://creativecommons.org/publicdomain/zero/1.0/deed.en.

Orders

Bookpoint Ltd, 130 Milton Park, Abingdon, Oxfordshire OX14 4SB
tel: 01235 827827
fax: 01235 400401
email: education@bookpoint.co.uk
Lines are open 9.00 a.m.–5.00 p.m., Monday to Saturday, with a 24-hour message answering service. You can also order through the Hodder Education website: www.hoddereducation.co.uk

Get the most from this book

Everyone has to decide his or her own revision strategy, but it is essential to review your work, learn it and test your understanding. These Revision Notes will help you to do that in a planned way, topic by topic. Use this book as the cornerstone of your revision and don't hesitate to write in it — personalise your notes and check your progress by ticking off each section as you revise.

Tick to track your progress

Use the revision planner on pages iv and v to plan your revision, topic by topic. Tick each box when you have:

● revised and understood a topic
● tested yourself
● gone online to check your answers.

You can also keep track of your revision by ticking off each topic heading in the book. You may find it helpful to add your own notes as you work through each topic.

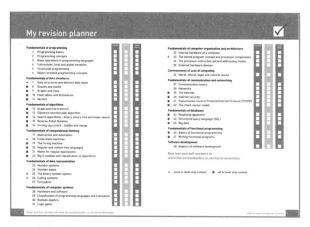

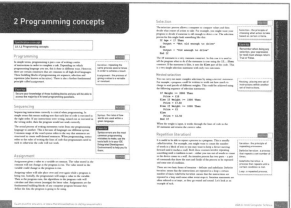

Features to help you succeed

A-level only

This marker means the content is only needed for the full A-level exam. The ✳ and ■ symbols on the revision planner indicate which chapters contain A-level only content.

Specification coverage

This feature lists which specification points are covered in each chapter.

Exam tips

Expert tips are given throughout the book to help you polish your exam technique in order to maximise your chances in the exam.

Definitions and key words

Clear, concise definitions of essential key terms are provided where they first appear. Key words from the specification are highlighted in bold throughout the book.

Summaries

The summaries provide a quick-check bullet list for each topic.

Now test yourself

Use these short, questions practice to consolidate your revision and practice your exam skills. Answers are given online at **www.therevisionbutton. co.uk/myrevisionnotes**.

Tasks

Further activities to test your understanding of the content of the chapter. They can be written exercises or computer tasks.

My revision planner

Now test yourself answers at
www.therevisionbutton.co.uk/myrevisionnotes

✳   some A-level only content   ■   all A-level only content

Countdown to my exams

6–8 weeks to go

- Start by looking at the specification — make sure you know exactly what material you need to revise and the style of the examination. Use the revision planner on pages iv and v to familiarise yourself with the topics.
- Organise your notes, making sure you have covered everything on the specification. The revision planner will help you to group your notes into topics.
- Work out a realistic revision plan that will allow you time for relaxation. Set aside days and times for all the subjects that you need to study, and stick to your timetable.
- Set yourself sensible targets. Break your revision down into focused sessions of around 40 minutes, divided by breaks. These Revision Notes organise the basic facts into short, memorable sections to make revising easier.

REVISED ☐

2–6 weeks to go

- Read through the relevant sections of this book and refer to the exam tips and key terms. Tick off the topics as you feel confident about them. Highlight those topics you find difficult and look at them again in detail.
- Test your understanding of each topic by working through the 'Now test yourself' questions in the book. Check your answers online at **www.therevisionbutton.co.uk/ myrevisionnotes**
- Make a note of any problem areas as you revise, and ask your teacher to go over these in class.
- Look at past papers. They are one of the best ways to revise and practise your exam skills.
- Try out different revision methods. For example, you can make notes using mind maps, spider diagrams or flash cards.
- Track your progress using the revision planner and give yourself a reward when you have achieved your target.

REVISED ☐

One week to go

- Try to fit in at least one more timed practice of an entire past paper and seek feedback from your teacher, comparing your work closely with the mark scheme.
- Check the revision planner to make sure you haven't missed out any topics. Brush up on any areas of difficulty by talking them over with a friend or getting help from your teacher.
- Attend any revision classes put on by your teacher. Remember, he or she is an expert at preparing people for examinations.

REVISED ☐

The day before the examination

- Flick through these Revision Notes for useful reminders, for example the exam tips, exam summaries, typical mistakes and key terms.
- Check the time and place of your examination.
- Make sure you have everything you need — extra pens and pencils, tissues, a watch, bottled water, sweets.
- Allow some time to relax and have an early night to ensure you are fresh and alert for the examinations.

REVISED ☐

My exams

Paper 1

Date:..

Time:..

Location:..

Paper 2

Date:..

Time:..

Location:..

1 Programming basics

Specification coverage

3.1.1.1 Data types
3.1.1.2 Programming concepts

3.1.1.6 Constants and variables in a programming language
3.5.1.2 Integers

Computer programs

In its simplest form a computer program can be seen as a list of instructions that a computer has to work through in a logical sequence in order to carry out a specific task. The instructions that make up a program are all stored in **memory** on the computer along with the data that is needed to make the program work.

Programs (also known as applications or apps) are created by writing lines of code to carry out algorithms. An **algorithm** is the steps required to perform a particular task and the programming code contains the actual instructions written in a programming language.

There are many different types of programming languages, each with their own vocabulary and rules that define how the words must be put together. These rules are known as the **syntax** of the language.

> **Memory**: the location where instructions and data are stored on the computer.
>
> **Algorithm**: a sequence of steps that can be followed to complete a specific task and that always terminates; independent of any programming language.
>
> **Syntax**: the rules of how words are used within a given programming language, i.e. the grammar of the programming language.

Exam tip

Make sure you can explain the difference between an algorithm and a computer program.

Naming and storing data

In addition to instructions, the computer program also needs data to work with. For example, to add two numbers together requires an **add** instruction and then the two numbers that need to be added. You need to give these two items names so that the computer will know which to use.

The data are stored in memory along with the instructions, each having a unique address, known as a **memory address**. It is a really good idea to use names that indicate the purpose of the data. Using meaningful names will help you when you are trying to trace bugs and it also allows other programmers to follow the code more easily. It is good practice to adopt a common naming convention. In the example below the first character is in upper case and the rest are in lower case.

> **Memory address**: a specific location in memory where instructions or data are stored.

This process of giving data values is called 'assigning', and it looks something like this:

```
Number1 = 23
Name = "Derek"
```

The = means 'becomes' or 'equals'. **Number1** is an example of a variable. In the example above it has been given a value of **23**, though this value will change while the program is being run. **Name** is another example of a variable and has been given the value **"Derek"**.

Constants and variables

REVISED

Data are stored either as **constants** or as **variables**. Constants (as you'd expect from the name) have values that are fixed for the duration of a program. The value of variables can change as a program is being run.

Declaring a constant or variable means that when you are writing code you describe (or declare) the variables and constants that you are going to use before you actually use them in your program.

There are two parts to a **declaration**. You need to supply a suitable name for the constant/variable and you need to specify the data type that will be used. The declarations might look something like this:

```
Dimension Age As Integer
Dimension Name As String
Dimension WearsGlasses As Boolean
```

`Dimension` or `Dim` is one of the command words used in Visual Basic to indicate that a variable is being declared. Once you have declared a variable it starts with a default value. In the above examples **Age** will start as zero, **Name** as nothing (also known as the empty string) and **WearsGlasses** will start with the value False. Other languages may use different default values so it is good practice to assign an initial value to the variable just to make sure it is correct.

> **Constant**: an item of data whose value does not change throughout the execution of a program.
>
> **Variable**: a named item of data whose value could change while the program is being run.
>
> **Declaration**: the process of defining variables and constants in terms of their name and data type.

Data types

REVISED

It is important to consider how you want your program to handle data. For example, to create a program that converts miles to kilometres, you have to tell the program that miles and kilometres both need to be stored as numbers.

There are lots of **data types** you might need to use and you need to think carefully about the best type to use. For example, if storing numbers, how accurate do you need the number to be? Will a whole number be accurate enough or will you need decimals? In addition to numbers, you will probably want to store other data such as a person's name, their date of birth or their gender.

All programming languages offer a range of data types but the actual name of the data type may vary from language to language. Here are some of the most common data types:

- **Integer**: This is the mathematical name for any positive or negative whole number.
- **Real/Float**: This is a number that has a fractional or decimal part, for example 3.5 or $3\frac{1}{2}$.
- **Text/String**: This data type is used to store characters, which could be text or numbers. House numbers and phone numbers are often stored as text/string as although they are numbers, you would never need to carry out any calculations on them and in the case of telephone numbers the leading zero is important and would be omitted if stored as a number.

> **Exam tip**
>
> The data type tells the program how to store the data in memory, what format to use and how much space to allocate. Your choice affects the efficiency of your program.

> **Data type**: determines what sort of data is being stored and how it will be handled by the program.
>
> **Integer**: any whole positive or negative number including zero.

> **Exam tip**
>
> Real numbers are known as floats due to being stored with a floating point – see section 4.5.4.4 on the A-level specification.

> **Exam tip**
>
> Remember that although strings can store what look like numbers, they are stored differently and cannot be compared, '4' != 4

- Boolean: The simplest data type is a simple yes/no or true/false. This is called a Boolean data type and can be used to store any kind of data where there are two possible values.
- Character: This data type allows you to store an individual character, which might be a letter, number or symbol. All computers have a defined character set, which is the range of characters that it understands.
- Date/Time: This will store data in a format that is easily identifiable as a date or time, e.g. 30.04.2014 or 12:30.
- **Pointer**/Reference: This data type is used to store a value that will point to or reference a location in the memory of the computer.
- Array: An **array** is a collection of data items of the same type. Each individual name in the array is called an **element**.

Built-in and user-defined data types

Built-in data types are those that are provided with the programming language that you are using. The list of built-in types varies from language to language, but all will include versions of the types listed above.

Most programming languages allow users to make up their own data types, usually by combining existing data types together. These are simply called user-defined data types. For example, if you were making a program to store usernames and IDs, you may create a user-defined data type called Logon made up of a set number of characters and numbers.

The reasons for creating user-defined types are mainly to do with efficiency. As you start to write your own programs you will find that they can get very long and complex and that **debugging** can be very time consuming. Most programmers try to make their code as organised and efficient as possible as this will save them time as the program develops. For example, it is easier to reuse a block of code rather than have to write it all over again.

Most programmers aim to create code that is 'elegant'. This means that it does exactly what it is supposed to do as efficiently as possible. Often this means writing as few lines of code as possible with no repeated coding.

> **Pointer**: a data item that identifies a particular element in a data structure – normally the front or rear.
>
> **Array**: a set of related data items stored under a single identifier. Can work in one or more dimensions.
>
> **Element**: a single value within a set or list – also called a member.
>
> **Record**: one line of a text file.

> **Exam tip**
>
> If you are using Python the nearest thing to an array is a list.

> **Debugging**: the process of finding and correcting errors in programs.

Summary

- Programming languages are used to write applications (apps).
- An algorithm is a sequence of instructions that can be followed to complete a task. Algorithms always terminate. Algorithms are independent of programming languages.
- Programming code is made up of algorithms that are implemented within a programming language.
- Instructions are stored in memory along with the data required by the program.
- It is best to have a naming convention to make your code easier to follow.
- Variables and constants are used to store data and must be declared in some languages.
- There are several data types built in to every programming language and the programmer can also define their own.

Now test yourself

TESTED

1 Define the term algorithm. [3]
2 Describe the difference between an algorithm and a program. [3]
3 Why is it important to utilise good coding practice such as naming conventions of variables? [2]
4 Name and describe four built-in data types. [4]
5 Explain the difference between a variable and a constant. [2]

Task

1 Research naming conventions in programming languages.

2 Programming concepts

Specification coverage

3.1.1.2 Programming concepts

Programming

REVISED

In simple terms, programming is just a case of writing a series of instructions in order to complete a task. Depending on which programming language you use, this is done in different ways. However, there are certain constructs that are common to all high-level languages. These building blocks of programming are sequence, selection and repetition (also known as **iteration**). There is also a further fundamental principle called **assignment**.

> **Iteration**: repeating the same process several times in order to achieve a result.
>
> **Assignment**: the process of giving a value to a variable or constant.
>
> **Selection**: the logical path through a program, usually by having 'if' statements.

Exam tip

Secure your knowledge of these building blocks and you will be able to access the majority of A-level programming questions.

Sequencing

REVISED

Sequencing instructions correctly is critical when programming. In simple terms this means making sure that each line of code is executed in the right order. If any instructions were wrong, missed out or executed in the wrong order, then the program would not work correctly.

The actual process of writing statements varies from one programming language to another. This is because all languages use different **syntax**. Common usage of the word syntax refers to the way that sentences are structured to create well-formed sentences. When programming, syntax refers to the rules of writing the lines of code that programmers need to stick to otherwise the code will not work.

> **Syntax**: the rules of how words are used within a given programming language, i.e. the grammar of the programming language.

Exam tip

Syntax errors are the most common programming mistakes to make; use the tools built in to your IDE (Integrated Development Environment) to help you fix them.

Assignment

REVISED

Assignment gives a value to a variable or constant. The value stored in the constant will not change as the program is run. The value stored in the variable could change as the program is run.

> **Initialisation**: setting the starting value for a variable.

Assigning values will take place over and over again while a program is being run. Initially, the programmer will assign a value to the variable. Then as the program runs, the algorithms in the program code will calculate and then return (reassign) the latest value. Assignments are the fundamental building blocks of any computer program because they define the data the program is going to be using.

Selection

The **selection** process allows a computer to compare values and then decide what course of action to take. For example, you might want your program to decide if someone is old enough to drive a car. The selection process for this might look something like this:

```
If Age < 17 Then
    Output = "Not old enough to drive"
Else
    Output = "Old enough to drive"
End If
```

The `If` statement is a very common construct. In this case it is used to tell the program what to do if the statement is true using the `If...Then` construct. If the statement is false, it uses the `Else` part of the code. This is a very simple selection statement with only two outcomes.

> **Selection**: the principle of choosing what action to take based on certain criteria.

> **Exam tip**
>
> Remember when doing any selection, your expression (or test) must always return True or False.

Nested selection

You can carry out more complex selections by using a **nested** statement. For example, a program could be written to work out how much to charge to send parcels of different weights. This could be achieved using the following sequence of selection statements:

```
If Weight >= 2000 Then
    Price = £10
Else If Weight >= 1500 Then
    Price = £7.50
Else If Weight >= 1000 Then
    Price = £5
Else
    Price = £2.50
End If
```

> **Nesting**: placing one set of instructions within another set of instructions.

When the weight is input, it works through the lines of code in the `If` statement and returns the correct value. The nested `If` statements combine the conditions together progressively as above.

Repetition (iteration)

It is useful to be able to repeat a process in a program. This is usually called **iteration**. For example, you might want to count the number of words in a block of text or you may want to keep a device moving forward until it reaches a wall. Both these routines involve repeating something until a condition is met – either you run out of words to count or the device comes to a wall. An iterative process has two parts – a pair of commands that show the start and finish of the process to be repeated and some sort of condition.

There are two basic forms of iteration – definite and indefinite. **Definite iteration** means that the instructions are repeated in a loop a certain number of times. **Indefinite iteration** means that the instructions are repeated in a loop until some other event stops it. Iteration statements are often referred to as **loops**, as they go round and round. Let's look at an example of each.

> **Iteration**: the principle of repeating processes.
>
> **Definite iteration**: a process that repeats a set number of times.
>
> **Indefinite iteration**: a process that repeats until a certain condition is met.
>
> **Loop**: a repeated process.

Definite iteration

If you want a process to be carried out a set number of times you will need to use definite iteration. For example, the following code could be used to operate a robotic device. It will move a device forward 40 units:

```
For Counter = 1 To 40
    Move forward 1 unit
Next
```

This is known as a **For...Next** loop as it will carry out the instruction for a set number of times.

Indefinite iteration

In this case the loop is repeated until a specified condition is met – so it uses a selection process to decide whether or not to carry on (or even whether to start) a process.

This routine moves a device forward until the sensor detects an obstacle:

```
Repeat
    Move forward 1 unit
Until Sensors locate an obstacle
```

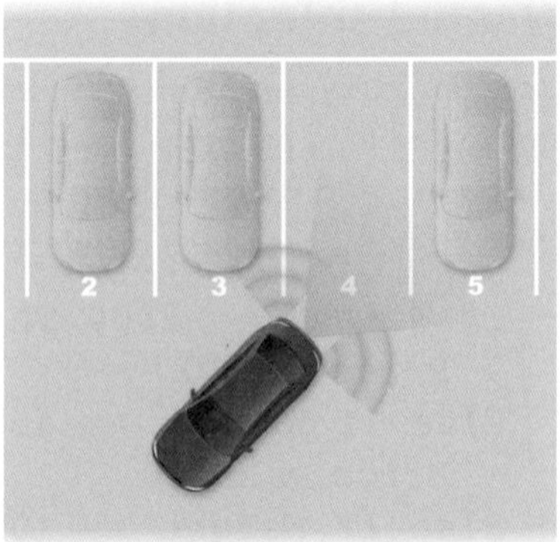

There is no way of knowing how many times this loop will be repeated so potentially it could go on for ever – a so-called infinite loop. This example is also known as a **Repeat...Until** loop as it repeats the instruction until a condition is met.

To check for a condition before the code is run, you can use what is commonly called a **While** loop. For example, a program that converts marks to grades might use the following line of code:

```
While Mark <=100
    Convert Mark to Grade
End While
```

In this case, it checks the condition before the code is run. If the mark is over 100, then the code inside the **While** loop will not even start.

Figure 2.1 Parking sensor

> **Exam tip**
>
> When deciding what type of loop to use, ask yourself two questions: Do you know how many loops there should be? If so, use a **For** loop. Do you always want to run the loop at least once? If so, use a **Repeat** or **Do...While** loop. If not, use a **While** loop.

Nested loops

In the same way that you can nest selection statements together, it is also possible to have a loop within a loop. For example, an algorithm to create a web counter on a web page may have 8 digits allowing for numbers up to 10 million. Starting with the units, the program counts from 0 to 9. When it reaches 9, it starts again from 0, but it also has to increment the value in the tens column by 1. The units will move round 10 times, at which point the tens will move around once. The tens column moves around 10 times and then the hundreds increments by 1 and so on.

> **Exam tip**
>
> A nested loop is often used when working with two-dimensional arrays. Make sure you practise with them.

					Tens	Units	
0	0	0	0	3	5	2	8

Figure 2.2 A web counter

The same algorithm can therefore be used for each digit and can be nested together so that the code is carried out in the correct **sequence**. The code below shows a nested loop just for the units and tens.

```
Tens = 0
Units = 0
While Tens < 10
    While Units < 10
        Output Tens and Units to web counter
        Units = Units + 1
    End While
    Tens = Tens + 1
    Units = 0
End While
```

Sequence: the principle of putting the correct instructions in the right order within a program.

Notice that the way the code is indented indicates the sequence of events. This shows that for every iteration of the outer loop, the inner loop will be completed.

Summary

- Programming statements are built up using four main constructs: sequence, selection, repetition (also known as iteration) and assignment.
- Sequencing is putting the instructions in the correct order to perform a task.
- Selection statements choose what action to take based on specified criteria. For example, If...Then statements.

- Iteration is where a particular step or steps are repeated in order to achieve a certain task. For example, For...Next statements.
- Assignment is the process of giving values to variables and constants. For example, Age = 25.

Now test yourself

TESTED ☐

1 Describe the difference between definite and indefinite iteration. [2]
2 Describe the four main constructs of computer programs. [4]
3 Describe a time in programming when you encountered a syntax error, and what you did to correct it. [2]

Tasks

1 Investigate the CASE or SWITCH method of selection in your chosen programming language.
2 Using a nested loop, write a program to output the 1 to 12 times tables.

3 Basic operations in programming languages

Arithmetic operations

REVISED

Most of these are the standard mathematical operations that you use every day such as add, subtract, multiply and divide.

- Addition: The sum of two or more values. Example: $5 = 3 + 2$ or
  `Answer = FirstNumber + SecondNumber`.
- Subtraction: One value minus another. Example: $2 = 5 - 3$ or
  `Answer = FirstNumber - SecondNumber`.
- Multiplication: The product of two values. Example: $6 = 3 * 2$ or
  `Answer = FirstNumber * SecondNumber`.
- Division of real numbers: A real number is one with a fractional part so may result in an answer with a fractional part. Example: $3.1 = 6.2/2$ or
  `Answer = FirstNumber/SecondNumber` (where all **variables** have been declared as Real or Float).
- Division of integers: An integer is a whole number and therefore may generate a number with a remainder. Example: $3r1 = 7/2$ or
  `Answer = FirstNumber / SecondNumber` (where all variables have been declared as Integer). The DIV operation can also be used in the format `Answer = FirstNumber DIV SecondNumber` in which case the quotient and remainder are calculated simultaneously.
- Modulo operation: The modulo or MOD operator is used to divide one number by another to find the remainder. Example: $1 = 7$ MOD 2 or `Answer = FirstNumber MOD SecondNumber` as $7/2 = 3r1$.
- Exponentiation: Repeated multiplication of a base number in the form B^n where B is the base number and n is the number of times to repeat the multiplication. For example 2^4 is $2 \times 2 \times 2 \times 2$.
  Example: $16 = 2 \wedge 4$ or `Answer = FirstNumber ∧ SecondNumber`.
- Rounding: Replacing the real value with a simpler representation that is close to the original value. For example, 2.315432 becomes 2.3. There are various methods for **rounding** within each programming language such as rounding up and down, or rounding to a specific number of decimal places. Example: $2 = $ Round(2.3) or
  `Answer = Round(FirstNumber)`.
- Truncating: Shortening a value by cutting it off after a certain number of digits. It is the equivalent of rounding down. There are various methods for **truncating** within each programming language. Example: $2 = $ Truncate (2.345) or `Answer = Truncate(FirstNumber)` where `FirstNumber` is a decimal value.

Arithmetic operation: common expressions such as +, –, /, *. (Note: * means multiply.)

Variable: a data item whose value will change during the execution of the program.

Operand: a number or variable in an arithmetic expression.

Operator: an arithmetic symbol, such as +, –, /, or *.

Exam tip

Make sure you can differentiate between real division and integer/modulo division; this is commonly tested and produces very different results.

Rounding: reducing the number of digits used to represent a number while maintaining a value that is approximately equivalent.

Truncating: the process of cutting off a number after a certain number of characters or decimal places.

- **Random number generation**: Creating a number that is random to be used in a program. There are several methods of doing this. Often the number is set to be generated between two fixed values. There are various methods within each programming language. For example: `0.123 = Rnd ()` or `Answer = Rnd().`
Random numbers are a very useful tool for programmers. Typical applications include:
  - ○ creating a range of test data to be used on a new program
  - ○ producing data to use in computer simulations
  - ○ creating random events and movements in computer games
  - ○ selecting a random sample from a dataset.

Random number generation: a function that produces a completely random number.

Relational operations

REVISED

Relational operations work by making comparisons between two data items. They consist of operands and operators where the operands are the values and the operator is the comparison being made.

Relational operations: expressions that compare two values such as equal to or greater than.

Table 3.1 Table of relational operators

Relational operator	Sign
Equal to	= or ==
Not equal to	< > or !=
Less than	<
Greater than	>
Less than or equal to	≤ or <=
Greater than or equal to	≥ or >=

Relational operations are often performed in order to create selection statements. For example: `If A > 1 Then...` means if A is 2 or more then the next action is carried out. In common with all operations, the comparisons could also be made between textual data as well as numerical data.

Exam tip

Even though we write 'if A > B', we can read this as 'if A > B is true'.

Boolean operations

REVISED

Boolean operations are those that carry out a comparison which results in either a TRUE or a FALSE answer. Boolean algebra is used in logic circuits and is an underlying principle to how modern computers work. It is also fundamental to the process of searching data, whether that is in a database or on the web. Once the Boolean operation has been evaluated, a further action is then taken. For example, on a database search, a subset of data would be created containing records that meet the search criteria. The examples below are based on a scenario where an online dataset is being searched to find a new car. The four basic operations are:

Boolean operations: expressions that result in a TRUE or FALSE value.

- **AND**: This is known as a conjunction as it adds together the data. For example, using the search phrase 'Four Door AND Less than 3 years old' would return a value of TRUE only if both conditions were met, so the car would need to have four doors AND be less than 3 years old.
- **OR**: This is known as a disjunction, which means that a TRUE result is produced if any of the conditions are met. For example, in the search phrase 'Four Door OR Three Door', only one of the conditions needs to be met to get a TRUE result, so all three- and four-door cars would be listed.

AND: Boolean operation that outputs true if both inputs are true.

OR: Boolean operation that outputs true if either of its inputs are true.

- **NOT**: This is known as a negation as it reverses the input. For example, 'NOT Ford' would result in data that did NOT contain the word Ford.

> **NOT**: Boolean operation that inverts the result so true becomes false and false becomes true.
>
> **XOR**: Boolean operation that is true if either input is true but not if both inputs are true.

> **Exam tip**
>
> NOT is the only Boolean operation which only needs a single parameter to act upon.

- **XOR**: This is known as an exclusive OR and means that a TRUE result is produced when one or the other condition is met but not both. For example, 'Sunroof XOR Air conditioning' would result in data where the car either had a sunroof or air conditioning, but not both. XOR operations are used extensively when creating logic gates and there is more on this in Chapter 30.

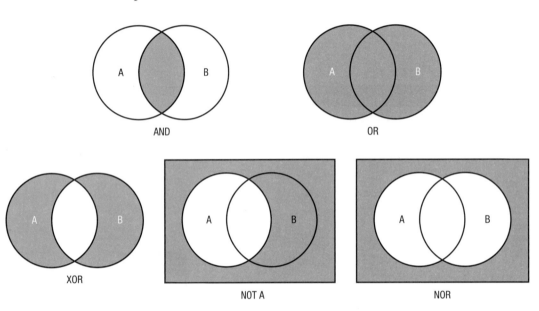

Figure 3.1 Venn diagrams to represent the five basic Boolean operations

It is possible to embed relational operators within Boolean operations. For example, 'Four Door AND Less than 3 years old' uses the **less than** operator. It is also possible to join lots of Boolean operations together to produce the desired outcome. For example, a very specific search might be: 'Four Door AND Less than 3 years old AND Ford OR Vauxhall NOT Fiat'.

> **Exam tip**
>
> Use brackets to ensure Boolean operations work in the order you desire.

String-handling functions

A string is a sequence of characters and can actually be made up of text, numbers and symbols. There are many situations where you will need to work with strings to produce the desired outcome; for example, searching for strings of characters or combining strings together.

- Length: The length of the string is how many characters are used to store a particular item of data.
- Position: Within a text string it is possible to identify the position of every character.
- Substring: A substring is a string contained within another string.
- Concatenation: This is the process of joining strings together to create another string.

> **String-handling functions**: actions that can be carried out on sequences of characters.

> **Exam tip**
>
> In many languages, a string works just like an array of characters, so individual characters can be accessed using square brackets.

- Character codes: Every character that you can use on a computer including all the keyboard characters has a corresponding **character code**, which is used to identify it. This might be an ASCII code or Unicode (see Chapter 26). This can be used in various ways; for example, if you need to convert a text value to a numeric value in order to carry out a calculation on it. You might do this when encrypting data.

In addition to converting strings to character codes, there are a number of other conversions that a programmer might need to do in order to manipulate the data further. Most programming languages include specific functions to carry out these conversions:
- String to Integer / Integer to String
- String to Float / Float to String
- String to Date-time / Date-time to String.

> **Character code**: a binary representation of a particular letter, number or special character.

> **Exam tip**
>
> Converting from one data type to another is known as type-casting. Always be careful, this can often go wrong and data should be checked before being converted.

Summary

- The syntax of a language describes the rules that you must follow.
- Arithmetic operations include common processes such as add, subtract, multiply and divide.
- Other arithmetic operations include rounding, truncating and exponentiation.
- Most languages include a random number generator.

- Relational operations compare two or more values to produce a result.
- Boolean operations return a true or false value and include AND, OR, NOT and XOR.
- Different types of operations can be combined to create more complex expressions.
- String handling is the process of identifying and extracting sequences of characters from a string of characters.

Now test yourself

TESTED

1 Describe the difference between a relational operator and a Boolean operator. [4]
2 Describe a situation when you might want to use integer division instead of real number division. [2]

Tasks

1 Investigate the use of character codes to create a Caesar cipher.
2 Find out why random numbers in computers are often known as pseudo-random numbers.

4 Subroutines, local and global variables

Specification coverage

3.1.1.9 Exception handling
3.1.1.10 Subroutines (procedures/functions)
3.1.1.11 Parameters of subroutines
3.1.1.12 Returning a value/values from a subroutine
3.1.1.13 Local variables in subroutines
3.1.1.14 Global variables in a programming language

Subroutines

REVISED

In programming a **subroutine** is a named block of programming code that performs a specific task. All programs therefore are made up of a series of subroutines. They provide structure to programs in the same way that chapters provide structure to a book. Subroutines are also called **procedures**, **subprograms** or **routines**.

Subroutines use variables that can either be local or global. **Local variables** are those that can only be used within that subroutine whereas **global variables** are accessible throughout the program.

A subroutine is self-contained and it carries out one or more related processes. These processes are sometimes called algorithms, which in turn are made up of lines of code. Subroutines must be given unique identifiers or names, which means that once they have been written they can be called using their name at any time while the program is being run.

You may want to write a program to maintain the contents of a file. For example, if the variable `Selected` is set to `Add` then the procedure `AddRecord` would be called.

> **Subroutine**: a named block of code designed to carry out a specific task.
>
> **Procedure**: another term for a subroutine.
>
> **Subprogram**: another term for a subroutine.
>
> **Routine**: another term for a subroutine.
>
> **Local variable**: a variable that is available only in specified subroutines and functions.
>
> **Global variable**: a variable that is available anywhere in the program.

```
Subroutine MainMenu
   Input Selected
   If Selected = "Add" Then Subroutine AddRecord
   If Selected = "Amend" Then Subroutine AmendRecord
   If Selected = "Delete" Then Subroutine DeleteRecord
End Subroutine
:
Subroutine AddRecord
'Code to add a new record to a file
End Subroutine
:
Subroutine AmendRecord
'Code to locate and amend an existing record
End Subroutine
:
Subroutine DeleteRecord
'Code to delete an existing record
End Subroutine
```

> **Exam tip**
>
> Make sure you remember the difference between local and global variables or your program could start doing odd things.

Breaking up a program into manageable blocks like this has many benefits:

- They can be called at any time using the subroutine's unique name.
- They allow you to gain an overview about how the program is put together.
- You can use a **top-down approach** to develop the whole project.
- The program is easier to test and debug because each subroutine is self-contained.
- Very large projects can be developed by more than one programmer.

> **Top-down approach**: breaking a problem into logical manageable chunks and then doing the same with each chunk. Also known as decomposition.

Functions

Functions are similar to subroutines but return a value. A function in a computer program performs much the same task as the buttons on a calculator. The user supplies the function with data and the function returns a value. For example, you could create a function that calculates the volume of a cylinder – you supply the height and radius and the function returns the volume.

> **Function**: a subroutine that returns a value.
>
> **Library**: a collection of pre-written and pre-tested functions and procedures for you to use.

This process is not limited to numeric data; for example, you could create a function to count the number of times the letter 'h' occurs in a given block of text, or to check to see if a file has read/write or read–only access restrictions in place.

There are two benefits of using functions in a program:

- Some processes are very complex and involve many lines of code, but in the end they produce a single result. Including all those lines of complex code in the middle of your program will probably make it harder to understand, so instead you could put the code in a function and put the function itself somewhere else in the program, away from the main body of the program. This means that if you want to alter the function, it is easier to find. It also makes the main body of the code easier to work through.
- If you have to carry out the same process in lots of different places in the program, then instead of having to rewrite the same code over and over again, you would create the code once as a function and call it from the various places through the program. This has the benefit of keeping programs smaller, and if you need to alter the way the function works, you only have to alter one version of it. You only have to test or debug it once.

Parameters and arguments

> **Exam tip**
>
> Remember that the name of an argument and the name of a parameter do not need to be the same.

In order for a subroutine or function to operate efficiently you need a way to control the data that it takes in. This is usually done by using **parameters** and arguments. A parameter works like a variable in that it identifies the data that you want a subroutine to take in and use. The **argument** is the actual value being passed to the subroutine.

A **block interface** is used, which is essentially a block of code that specifies the type and characteristics of the data being passed.

> **Parameter**: data being passed into a subroutine.
>
> **Argument**: an item of data being passed to a subroutine.
>
> **Block interface**: code that describes the data being passed from one subroutine to another.

Local and global variables

REVISED

As we have seen, it is highly likely that your program will be split up into lots of subroutines and functions. If you do this, then you have to decide on the scope of any variables created. This means you have to construct your program in a way that either:

● limits the existence of the variable to the subroutine or function in which it was declared – a local variable, or
● allows the variable to be used anywhere in the program – a global variable.

An important aspect of programming is keeping track of the state of variables and one of the main causes of program errors is when the value of a variable is changed within one subroutine, that then has an impact on another subroutine. This is known as a side effect.

It is good practice to use local variables wherever possible and using them has a number of advantages:

● You cannot inadvertently change the value being stored somewhere else in the program.
● You could use the same variable name in different sections, and each could be treated as a separate variable.
● You free up memory as each time a local variable is finished with, it is removed from memory.
● It makes your functions and procedures re-useable if they only use local variables.

Exception handling

REVISED

There are many situations where a subroutine has to stop because of an exceptional circumstance that causes an error. This is not necessarily an unexpected **event**, just one that causes the current subroutine to stop. When this happens, the subroutine has been 'thrown' an error, which it must deal with. If it is unable to 'catch' the error, the program could produce a fatal error, causing the program to stop running completely.

In the same way that subroutines are triggered by events, there need to be blocks of code that handle errors that are triggered whenever the error occurs. These are often referred to as catch blocks, which are specific blocks of code that are triggered in response to specific errors.

The normal procedure when this happens is:

● an error is thrown so the current subroutine stops or is paused
● the current state of the subroutine is saved
● the **exception handling** code (or catch block) is executed to take care of the error
● the normal subroutine can then be run again, picking up from where it was saved.

> **Event**: something that happens when a program is being run.
>
> **Exception handling**: the process of dealing with events that cause the current subroutine to stop.

> **Exam tip**
>
> Gaining confidence in using exception handling can allow you to make highly efficient and creative solutions to problems.

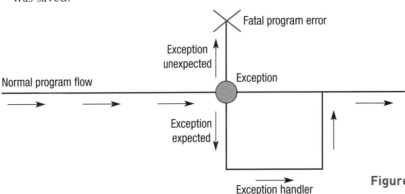

Figure 4.1 The exception handling process

Summary

- Subroutines or procedures are a way of breaking up code into manageable blocks, each of which performs a specific task.
- Subroutines are likely to have other related subroutines.
- Breaking a program up into subroutines is beneficial for several reasons, mainly related to being easier to manage and maintain the program.
- A function is a type of subroutine that returns a set value; for example, the square root function.

- Parameters and arguments are the data that are passed into the function on which it performs its computations.
- Local variables can only be used within the subroutine in which they were created.
- Global variables can be used anywhere in a program.
- Exception handling is the way in which the program deals with events that may cause it to stop.

Now test yourself

TESTED

1 Define what a subroutine is. [2]
2 Differentiate between a local variable and a global variable. [2]
3 Explain why the use of parameters and arguments is preferable to using global variables. [4]
4 Describe the relationship between decomposition and subroutines. [2]

Task

1 Investigate how the programming language of your choice deals with exception handling.

5 Structured programming

Specification coverage

3.1.2.1 Structured programming
3.3.1.2 Design

Hierarchy or structure charts

REVISED

Exam tip

The process of breaking problems down, or decomposition, is fundamental to Computer Science and can be applied to almost any problem you come across.

Hierarchy or **structure charts** use a **top-down approach** to explain how a program is put together. Starting from the program name, the programmer breaks the problem down into a series of steps.

Each step is then broken down into finer steps so that each successive layer of steps shows the subroutines that make up the program in more detail.

The overall hierarchy of a program might look like this:
- programs are made up of **modules**
- modules are made up of subroutines and functions
- subroutines and functions are made up of lines of code
- lines of code are made of up statements (instructions) and data.

In larger programs a module is a self-contained part of the program that can be worked on in isolation from all the other modules. This enables different programmers to work independently on different parts of large programs before they are put together at the end to create the program as a whole.

The text in a hierarchy chart at each level consists of only a few words – if you want more detail about what the process involves you need to move further down the diagram. The component parts for each section are organised from left to right to show how the system will work.

Figure 5.1 shows just part of a structure diagram of a program showing the program at the top, the modules beneath that and so on.

Hierarchy chart: a diagram that shows the design of a system from the top down.

Structure chart: similar to a hierarchy chart with the addition of showing how data are passed around the system.

Top-down approach: when designing systems it means that you start at the top of the process and work your way down into smaller and smaller sub-processes.

Module: a number of subroutines that form part of a program.

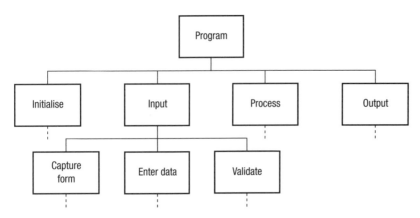

Figure 5.1 A simple hierarchy or structure chart

Flowcharts

> **Exam tip**
>
> Visual learners may find creating flowcharts an effective way of visualising the workings of code.

> **Flowchart**: a diagram using standard symbols that describes a process or system or algorithm.
>
> **System flowchart**: a diagram that shows individual processes within a system.

A **flowchart** uses a set of recognised symbols to show how the components of a system or a process work together. Some of the more common symbols are shown in Figure 5.2.

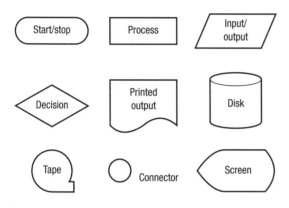

Figure 5.2 Flowchart symbols

A **system flowchart** shows the tasks to be completed, the files that will be used and the hardware that will be needed but only as an overview. It may be possible to create just one flowchart that shows the whole system, or it might be more advantageous to create a separate systems flowchart for each section of the project.

The system flowchart in Figure 5.3 shows the first few processes that are used when a person starts to use an ATM (Automated Teller Machine) at a bank.

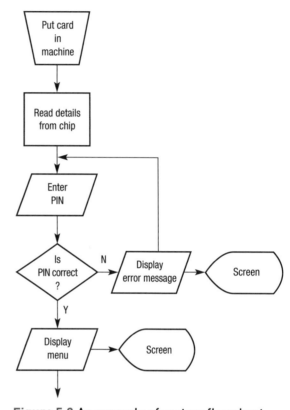

Figure 5.3 An example of system flowchart for an ATM

Pseudo-code

> **Exam tip**
>
> While there is no standard in pseudo-code, it should be less 'codey' than computer code and more formal than English. Try to make it clear and unambigious.

So far we have looked at diagrammatic ways of organising a program, but the code that a programmer creates does not use diagrams, it uses lines of code.

Pseudo-code is a way of writing code without having to worry too much about using the correct syntax or constructs. It consists of a series of commands that show the purpose of the program without getting bogged down with the intricacies of the chosen high-level language. The programmer will need to convert the pseudo-code into high-level code at a later date.

> **Pseudo-code**: a method of writing code that does not require knowledge of a particular programming language.

Pseudo-code can be used at many levels. It will be up to the programmer to decide how far down they need to break their pseudo-code before they can start to actually write the code.

Pseudo-code is very useful in that it allows a programmer to sort out the overall structure of the program as it will eventually appear.

Naming conventions

It is good practice to create a list of all the variables you intend to use, including details of the data types and whether they are going to be local or global variables, before you start coding.

Giving the variables, constants, modules, functions and subroutines in a program meaningful names is good practice.

In the same way that programmers should sort out the variables, they should also draw up a list of the functions and subroutines they intend to use along with details of what each will do, what it will be called, and what parameters it will need to have assigned to it.

> **Exam tip**
>
> Using a naming convention makes code easier to understand and maintain.

> **Naming conventions**: the process of giving meaningful names to subroutines, functions, variables and other user-defined features in a program.

Code layout and comments

The final step to good program construction is to use the features of the programming language to make the code as programmer-friendly as possible. This might include adding suitable comments, especially to more complex or unusual sections of code, and using gaps and indents to show the overall structure of the program. Indenting loops can help to identify where a loop begins and ends. It also helps when you are trying to debug a program. In Python, indenting code is essential as it indicates to the interpreter that the code is part of the loop.

The following two sets of code do the same thing – they place the first 12 values from the two times table in an array.

This first example provides no support for the programmer at all.

```
For X = 1 To 12
  W(X) = 2 * X
Next
```

This second example has made use of a number of features:

```
'routine to place multiples of 2 in array TwoTimes()
For Count = 1 To 12
    'counter counts from 1-12
    TwoTimes(Count) = 2 * Count
    'result in array TwoTimes
Next Count
'end loop
```

The helpful features are:
- comments to show the purpose of the algorithm itself
- comments to show the purpose of each line
- sensible variable names such as **Count** and **TwoTimes**
- the contents of the loop have been indented.

Dry runs and trace tables

Dry running is the process of following code through on paper in order to track down a bug. The variables that are used are written down in a **trace table**. Note that dry running can be done on pseudo-code or actual programming code. It is useful to dry run pseudo-code as any errors in the overall design of the algorithm can be identified before too much time has been spent programming it.

A programmer might also use techniques such as single stepping, where the program is executed one line a time. The programmer can see the values of the variables being used and may choose to insert breakpoints. A breakpoint stops the execution of a program either so the programmer can check the variables at that point or possibly just to show that the program has executed a particular section of code.

> **Dry run:** the process of stepping through each line of code to see what will happen before the program is run.
>
> **Trace table:** a method of recording the result of each step that takes place when dry running code.

Summary

- Hierarchy or structure charts use a top-down approach to explain how a program is put together.
- A flowchart uses a set of recognised symbols to show how the components of a system or a process work together.
- Pseudo-code is a way of writing code without having to worry too much about using the correct syntax or constructs.
- All the variables you intend to use including details of the data types and whether they are going to be local or global variables should be identified at the start.
- Good program construction is to use the features of the program to make the code as programmer-friendly as possible.
- Dry running is the process of following code through on paper. The variables that are used are written down in a trace table.

Now test yourself

1 Ask your teacher to provide you with code from the 2013 AQA COMP1 exam paper. Draw a hierarchy chart for this code. [5]
2 Using the same code as question 1, create a flowchart for the subroutine `Encrypt Using RailFence`. [5]
3 Using the same code as question 1, convert the code to pseudo-code. [5]
4 Look at the following algorithm.

```
SUBROUTINE myalgorithm (list)
    max = 0
    FOR x IN list
        IF x > max
        THEN max ← x
        NEXT x
        RETURN max
    mylist = [3,6,3,7,4,5]
    OUTPUT myalgorithm (mylist)
```

a) Dry run the algorithm and produce a trace table. [4]
b) What does the algorithm do? [1]

Tasks

1 Search the AQA website for their guidance on using pseudo-code. It may come under the GCSE sections.
2 Investigate the differences and similarities between pseudo-code and structured English.
3 Open the code from the 2013 AQA COMP1 exam paper (your teacher may need to provide this for you) in your chosen language and comment as fully as you are able.
4 One common naming convention is 'camel case'. Investigate this and other naming conventions.

6 Object-oriented programming concepts

A level only

Specification coverage

4.1.2.1 Programming paradigms
4.1.2.3 Object-oriented programming

Object-oriented programming

REVISED

Object-oriented programming can be thought of as an extension to the structured approach that we looked at in the previous chapter, as it is entirely modular.

The key difference between procedural and object-oriented programming is that in **procedural programming**, the lines of code and the data the code operates on are stored separately. An object-oriented program puts all the data and the processes that can be carried out on that data together in one place called an object and allows restrictions to be placed on how the data can be manipulated by the code.

> **Procedural programming languages**: languages where the programmer specifies the steps that must be carried out in order to achieve a result.

Object-oriented programming can be described as being organised in a way that reflects the real world. For example, in real life you may have an object, such as a bank. Inside that object there are various other objects such as customers and financial transactions. Inside each of those objects there are a number of data items and behaviours. For example, there are data about customers. These data are handled in a particular way and therefore have to be processed accordingly. For example, one process might be to add new customer data.

Another process might be that money withdrawn needs to be deducted from the balance.

In object-oriented programming, a banking application would be created to mirror these real-life relationships. So there might be one object for customers and another for transactions. The customer object will then contain customer data and all the processes needed for that data.

There are a number of advantages to this approach:
- Programs are written in modules, which means that it is easy to amend programs as only the affected module needs editing.
- It is also easier to add new functionality to a program by adding a new module.
- Most programs are written by teams of programmers so the **modular design** approach allows groups of programmers to work independently on self-contained modules.
- Objects can inherit attributes and behaviours, making code reusable throughout the program.
- Changes carried out to data are made within an object rather than in the program. This makes it less likely that changes made to code will inadvertently affect the results of another routine, which is a common cause of bugs in software programs.
- Libraries can be created, enabling code to be reused easily.

> **Modular design**: a method of system design that breaks a whole system down into smaller units, or modules.

Encapsulation

The concept of keeping the data and the code within the same object is called **encapsulation**. The code is known as **methods**, which are the subroutines contained within an object that are designed to perform particular tasks on the data within the object. This is the main concept behind object-oriented languages, meaning that the objects are self contained. The implication of this is that there are far fewer side effects than with procedural languages. A side effect is where a subroutine changes the value of a variable which then has implications for other parts of the program.

In theory this cannot happen in object-oriented programming as the data can only be directly manipulated by the methods contained within the object. This concept is sometimes called information hiding, which means that the data are directly available in the object that actually needs to use them. Code outside of the class can only access data through the defined methods.

> **Encapsulation**: the concept of putting properties, methods and data in one object.
>
> **Method**: the code or routines contained within a class.

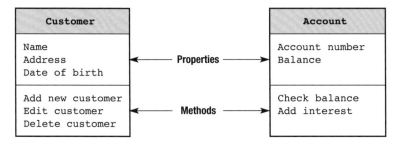

Figure 6.1 Classes containing properties and methods

Figure 6.1 shows two classes, `Customer` and `Account`, both containing their own **properties** and methods.

The two main building blocks of an object-oriented program are classes and objects:
- A **class** is a blueprint or master copy that defines a related group of things. It contains properties, which describe what the data are, and methods, which describe the way in which the data can behave. However, it does not store any data. Classes can be created based on other classes, these are known as **sub-classes**.
- **Objects** are created from a class. Every object is defined as an instance of a class so will have the same properties and methods as the class from which it is built. It will also contain the data on which the methods will be run.

> **Properties**: the defining features of an object or class in terms of its data.
>
> **Class**: defines the properties and methods of a group of similar objects.
>
> **Object**: a specific instance of a class.
>
> **Sub-class**: a class devided from another class (see inheritance).

When designing object-oriented programs, you can see how important it is to think carefully about the properties and methods of each object and how these might be organised into classes. Classes are fundamental to the design of object-oriented programs. Therefore they are stored where they can be reused either in the future, or by programmers working on other modules. The definitions of all classes are stored in a class library.

Inheritance

Inheritance in object-oriented languages acts in a similar way to the biological definition of inheritance. You start out with a set of characteristics and add to what already exists. You can add or change features and abilities but you cannot delete them directly.

When programmed the methods become the subroutines (procedures or functions) required.

The properties and methods defined in the base class are common to all classes. For example, whether the account was a current account or mortgage account it would still have the same properties and methods. In addition, the other account types would have additional properties and methods so these can now be set up as subclasses along with any properties and methods that are unique to the subclass.

This relationship between the classes and subclasses can be shown as an inheritance diagram as in Figure 6.2. Note that the direction of arrows shows the path of inheritance.

Inheritance produces a hierarchical structure. In this scenario, `Account` could be described as a base class, super class or parent class, as it is the main class from which other classes, `Current` and `Mortgage`, are created. Classes that inherit from others are called subclasses, derived classes or child classes.

> **Exam tip**
>
> Remember that these words are not specific to Computer Science – there is always a link between the meaning in CS and the meaning in ordinary English. Use this to help you remember what they mean.

> **Inheritance**: the concept that properties and methods in one class can be shared with a subclass.

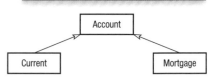

Figure 6.2 An inheritance diagram for Account

Class diagrams for inheritance

Class diagrams are a standard method for representing classes, their properties and methods and the relationships between the classes. There are different ways of representing the relationships between the classes. This section deals with inheritance:

- Class diagrams are hierarchical in structure with the base class at the top and the subclasses shown beneath.
- A subclass inherits the properties and methods of the base class.
- Arrows are used to shows the direction of inheritance.
- Each class is represented by a box made up of three sections to include the class name, properties and methods.

> **Class diagrams**: a way of representing the relationship between classes.

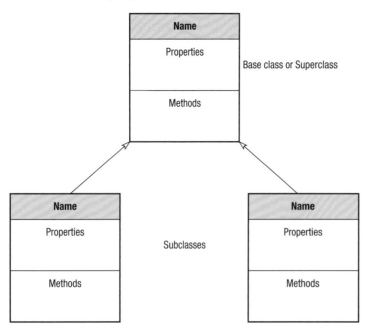

Figure 6.3 A basic class diagram

Now test yourself answers at www.therevisionbutton.co.uk/myrevisionnotes

A class diagram for the account example might look like Figure 6.4.

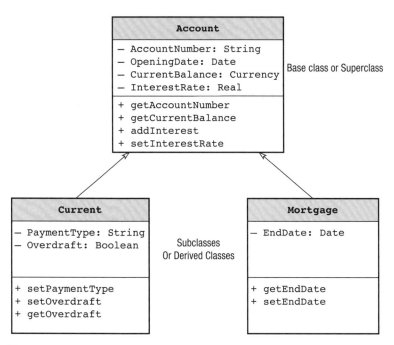

Figure 6.4 A class diagram for Account

The class diagram:

- Uses a + or − to indicate the visibility of the properties and methods to other classes. + means that the properties and methods are public to all classes. − means that the properties and methods are private and can only be used in that class.
- Uses a # to indicate that the properties and methods are protected so they can be used in that class and any of its subclasses.
- Uses arrows with the arrow pointing to the base class to show where the subclass is inheriting its properties and methods from.
- Defines the data types to be used for each variable.

> **Protected methods**: these can only be called with class or sub-class themselves and not on objects.

Instantiation

REVISED

Instantiation is the process of creating an object from a class. In other words, you are creating an actual instance of an object using the properties and methods described in the class.

When programming, there is a method called a constructor, which is called when an object is instantiated from a class to initialise the object.

> **Instantiation**: the process of creating an object from a class.

Polymorphism and overriding

REVISED

The literal meaning of **polymorphism** is to take on many shapes. In object-oriented programming it describes a situation where a method inherited from a base class can be redefined and used in different ways depending on the data in the subclass that inherited it.

It is related to the hierarchy of classes and the way in which classes inherit properties from other classes. For example, there may be a common method that you want to carry out as part of your program. As this method is critical to the program, it could be defined in a base class, which is then inherited by other classes. However, the data contained in these new classes is perhaps of a different type. Rather than having to

> **Polymorphism**: the ability of different types of data to be manipulated with the same method.

define a new method, polymorphism enables the original method to be redefined so that it will work with the new data.

When the subclass implements the method it is called **overriding** because it overrides (or replaces) the method in the base class.

> **Overriding**: where a method described in the subclass takes precedence over a method with the same name in the base class.

Abstract, virtual and static methods

Object-oriented languages handle objects in three different ways. You can think of the code inside an object as subroutines, which are a series of instructions that it will carry out on the data. Due to the nature of the relationships between objects and classes, it means that methods in one object may be used on data contained within another object.

In order to define the behaviour of the methods, they can be set up in three different ways:
- Static: the method can be used without an object of the class being instantiated.
- Virtual: the method is defined in the base class but can be overridden by the method in the subclass where it will be used. This is a feature of polymorphism.
- Abstract: the actual method is not supplied in the base class, which means that it must be provided in the subclass. In this case, the object is being used as an interface between the method and the data.

Which one you use depends on the nature of the methods and the data contained within the class and at what point you want the method to run.

> **Abstract class**: this can only be used to create sub-classes from, through inheritance. You can never have an object for an abstract class directly.

Aggregation

Aggregation is a method of creating new objects that contain existing objects, based on the way in which objects are related. Object-oriented programming is concerned with recreating real-life objects as programming objects. In real life, objects are related to each other. For example, in a business you might have an object called **Workforce** and another called **Job Roles**. Under **Workforce** there may be further objects called **Manager** and **Employee**. All of these objects exist in their own right, but there is also relationship between them. For example:
- Managers and employees make up the workforce.
- Job roles can be taken on by managers or employees.
- Job roles define what the managers and employees do as part of the workforce.

Composition aggregation

Workforce is made up of **Manager** and **Employee**. If you deleted **Workforce** you would by definition be deleting **Manager** and **Employee**. This is an example of **composition aggregation**, sometimes just called composition and it is where one object is composed (or made up of) two or more existing objects. You could say that **Workforce** is instantiated (created) when **Manager** and **Employee** are combined.

This can be shown as a class diagram as in Figure 6.5. Notice the shape of the arrow head, which indicates that **Manager** and **Employee** cannot exist unless **Workforce** does.

> **Composition aggregation**: creating an object that contains other objects, and will cease to exist if the containing object is destroyed.

Figure 6.5 Class diagram showing composition aggregation

Association aggregation

You could now extend the **Workforce** object to include a **Job Role** object. There is a relationship between **Manager**, **Employee** and **Job Role** in that the managers and employees all have specific job roles that they carry out. However, if you deleted **Job Role**, the **Manager** and **Employee** objects would still be retained and still be usable objects as would the **Workforce** object. This is due to the nature of the relationship in the real world in that a job role is not fixed and therefore any manager or employee could be given any job role. This is an example of **association aggregation** where an object is made up of one or more objects but is not entirely dependent on those objects for its own existence.

This can be shown as a class diagram as in Figure 6.6. Notice the shape of the arrow head, which indicates that **Manager** and **Employee** can still exist even if **Job Role** does not.

> **Association aggregation**: creating an object that contains other objects, which can continue to exist even if the containing object is destroyed.

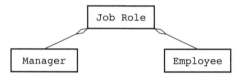

Figure 6.6 Class diagram showing association aggregation

Design principles

REVISED

There are three key design principles that are recognised as producing the most elegant solution when programming using an object-oriented language.

- **Encapsulate what varies**: This is related to the concepts of encapsulation and information hiding and the basic concept is that everything that varies should be put into its own class. This means that properties and methods are subdivided into as many classes as needed to reflect the real-life scenario.
- **Favour composition over inheritance**: This principle refers to the way in which classes and objects are instantiated (created). As we have seen, objects can be created from a base class and inherit its properties and methods. The alternative is to use aggregation or composition to combine existing objects to make new ones. This method is less error prone and enables simpler maintenance.
- **Program to interfaces, not implementation**: In object-oriented programming, an interface defines methods to be used, which are then applied when classes are defined. In this sense an interface is an abstract type which is implemented when a class is created. When a class is created that adheres to the methods in the interface, it can be seen as an implementation of the interface. Programs can then be written based on the interfaces rather than each individual implementation of a class. Using this methodology, if classes need to be added to or amended, this can be done with reference to the interface, meaning there will be little or no impact on the other classes in the program.

Summary

- Object-oriented programming can be described as being organised in a way that reflects the real world.
- An object-oriented program puts all the data and the processes (methods) that can be carried out on that data in one place called an object.
- The concept of keeping the data and the code within the same object is called encapsulation.
- Class diagrams are a standard method for representing classes, their properties and methods and the relationship between the classes.
- Inheritance in object-oriented languages acts in a similar way to the biological definition of inheritance.

- Instantiation is the process of creating a real instance of a class, which is an object.
- Polymorphism describes a situation where a method inherited from a base class can be used in different ways depending on the data in the subclass that inherited it.
- When the subclass implements the method it is called overriding because it overrides (or replaces) the method in the subclass.
- Aggregation is a method of creating objects that contain other sorts of object.

Now test yourself

TESTED ☐

1 Define object-orientation. [1]
2 Describe the difference between an object and a class. [2]
3 Describe inheritance, polymorphism and overriding. [3]
4 Describe the difference between composition and association aggregation. [2]
5 An object-oriented program is being written to store details about network appliances. An **appliance** class has been created, which will have three subclasses: **printer**, **tablet** and **computer**. The **printer** class will have four subclasses: **inkjet**, **laserjet**, **inkjet-multifunction** and **laserjet-multifunction**.

   (a) Draw an inheritance diagram for the eight classes. [4]

   (b) The **appliance** class has the following definition:

```
appliance = class
public
procedure AddDevice
procedure GetIPAddress
procedure GetRoom
private
IPAddress: String
Room: Integer
```

   The **printer** class has the following additional fields:
   Manufacturer, BlackCartridgeCode, PurchaseDate
   Write the class definition for **printer**. [4]

   (c) The **inkjet-multifunction** class also has the additional field **isWifi**. Write the class definition for **inkjet-multifunction**. [2]

Tasks

1 Using the language of your choice, create an object 'mymaths' that has three properties, 'input1', 'input2' and 'output1' and methods 'set1', 'set2', 'getOutput' as well as 'add', 'subtract' and 'multiply'. The set methods should set a value to the input1 or input2 properties, and the getOutput method should output whatever is in the output1 property. The add, subtract and multiply methods should take the two properties 'input1' and 'input2' and perform the relevant calculation on them, saving the result in 'output1'. Also create a program to test your object.

2 Most languages used at A-level can produce either object-oriented code or procedural code. Using the Internet, search for some object-oriented code in your language and investigate the differences and similarities.

7 Data structures and abstract data types

Data structure and abstract data type

REVISED

A **data structure** is any method used to store data in an organised and accessible format. Data structures normally contain data that are related and the way that the data are organised enables different programs to manipulate them in different ways. Different data structures tend to lend themselves to different types of applications. For example, a text **file** may be suitable for a database whereas a stack is suitable for handling exceptions.

An **abstract data type** is a conceptual model of how the data are stored and the operations that can be performed upon them. The data structure is an implementation of this in a particular programming language.

> **Data structure**: a common format for storing large volumes of related data, which is an implementation of an abstract data type.
>
> **Abstract data type**: a conceptual model of how data can be stored and the operations that can be carried out on the data.
>
> **File**: a collection of related data.

Arrays

REVISED

> **Exam tip**
>
> If you are using Python, the nearest thing to an array is a list.

An **array** is a list or table of data that has a variable name that identifies the list or table. Each item in the table is called an element. An array can have many dimensions but most arrays are either one-dimensional, in which case they form a list, or can be visualised as a two-dimensional table.

Lists and arrays are static data structures that are created by the programmer to store tables of data. In some programming languages programmers need to define just how big an array is going to be at the start of their program. This means that the size of the array and the amount of memory put aside for it does not change.

You might find that you want to store a sequence of data in some way. For example, you might want to store the names of pupils in a class:

> **Array**: a set of related data items stored under a single identifier. Can work on one or more dimensions.

> **Exam tip**
>
> In most languages a two-dimensional array is actually a one-dimensional array with each element in itself being an array.

```
Name1 = "Derrick"
Name2 = "Peter"
Name3 = "Jill"
Name4 = "Lynn"
```

In the example above, we could call the array **StudentName**. Each element of the array can now be accessed using its position. For example, the third element in the array is Jill (assuming indexing starts at 1 and not 0). This would be shown as: StudentName(3) = "Jill"

Another example could be to set up a one-dimensional array called DaysInMonth. The third element would be set to 31 as that is the number of days in March. As this table contains just one row of data it could also be described as a list.

Element in DaysInMonth	1	2	3	4	5	6	7	8	9	10	11	12
Contents of that element	31	28	31	30	31	30	31	31	30	31	30	31

Figure 7.1 A one-dimensional array or list

An array has one or more dimensions – for example you might want to store the mock exam results of a group of pupils. The array then might be called Results and it would have two dimensions, one for the pupils and the other for the subjects and might look something like Figure 7.2.

	1	2	3	4	5	6	7
1	54	67	76	65	75	32	19
2	32	45	98	32	53	14	88
3	12	32	54	56	59	95	71
4	32	21	12	43	22	26	16
5	15	47	65	35	99	82	41

Figure 7.2 A two-dimensional array

You will note that the rows/columns are not labelled – it is up to the programmer to remember which axis refers to the pupil and which to the subject. In this diagram the 65 might represent the mark obtained by Hilary in the French exam. If the table were called Results then Hilary's French mark would be stored in Results(4, 1) where the 4 identifies the pupil and the 1 identifies the subject.

Files

REVISED

You will already be familiar with the concept of a file to store data. There are hundreds of different file types, all of which have their own structure depending on the specific use of the file. Some files are very specific in that they can only be used on certain applications. Many file formats however are portable, which means they can be used in a wide range of programs. Two common portable formats that can be used when programming are **text files** and **binary files**.

A text file is one that simply contains lines of text or other human-readable characters, where each line is usually referred to as a **record**. There may be different items of data stored and these are referred to as **fields**.

The two main actions you might want to carry out when working with text files are:
● to write data from the program into a text file
● to read data into the program from a text file.

A binary file is one that stores data as a series of 0s and 1s. Binary representation is one of the cornerstones of how computers work and is covered in detail in Chapter 25. At this stage it is important to understand that all program code and all of the data that you might use in a program including text, graphics and sound are all made up of 0s and 1s. These are usually organised into groups of 8 bits, called bytes.

Binary files contain binary codes and usually contain some header information that describes what these represent. As you can see from Figure 7.3, binary files are not easily readable by a human, but can quickly be interpreted by a program.

```
11101111 10111011 10111111 00111100 01101110 01101111 01100100 01100101
00100000 01101001 01100100 00111101 00100010 00110001 00110000 00110111
00110000 00100010 00100000 01110110 01100101 01110010 01110011 01101001
01101111 01101110 00111101 00100010 01100101 01100010 01100011 00110111
01100010 00100011 01100001 00101101 00110011 00110011 01100001 01100110
01100010 00101101 00110100 01100001 01100001 00110010 00101101 00110110
01100001 00110100 01100101 00101101 01100110 01100100 00110000 01100100
00110110 00110011 00110110 00110011 01100001 01100010 01100001 00110110
00100010 00100000 01110010 01110010 01110010 01100101 01101110 01110110
01001001 01000100 00111101 00100010 00101101 00110001 00100010 00100000
01101100 01100101 01110110 01100101 01101100 00111101 00100010 00110001
00100010 00100000 01110111 01110010 01101001 01110100 01100101 01110010
01001001 01000100 00111101 00100010 00110000 00100010 00100000 01100011
01110010 01100101 01100001 01110100 01101111 01110010 01001001 01000100
00111101 00100010 00110000 00100000 01101110 01101111 01110000
01100101 01010100 01111001 01110000 01100101 00111101 00100010 00110001
00100000 00110101 00110110 00100000 00100000 01110100 01101101 01101001
01110000 01101100 01100001 01110100 01100101 00111101 00100010 01100111
00110000 00110100 00110010 00100010 00100000 01110011 01101111 01110010
01110100 01001111 01110010 01100100 01100101 01110010 00111101 00100010
00110010 00100010 00100000 01100011 01110010 01100101 01100001 01110100
01100101 01000100 01100001 01110100 01100101 00111101 00100010 00110010
00100000 00110000 00110111 00101101 00110010 00110110 00101101 00110010
00110101 01010100 00110001 00111000 00111010 00110010 00111000 00111010
00110010 00110110 00100010 00100000 01110101 01110000 01100100 01100001
01110100 01100101 01000100 01100001 01110100 01100101 00111101 00100010
```

Figure 7.3 Output from a binary file

For example, the PNG image file is a binary file, can be used in a range of applications and requires less memory than some other image formats. Many program files (executables) are created as binary files so that they can be used on other platforms.

The two main actions you might want to carry out when working with binary files are:
● to write data from the program into a binary file
● to read data into the program from a binary file.

Static and dynamic data structures

A-level only

REVISED ☐

The way that data can be stored can be split into two broad categories – dynamic and static. This reflects the fact that sometimes the programmer will know how big a data structure will get and therefore how much memory is needed to store it. More often than not, the amount of data stored within a data structure will vary while the program is being run. Different data structures such as **queues** and **stacks** can be implemented either as static or dynamic structures.

● Static: A **static data structure** stores a set amount of data which is usually defined by the programmer. This is done by allocating a set amount of memory to the data structure. Accessing individual elements of data within a static structure is very quick as their memory location is fixed. However, the data structure will take up memory even if it doesn't need it. Records and some arrays are examples of static data structures.

> **Queue**: a data structure where the first item added is the first item removed.
>
> **Stack**: a data structure where the last item added is the first item removed.
>
> **Static data structure**: a method of storing data where the amount of data stored (and memory used to store it) is fixed.

- Dynamic: The word 'dynamic' means changeable. **Dynamic data structures** can use more or less memory as needed through the use of a **heap**. In basic terms, unused blocks of memory are placed on a heap, which are then usable within a program. A dynamic data structure is able to take more memory off the heap if it is needed and also put blocks of unused memory back onto the heap if it is not needed. This is a more efficient use of resources and a more flexible solution as elements can be added and removed much more easily. Stacks, queues and binary trees are often implemented as dynamic structures.

The programmer will normally put a limit on the maximum amount of memory that any one data structure needs. However, it can lead to errors if elements are removed from empty structures or added to full ones. There is more on this in the following chapters.

Dynamic data structure: a method of storing data where the amount of data stored (and memory used to store it) will vary as the program is being run.

Heap: a pool of unused memory that can be allocated to a dynamic data structure.

Table 7.1 Comparison of static and dynamic data structures

Static data structures	Dynamic data structures
Inefficient as memory is allocated that may not be needed.	Efficient as the amount of memory varies as needed.
Fast access to each element of data as the memory location is fixed when the program is written.	Slower access to each element as the memory location is allocated at run time.
Memory addresses allocated will be contiguous so quicker to access.	Memory addresses allocated may be fragmented so slower to access.
Structures are a fixed size, making them more predictable to work with. For example, they can contain a header.	Structures vary in size so there needs to be a mechanism for knowing the size of the current structure.
The relationship between different elements of data does not change.	The relationship between different elements of data will change as the program is run.

Summary

- A data structure is any method used to store data in an organised and accessible format.
- An abstract data type is a conceptual model of how data are organised and the operations on them.
- An array is a data structure that contains data of the same type using a single identifier.
- A one-dimensional array is also known as a list.
- Arrays can be multi-dimensional.
- Files are used to store data.
- A text file is one that simply contains lines of text or other human-readable characters.
- A binary file is one that stores data as a series of 0s and 1s.
- Static data structures store a set amount of data which is usually defined by the programmer.
- Dynamic data structures can use more or less memory as needed through the use of a heap.

Now test yourself

TESTED ☐

1 Describe the differences between static and dynamic data structures. [4]
2 Create a flowchart to fill a two-dimensional 4 × 4 array with random numbers. [5]
3 Identify an occasion when you would choose to use a text file, and a binary file. Explain why on each occasion your choice is correct. [4]

Task

1 Create a program to write a string and a number to both a text file and a binary file. Open the files in Notepad and compare the results.

Now test yourself answers at www.therevisionbutton.co.uk/myrevisionnotes

8 Queues and stacks

Specification coverage

3.2.1.4 Abstract data types/data structures
3.2.2 Queues
3.2.3 Stacks

How stacks work

REVISED

A **stack** is an example of a **LIFO** (last in first out) structure that means that the last item of data added is the first to be removed. A stack in a computer works in exactly the same way as a stack of books waiting to be marked or a stack of dishes waiting to be washed up – whichever item was added to the top of the stack last will be the first one to be dealt with.

However, unlike the washing up where items are literally taken off the stack as they are needed, the data in a computer stack is not actually removed. What happens is that a variable called the stack pointer keeps track of where the top of the stack is.

The process of adding a new item of data to the stack is called pushing and taking an item off the stack is called popping. A further action called peeking is used to identify the top of a stack. When an item is pushed onto the stack the stack pointer moves up and when an item is popped off the stack the pointer moves down, but a copy of the data is still left on the stack.

Here is a simplified example of a stack in use. Note that this stack can only store six data items.

> **Stack**: a LIFO structure where the last item of data added is the first to leave.
>
> **LIFO**: last in first out refers to a data structure such as a stack where the last item of data entered is the first item of data to leave.

The stack pointer is used to show where the top of the stack is.

"Linda" has been pushed to the top of the stack so the pointer moves up.

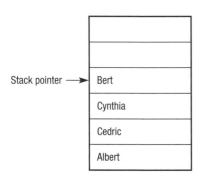

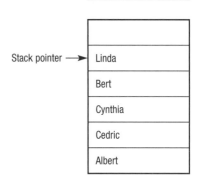

The stack is popped so the data at the **pointer** ("Linda") is read and the pointer moves down.

It is possible for the stack to need more memory than has been allocated to it. In the example given above, assuming that the stack had been set up as a static data structure, if the CPU tried to push on three more data items, the last one would have nowhere to go. In this case a stack overflow error would occur. Similarly if the stack was empty and the CPU tried to pop an item, this would result in a stack underflow as there is no data to be popped.

> **Pointer**: a data item that identifies a particular element in a data structure – normally the front or rear.

Implementing a stack

In the following two routines a single-dimension array called `StackArray` has been used to represent the stack. The variable `StackPointer` is being used to keep track of how far up or down the stack the pointer should be and `StackMaximum` stores the maximum number of values that can be stored on the stack.

> **Exam tip**
>
> It's worth memorising the **algorithm** for pushing and popping stack items. Don't forget the error checking!

The stack will only be allocated a limited number of memory locations. An error trapping routine is required to catch the overflow, so that the stack cannot overflow. Similarly, an error trapping routine is needed to catch any underflow.

Uses of stacks

There are many uses for stacks. Due to their LIFO nature they can be used anywhere where you want the last data item in to be the first one out. A simple application would be to reverse the contents of a list as shown on the right.

1	2	3	4
Andrew	Jane	Mark	Wendy

This list would go into the stack as follows:

Wendy
Mark
Jane
Andrew

If you now pull the names off the stack in order you would get:

1	2	3	4
Wendy	Mark	Jane	Andrew

Stack frames

Stacks can be used to store information about a running program. In this case it is known as a **stack frame** and a pointer is used to identify the start point of the frame. This is used as a **call stack** when running programs as it can be used when a subroutine is running to call functions and pass parameters and arguments.

Function call and argument data	The function is called and data passed to it. The return address is placed on the stack so that when the function is finished, it will look at the return address so it knows where to go back to.
Return address	
Saved frame pointer	The subroutine is running using local variables. When a function is called, the current position is saved in the stack as a saved frame pointer.

> **Stack frame**: a collection of data about a subroutine call.
>
> **Call stack**: a special type of stack used to store information about active subroutines and functions within a program.

This is the same mechanism that is used for handling interrupts and exceptions in programs. **Interrupts** and exceptions are events where hardware or software demand the attention of the processor and cause the

> **Interrupt**: a signal sent by a device or program to the processor requesting its attention.

current program to stop. This could be something happening inside the program that is running or it could be an external event, such as a power failure, or a printer running out of paper.

When this happens, special blocks of code called interrupt handlers and exceptions handlers are loaded into memory and executed. While the new demand is being dealt with, the details of the first program are stored on a stack. As soon as the interrupt or exception has been dealt with, the details are taken back off the stack and the first program can carry on wherever it left off.

Nesting and recursion

It is common practice to **nest** program constructs. For example, you might want to put one selection process inside another, or you might have a selection process being carried out inside an iterative loop. In this case the details of the successive nested loops are stored on the stack. Stacks also play a vital role in a process called **recursion**. This is where a subroutine calls itself in order to complete a task.

> **Nesting**: the process of putting one statement inside another statement.
>
> **Recursion**: the process of a subroutine calling itself.

```
def factorial (n)
   if n == 1;
      return 1
   else:
      return n*factorial (n-1)
```

Queues

A **queue** is called a **FIFO** (first in first out) structure. A queue in a computer acts just like people queuing for a bus – the first person in the queue is going to be the first person to get on the bus and the first item of data to be put into the queue in a computer will be the first to be taken out.

> **Queue**: a FIFO structure where data leaves in the order it arrives.
>
> **FIFO**: first in first out refers to a data structure such as a queue where the first item of data entered is the first item of data to leave.

A common use of queues is when a peripheral such as a hard disk or a keyboard is sending data to the CPU. It might be that the CPU is not in a position to deal with the data straight away, so they are temporarily stored in a queue. Data being sent from the CPU might also need to be stored, and this is certainly the case when a document is sent to a printer. In this case your document is placed in the queue until the printer (which is a very slow device compared with the CPU) has the time to deal with the job. Queues that are used in this way are also known as buffers.

Here is a simplified example of how a queue is used. This queue can only store six data items.

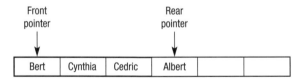

The queue has already been sent four data items, but none has yet been removed. The first item in the queue is "Bert" indicated by the front pointer. The last item in the queue is "Albert" indicated by the rear pointer.

When an item is added to the queue it is added at the end. If a new item ("Linda") is added, notice that the rear pointer has moved and now points to the new item "Linda". The front pointer has not moved.

When a name is taken from the queue it is taken from the front. In this case "Bert" is removed from the queue and the pointer moves to the next item in the queue. The rear pointer does not move.

Exam tip

Head and tail are often used instead of front and rear.

Linear, circular and priority queues

REVISED

The examples above show a **linear queue**, that is, where you can envisage the data in a line. The first item in is the first item out. The maximum size of the queue is fixed in this case, although it could be dynamic. A typical method for storing data in a queue is to use a one-dimensional array.

A **circular queue** can be envisaged as a fixed-size ring where the back of the queue is connected to the front. This is often referred to as a circular buffer. As with a linear queue, it is the pointers that move rather than the data. However, with a circular queue the first items of data can be seen as being next to the last item of data in the queue.

A common implementation is for buffering, when items of data need to be stored temporarily while they are waiting to be passed to/from a device.

Linear queue: a FIFO structure organised as a line of data, such as a list.

Circular queue: a FIFO data structure implemented as a ring where the front and rear pointers can wrap around from the end to the start of the array.

Priority queue: a variation of a FIFO structure where some data may leave out of sequence where it has a higher priority than other data items.

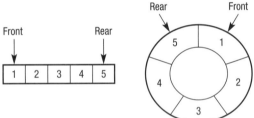

Figure 8.1 Linear and circular queues

A **priority queue** adds a further element to the queue which is the priority of each item. For example, if documents are being sent to print on a network printer then it might be possible for the user or systems manager to control the queue in some way. They may be able to force print jobs to the top of the queue or to put print jobs on hold while others are pushed through. This is known as a 'priority' queue and requires the programmer to assign priority ratings to different jobs. Higher priority jobs are effectively able to jump the queue. Where two jobs have the same priority, they will be handled according to their position in the queue.

Implementing a linear queue

A queue is typically made up of a number of data items of the same type. Therefore, a common implementation is to use an array. To demonstrate the principle, this example shows a queue with a fixed size of nine elements. There are currently five items in the queue and FP shows the front pointer and RP shows the rear pointer.

Exam tip

Practise drawing diagrams or illustrations for moving data through stacks, linear queues and circular queues.

FP				RP				
0	1	2	3	4	5	6	7	8
Alice	Belinda	Carly	Daphne	Erica				

Note that it is possible for the queue to become empty or full as data are added and removed, and that not every element has to have data in it. Therefore, when the queue is implemented we need to know:

- the name of the array
- the maximum size of the queue
- whether the queue is full or empty
- where the front of the queue is
- where the rear of the queue is.

Assuming that element 0 is the front of the queue and element 4 is the rear, when an item is removed, the queue will then look like this:

	FP			RP				
0	1	2	3	4	5	6	7	8
	Belinda	Carly	Daphne	Erica				

The front pointer has moved +1 so that the front is now pointing at element 1. The rear pointer does not change so remains on position 4.

Any item of data added to the queue is added to the rear. In this case it would be added in position 5 as this is the next available position. For example, if we add "Beth":

	FP				RP			
0	1	2	3	4	5	6	7	8
	Belinda	Carly	Daphne	Erica	Beth			

The front pointer is now on position 1 and the rear pointer is on position 5. Items can now be added and removed with the front and rear pointers moving accordingly. For example, if we removed the next two elements and added a new name "Jessica", the queue would look like this:

			FP			RP		
0	1	2	3	4	5	6	7	8
			Daphne	Erica	Beth	Jessica		

The front pointer will have moved forward to position 3 and the rear pointer will have moved to position 6.

Eventually, if data items keep being added, the rear pointer will reach the end of the array and there will be no more room in the array to add new elements, despite some earlier locations in the array being empty, because elements have been removed from the front of the queue. The simplest way to deal with this is to always keep the front pointer pointing at index 0 in the array, and to move elements forward in the array each time an item is removed. This method is simple, but it can be time consuming to move the elements along in the array, especially if the queue is a long one. Therefore a more efficient method of dealing with this problem, known as a circular queue, is more common.

Implementing a circular queue

A circular queue works in a similar way to a linear queue except the front and rear pointers move when an item is added or removed, making more efficient use of memory. For example, in the linear queue above, items 1, 2 and 3 have all been removed. However, there is no way of adding items into those empty elements in the array as the front pointer has moved to element 3.

The circular queue makes use of the spaces that are freed up at the front of a queue after they have been removed. It does this by wrapping the rear pointer around the array, starting again at element 0 once the queue becomes full. If we start with the same queue as before, the front pointer is 0 and the rear pointer is 4.

FP				RP				
0	1	2	3	4	5	6	7	8
Alice	Belinda	Carly	Daphne	Erica				

If two items are removed, the queue will then look like this:

		FP		RP				
0	1	2	3	4	5	6	7	8
		Carly	Daphne	Erica				

Four new items are now added to the queue: "Jane", "Davina", "Yvonne" and "Kelly". Notice that the rear pointer is now on 8.

		FP						RP
0	1	2	3	4	5	6	7	8
		Carly	Daphne	Erica	Jane	Davina	Yvonne	Kelly

As this is a circular queue, the rear pointer can now wrap back around to the beginning. If a further item is added, the rear pointer would move to position 0 as this free. To add "Maria":

RP		FP						
0	1	2	3	4	5	6	7	8
Maria		Carly	Daphne	Erica	Jane	Davina	Yvonne	Kelly

Implementing a priority queue

A priority queue can also be implemented using an array by assigning a value to each element to indicate the priority. Items of data with the highest priority are dealt with first. Where the priority is the same, then the items are dealt with on a FIFO basis like a normal queue.

There are two possible solutions using an array. One option is to use a standard queue where items are added in the usual way at the end of the queue. When items are removed, each element in the array is checked for its priority to identify the next item to be removed. Where this method is used, adding data is straightforward but removing it is more complex.

Starting with the same queue, this time a priority is included shown here in subscript and assuming that 1 is highest priority.

FP   RP

0	1	2	3	4	5	6	7	8
Alice$_2$	Belinda$_1$	Carly$_2$	Daphne$_3$	Erica$_4$				

If an item is added, it is simply added with its priority at the end and the rear pointer is moved. If "Jane" were added with a priority of 1:

FP   RP

0	1	2	3	4	5	6	7	8
Alice$_2$	Belinda$_1$	Carly$_2$	Daphne$_3$	Erica$_4$	Jane$_1$			

When data is removed, it is done so in order of priority. There are two items with a priority of 1. In this case, "Belinda" would be removed first as she is closest to the front of the queue. "Jane" would be the next item to be removed. In this example it shows how the principle of FIFO is still being used as "Belinda" entered the queue before "Jane".

An alternative is to maintain the queue in priority order, which means that when a new item is added, it is put into the correct position in the queue. Removing items can then be done in the usual way by taking the item at the front of the queue. Where this method is used, removing data is straightforward but adding it is more complex.

Working on the same list, this time the names would be in priority order. To remove the next item is just a case of removing the item at the front of the queue.

FP   RP

0	1	2	3	4	5	6	7	8
Belinda$_1$	Alice$_2$	Carly$_2$	Daphne$_3$	Erica$_4$				

Therefore the first item to be removed would be "Belinda" as she has the highest priority:

  FP   RP

0	1	2	3	4	5	6	7	8
	Alice$_2$	Carly$_2$	Daphne$_3$	Erica$_4$				

If a new item is added, it will be put into the correct position based on its priority. Where it has the same priority it will be added after the existing items of the same priority. For example, if "Yvonne" is added with a priority of 1:

  FP   RP

0	1	2	3	4	5	6	7	8
	Yvonne$_1$	Alice$_2$	Carly$_2$	Daphne$_3$	Erica$_4$			

If "Kelly" is added with a priority of 2:

  FP   RP

0	1	2	3	4	5	6	7	8
	Yvonne$_1$	Alice$_2$	Carly$_2$	Kelly$_2$	Daphne$_3$	Erica$_4$		

Summary

- Queues and stacks are dynamic data structures.
- A stack is an example of a LIFO (last in first out) structure, which means that the last item of data added is the first to be removed.
- A queue is called a FIFO (first in first out) structure, which means that the first item of data added is the first to be removed.
- There are three types of queues: linear, circular or priority.

Now test yourself

1 Joe has made a set of 40 Computer Science revision cards. He takes a card, reads it and tests himself. If he is happy he returns the card to the bottom of the pack, if he wants to go over it again soon he puts the card on his desk. Joe wants to digitise his cards into a computer program.

(a) Explain why a queue is a suitable data structure to represent the pack of revision cards. [1]

(b) Joe has created a circular queue with an index running from 1 to 40 and called the queue **RevisionCards**. The table below represents the queue and associated variables at the start of the program. QSize represents the number of cards currently in the queue.

Index	Data
1	Variable: A named piece of memory that can be changed.
2	Constant: A named piece of memory that cannot be changed.
3	Procedure: A subroutine that executes instructions.
4	Function: A subroutine that executes instructions and returns a result.
...	...
40	Queue: A FIFO or LILO data structure.

```
FrontPtr = 1
RearPtr = 40
QSize = 40
```

(i) If Joe takes the first seven cards from the top of the pile, what values are now stored in the three variables? [1]

(ii) Joe is happy with his knowledge of three cards and puts them back. What values are now stored in the three variables? [1]

(iii) Write an algorithm in pseudo-code to take the top card from the pile. Your algorithm should print the card contents to screen and make any modifications needed to the variables. It should cope effectively with any situations that may occur while the program is being run. [6]

2 A stack is a LIFO data type – a stack with a single element may look like this:

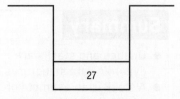

(a) What is meant by the term LIFO? [1]

(b) Draw diagrams (as above) to show the effects of:

(i) Push 5 [1]

(ii) Push 9 [1]

(iii) Pop [1]

(iv) Push 6 [1]

(c) Give one example of the use of a stack. [1]

3 Differentiate between a linear queue, a circular queue and a priority queue. [3]

Task

1 Ignoring any built-in stacks or queues, use your chosen language to implement:

(a) a stack   (c) a circular queue

(b) a linear queue   (d) a priority queue.

You may want to revisit object-oriented programming to add extra challenge.

9 Graphs and trees

A-level only

Specification coverage

3.2.4 Graphs

Graphs

REVISED

A **graph** is a mathematical structure that models the relationship between pairs of objects. The pairs of objects could be almost anything including places, people, websites, numbers, physical components, biological or chemical data, or even concepts. The study of the use of graphs is called **graph theory** and it is useful in computing as it allows the programmer to model real-life situations that would otherwise be abstract.

To start with an example, a graph could be used to model the relationship between two places and how they are connected via a train line. In graph theory, objects are called nodes or **vertices** and each connection is called an edge or **arc**. In this simple example, we have two vertices, one for each town and one edge, which in this case will be the train connection between the two towns. A simple graph may look like this:

A **weighted graph** can be created by adding values to the edges. In this example, we might add the travel time between the two towns, so the weighted graph would look like this:

To extend this example, you might add in all of the towns on a particular network, with the travel time between each point. Figure 9.1 shows a graph that models the real-life situation so you can see that there is no direct connection between some of the towns, therefore there is no edge between some of the vertices.

> **Graph**: a mathematical structure that models the relationship between pairs of objects.
>
> **Graph theory**: the underlying mathematical principles behind the use of graphs.
>
> **Vertex/vertices**: an object in a graph – also known as a node. (Vertices is the plural.)
>
> **Arc**: a join or relationship between two nodes – also known as an edge.
>
> **Weighted graph**: a graph that has a data value labelled on each edge.

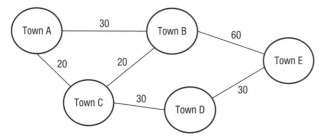

Figure 9.1 A graph structure to show journey times between towns

The graph now becomes quite useful as it could be used, for example, to find the quickest journey times between two towns. For example, to travel by train from Town A to Town E would be quicker via Town C and Town D than via Town B.

Graphs can also be directed or undirected, which refers to the direction of the relationship between two vertices.

An **undirected graph** is when the relationship between the vertices can be in either direction. In this example, the train will go in either direction between the towns, which means there is a two-way direction between the vertices in the graph.

A **directed graph** (also known as a digraph) is where there is a one-way relationship between the vertices. For example, we may produce a digraph to represent a real-life situation where we are creating a family tree. Figure 9.2 is a graph that shows parents and siblings.

In this case, Charles is the parent of Dave and Pauline, Pauline is the parent of Jack and Harry. The arrows indicate that this is a one-way relationship.

> **Undirected graph**: a graph where the relationship between vertices is two-way.
>
> **Directed graph**: a graph where the relationship between vertices is one-way.

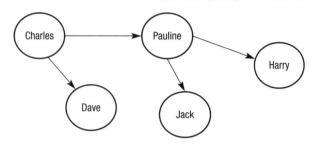

Figure 9.2 Graph to show parents and siblings

Uses of graphs

Graphs have a wide range of uses in computing, as they are able to model complex real-life problems including human networks, transport networks, the Internet and web, computer networks, medical research, project management and game theory.

Graph theory is also an important concept in relation to Dijkstra's algorithm. This calculates the shortest path between nodes. It has been used for applications such as working out shortest distances between cities and calculating shortest distances between vertices in computer networks. This is covered in detail in Chapter 13.

> **Exam tip**
>
> Once you have a thorough understanding of graph theory you can apply the skills to a multitude of problems.

> **Exam tip**
>
> Make sure you can apply Dijkstra's shortest path algorithm to a variety of graph problems.

Adjacency list

A graph is an example of an abstract data type. So far we have considered the graph in graphical form, but we need to represent it in a way that can be stored and manipulated by the computer. The first method is to use a list, called an **adjacency list**. There are three basic formats for the list depending on whether the graph is directed or undirected and whether it is weighted.

> **Adjacency list**: a data structure that stores a list of nodes with their adjacent nodes.

Undirected graph

Vertex	Adjacent vertices
A	B,C
B	A,C,E
C	A,B,D
D	C,E
E	B,D

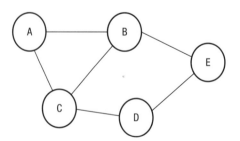

The list shows each vertex and each vertex that it is adjacent to. All adjacencies are shown as this is a two-way relationship.

Directed graph

Vertex	Adjacent vertices
A	B,D
B	E
C	
D	C,E
E	

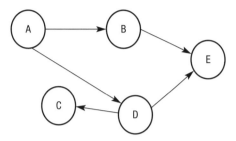

The list only shows the one-way relationship between the vertices. For example, D is connected to C but C is not connected to D.

Weighted graph

Vertex	Adjacent vertices
A	B,20,C,30
B	A,20,C,30,E,25
C	A,30,B,30,D,35
D	C,35,E,40
E	B,25,D,40

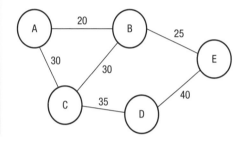

The list shows the value of each edge after each adjacent vertex. For example, A is adjacent to B with a weighted value of 20, A is adjacent to C with a weighted value of 30 and so on. Notice that this example is an undirected weighted graph.

Adjacency matrix

The second method for storing the data is to use an **adjacency matrix**. This method uses a two-dimensional array or grid populated with 1s and 0s.

> **Adjacency matrix**: a data structure set up as a two-dimensional array or grid that shows whether there is an edge between each pair of nodes.

Undirected graph

	A	B	C	D	E
A	0	1	1	0	0
B	1	0	1	0	1
C	1	1	0	1	0
D	0	0	1	0	1
E	0	1	0	1	0

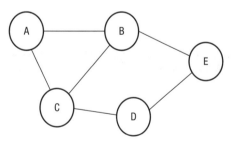

This works by putting a 1 in each cell where there is an edge and a 0 in each cell where there is not an edge. For example, A is adjacent to B so there will be a 1 in the grid where A and B intersect in the matrix. A is not adjacent to D so there will be a 0 in the grid where A and D intersect in the matrix.

Directed graph

	A	B	C	D	E
A	0	1	0	1	0
B	0	0	0	0	1
C	0	0	0	0	0
D	0	0	1	0	1
E	0	0	0	0	0

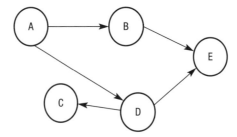

In this case, you read the matrix row by row, inserting a 1 where there is a one-way relationship between two vertices and 0 where there isn't. For example, A has a one-way relationship to B so there is a 1 in the cell where A and B intersect in the matrix. B does not have a one-way relationship to A, so there is a 0 in the cell where B and A intersect in the matrix.

Weighted graph

	A	B	C	D	E
A	∞	20	30	∞	∞
B	20	∞	30	∞	25
C	30	30	∞	35	∞
D	∞	∞	35	∞	40
E	∞	25	∞	40	∞

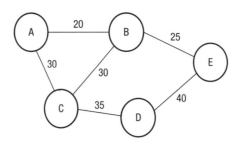

> **Exam tip**
>
> Common mistakes include using inappropriate symbols for indicating no link, and not checking for symmetry in non-directional graphs.

In this case, you follow the same process for an undirected graph, but this time you input the weighted value rather than a 1. Instead of the 0, the infinity sign is used.

Adjacency list vs adjacency matrix

REVISED

When deciding on which implementation to use it usually comes down to two factors: speed and memory. Speed refers to how quickly the program will be able to access the data structure and produce a result. Memory refers to the amount of memory that each implementation will use. Bear in mind that the graph structure is likely to be used with very large datasets, making these issues critical. Table 9.1 shows the main factors.

> **Exam tip**
>
> You may be asked to consider and contrast between the choice of an adjacency list or adjacency matrix.

Table 9.1 Comparison of adjacency list and adjacency matrix

Adjacency list	Adjacency matrix
Only stores data where there is an adjacency (edge) so requires less memory.	Stores a value for every combination of node adjacencies so requires more memory.
The list has to be parsed to identify whether particular adjacencies exist, which increases the time taken to process the data.	Adjacencies can be identified more quickly as every combination is already stored. Effectively the matrix forms a look-up table of each node to every other node.
Where there are not that many edges (few adjacencies), this method would be more suitable for the reasons stated above. This is known as a sparse graph.	Where there are many edges (lots of adjacencies), this method would be more suitable for the reasons stated above. This is known as a dense graph.

Trees

A **tree** is an abstract data structure that is very similar to a graph in that it has **nodes** and **edges**. It is called a tree because it is visualised as a hierarchical structure (like a family tree) with branches. Trees can have a root node, with all the other nodes branching away from the root.

The key difference with a tree compared to a graph is that it is connected and undirected and can contain no cycles or loops. For example, A goes to B and C, but you could not go from A to B to C or from A to C to B and back to A.

A tree could be visualised as follows:

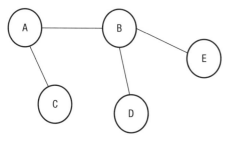

Figure 9.3 A tree structure

In this example, there are five nodes and four edges:
- A is the **root** node as all the other nodes branch away from it.
- A is also a **parent** node as it has two **child** nodes B and C.
- B is also a parent node and has two child nodes, D and E.
- C, D and E have no child nodes. These are sometimes called **leaf** nodes.
- You can see that there are no cycles. For example, A has an edge with C forming a single path. It would not be possible, for example, to go from A to C to D and back to A.

Trees have a number of uses. They:
- can be used to store data that has an inherent hierarchical structure. For example, an operating system may use a tree for directories, files and folders in its file management system
- are dynamic, which means that it is easy to add and delete nodes
- are easy to search and sort using standard traversal algorithms. There is more on this in Chapter 16
- can be used to process the syntax of statements in natural and programming languages so are commonly used when compiling programming code.

Binary search trees

A common implementation of a tree is the binary search tree. This is a directed and rooted tree, which can have no more than two branches off each node and is commonly used to store data that are input in a random order. The nature of the structure means that data are automatically sorted as they are entered and the tree can be 'traversed' in order to search for and extract data from it.

> **Tree**: a data structure similar to a graph, with no loops.
>
> **Node**: an object in a graph – also known as a vertex.
>
> **Edge**: a join of relationship between nodes – also known as an arc.

> **Exam tip**
>
> Ensure you can differentiate between trees and non-tree graphs.

> **Root**: the starting node in a rooted tree structure from which all other nodes branch off.
>
> **Parent**: a type of node in a tree, where there are further nodes below it.
>
> **Child**: a node in a tree that has nodes above it in the hierarchy.
>
> **Leaf**: a node that does not have any other nodes beneath it.

> **Exam tip**
>
> Practise entering and adding data to binary search trees as this is frequently muddled up in exams.

The first item of data to be used is stored in the root node. The next (and any subsequent) data item is dealt with by the following routine:

- If the value of the new data item is less than the value in the current node then branch left, otherwise branch right.
- Keep repeating this process until you come to an 'empty' branch, then put the new value in the node at the end of the branch.

This sounds awkward but look at Figure 9.4 and try to follow through how the name "Fred" has been added to the **binary tree**.

Binary tree: a tree where each node can only have up to two child nodes attached to it.

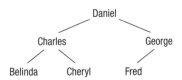

Figure 9.4 An example of a binary tree

Daniel is the root node. Belinda, Cheryl and Fred can be classed as leaf nodes because they have no nodes below them. Charles can be described as the parent and Cheryl the child.

Summary

- Graphs are a data structure made up of vertices (nodes) and edges, which are the connections between the vertices.
- Graphs can be used to analyse the connections and relationships between data items and are a useful tool for modelling real-life situations.
- Graphs can be directed or undirected, meaning that there may be a one-way or two-way connection between each vertex.
- Graphs can be weighted, meaning that a value can be applied to the edges between nodes.
- An adjacency list or matrix can be used to identify which vertices are connected to which others and whether there is any weight associated with the edge.
- A tree structure is a connected, undirected graph that contains no cycles.
- A binary tree structure is a special type of tree where each vertex can have no more than two children.

Now test yourself

TESTED ☐

1 This table shows an adjacency matrix for a directed graph:

		1	2	3	4	5
FROM	**1**	0	1	1	0	1
	2	0	0	1	0	0
	3	1	1	0	1	1
	4	0	0	1	0	0
	5	0	1	1	1	0

(a) Create a diagram of the matrix. [3]
(b) Is this a weighted or an unweighted graph? [1]
(c) Explain under what circumstances an adjacency matrix would be the most effective method of representing a graph, and in what circumstances an adjacency list would be preferable. [2]
(d) What properties would be required for this graph to be a tree? [2]

2 'Foo Fighters' is to be the root of an alphabetically organised binary tree. Insert the following super-bands into the tree in the order they are listed:
Bon Jovi, AC/DC, Iron Maiden, Metallica, Green Day, Rolling Stones, Pink Floyd. [3]

10 Hash tables and dictionaries

Specification coverage

3.2.6 Hash tables
3.2.7 Dictionaries

Hash tables

A **hash table** is a data structure made up of two parts, a table (or array) of data, and a **key**, which identifies the location of the data within the table. A **hashing algorithm** is carried out on the key, which then acts as an index to the specific location of that data item within the array. You could think of it as a look-up table that uses a key/value combination.

When the data need to be retrieved, for example, if a search is carried out on the data, the same hashing algorithm is used on the key being searched to calculate the index and therefore retrieve the data in one step. This is a very efficient search technique and it is why hashing tables are used extensively in applications where large datasets need to be accessed or where speed of access is critical. This could be visualised as shown in Figure 10.1.

> **Hash table:** a data structure that stores key/value pairs based on an index calculated from an algorithm.
>
> **Key/value pair:** the key and its associated data.
>
> **Hashing algorithm:** code that creates a unique index from given items of key data.

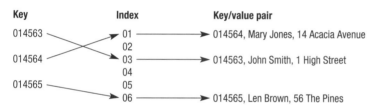

Figure 10.1 Visualisation of a hash table

The array into which the data are being stored can be envisaged as a series of slots, each of which has a unique index. The index can then be used to access all of the data stored in the record. Note that the key/value pair is the key and all of the data stored is in relation to that key. In this case it would be a customer record.

Uses of hashing algorithms

Hashing algorithms have many applications:
- Databases: Used to create indices for databases enabling quick storage and retrieval of data.
- Memory addressing: Used to generate memory addresses where data will be stored. It is particularly useful for cache memory, where data is placed temporarily allowing the user fast access to programs and data stored in the **cache**.
- Operating systems: As an example of memory addressing, some operating systems use hashing tables to store and locate the executable files of all its programs and utilities.
- Encryption: Used to encrypt data, hence the term 'encryption key'. In this case the algorithm must be complex so that if data is intercepted it is not possible to reverse-engineer it.

> **Cache:** a high-speed temporary area of memory.

- Checksums: A value calculated from a set of data that is going to be transmitted. On receipt the algorithm is run again on the data and the two results are compared as a way of checking whether the data has been corrupted during transmission.
- Programming: Used to index keywords and identifiers as the compiler will need access to these quickly as it compiles the program.

Generating hashing algorithms

REVISED

To generate the index, you need a suitable algorithm. To start with we will look at a very simple example to show the concept. You might have an array with six elements used to store six values. We could calculate the index using an algorithm that adds the numbers (digits) in the key together and then performs a modulo 6 sum on the result, as there are six slots in our hash table.

- For the first data item the value of the key might be 25463.
- Add the numbers (digits) together $2 + 5 + 4 + 6 + 3 = 20$.
- Perform modulo 6 calculation so divide by 6 = 3 r 2.
- Therefore the Index = 2.
- The data is placed in slot 2.
- The second data item might have a key with the value 34255.
- Add the numbers (digits) together $3 + 4 + 2 + 5 + 5 = 19$.
- Perform modulo 6 calculation so divide by 6 = 3 r 1.
- Therefore the Index = 1.
- The data is placed in slot 1.

0	
1	34255
2	25463
3	
4	
5	

This process then continues for every key. You can see from this how the index is created from the data in the key. The real benefit of using an algorithm is that it is used to store the data in the first place and then used to locate the data when it is needed. The indices therefore are created and recreated when they are needed.

Choosing a hashing algorithm

The basic example above demonstrates a few features and associated problems when creating a suitable algorithm:

- A numeric value needs to be generated from the data in order to perform the calculation. For non-numeric keys such as text and other characters, the ASCII or Unicode value of each character is normally used.
- It must generate unique indices to avoid **collisions**. A good algorithm will create as few as possible and needs a mechanism to cope with collisions as they occur.
- It needs to create a uniform spread of indices. For example, if you were storing millions of items of data into millions of slots, the algorithm needs to provide an even spread of index values from the data and avoid **clustering**. This cuts down the possibility of collisions.
- There must be enough slots to store the volume of data. For example, if a database is going to store 1 million records, the algorithm must be capable of producing at least 1 million indices. In fact it would need more than this to avoid collisions as the table fills up. Hash tables have a **load factor** which is the number of keys divided by the number of slots. A high load factor means that it will become increasingly difficult for the algorithm to produce a unique result.
- It has to balance the issues of speed with complexity. For example, an algorithm for a database needs to calculate the index very quickly. An algorithm for encryption needs to be very complex, but may not need to calculate the index quickly.

Exam tip

When exam questions about hashing discuss complexity, they are not interested in the difficulty of coding and using this as a point in an answer may not gain a mark.

Collision: when a hashing algorithm produces the same index for two or more different keys.

Clustering: when a hashing algorithm produces indices that are not randomly distributed.

Load factor: the ratio of how many indices are available to how many there are in total.

Collisions

One of the main features of a hashing algorithm is that it must produce a unique **index**. Where a collision occurs, there must be some way of handling it so that a unique index can be assigned to the key.

There are two main methods:

- **Chaining**: In this case, if a collision occurs, a list is created in that slot and the key/value pair becomes an element of the list. If another collision occurs, that key/value pair becomes the next element in the list and so on. Figure 10.2 shows the concept.

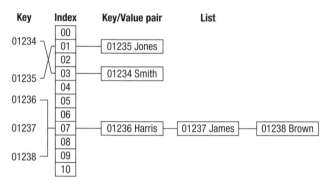

Figure 10.2 Chaining of key/value pairs when there is a collision

Where the index is unique, the key/value pairs work in the normal way. Where two or more keys generate the same index, a list is formed. It is called chaining as the additional key/value pairs get chained together inside a list. Each key/value pair is uniquely identified by its position within the list. In this example the keys 01236, 01237 and 01238 all produced the same index so their key/values have been chained together.

- **Rehashing**: In this case, if a collision occurs, the same algorithm is run again, or an alternative algorithm is run until a unique key is created. This normally uses a technique called probing, which means that the algorithm probes or searches for an empty slot. It could do this by simply looking for the next available slot to the index where there was a clash.

Figure 10.3 shows a simple linear probe where the next available slot is used. This is not very sophisticated because if the hashing algorithm is leading to clustering as in this example, the results are still going to be clustered around the same slots. A more sophisticated method is to apply another hashing function to the index where the clash occurred, in order to generate another one.

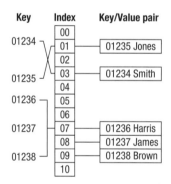

Figure 10.3 Probing as a result of a collision

Dictionaries

A **dictionary** is an abstract data type that maps keys to data. It is called an **associative array** in that it deals with two sets of data that are associated with each other. The dictionary data structure is analogous with a real-life dictionary in that there is a word (the key) associated with a definition (the data). This is similar to a hash table in that it has key/value pairs.

In the same way that a real-life dictionary is accessed randomly, a dictionary data structure also requires random access. The common procedures that you would need to carry out on a dictionary would be to add, retrieve and delete data. Unlike a real-life dictionary however, the data inside a dictionary data structure is unordered.

> **Exam tip**
>
> Study past paper mark schemes very carefully to identify the nuances that examiners are looking for when dealing with collisions.

> **Index**: the location where values will be stored, calculated from the key.
>
> **Chaining**: a technique for generating a unique index when there is a collision by adding the key/value to a list stored at the same index.
>
> **Rehashing**: the process of running the hashing algorithm again when a collision occurs.

> **Dictionary (data structure)**: a data structure that maps keys to data.
>
> **Associative array**: a two-dimensional structure containing key/value pairs of data.

10 Hash tables and dictionaries

For example, in a customer database each record has a key, which might be the **CustomerID**. This key links to all of the data that is stored about the customer. At any time we may want to retrieve, add or delete a customer record. Dictionary data structures are often used to implement databases due to the fact that there will be inherent associations within the data and that they need to be searched and sorted as a matter of routine in order to retrieve data.

In simple terms the dictionary data structure can be envisaged as a two-dimensional array:

Table 10.1 A two-dimensional array

Key e.g. CustomerID	Associated data
01234	James Cochran, 12 Harbour Mews, Leicester
01235	Mary Abbot, 56 Eagle Street, Manchester
01236	Keith Fletcher, 3 Yarborough Road, Leeds
01237	Hussain Khan, 68 Lemon Street, Derby
01238	David Lui, 87 Threddle Lane, Northampton
01239	Rachel Young, The Forest Lodge, Kettering

As you can see from this example, dictionaries and hash tables are very similar and in fact a hash table is one way of implementing a dictionary. Dictionaries can also be created using binary trees (see Chapter 9).

Summary

- A hash table is a data structure made up of two parts, a table (or array) of data, and a key, which identifies the location of the data within the table.
- A hashing algorithm is carried out on the key, which then acts as an index to the specific location of that data item within the array.
- Hashing algorithms must create a range of keys sufficient to assign unique values to each item of data.
- Collisions occur when the hashing algorithm generates the same key from two different items of data.
- Chaining or rehashing must be carried out in the event of a collision.
- A dictionary is an abstract data type that maps keys to data.
- Dictionaries and hash tables are similar data structures.

Now test yourself

TESTED ☐

1 National Insurance (NI) numbers are of the form **Two Letters, Six Numbers, One Letter**. A program is being developed to store details of 800 people identified by NI number.
   (a) Discuss the advantages of organising a list of NI numbers by hashing rather than in alphabetical order. [2]
   (b) Define the term collision. [1]
   (c) The developer has found two NI numbers that produce the same hash value. In the context of storing data in files using hashing, explain the effect of this collision and how this might be dealt with. [2]
2 Discuss how an array differs from a dictionary. [2]

11 Vectors

Specification coverage

3.2.8 Vectors

Vectors

REVISED

Vectors can be represented and applied in various ways, both mathematically and geometrically. They are used in different ways in computing, for example:

- as a data structure
- as a method for mapping one value to another
- as a method of defining geometric shapes.

In this chapter we will look at all three interpretations of vectors.

Representing vectors as a data structure

REVISED

When programming, vectors can be implemented as values stored in a list. For example, the first six values of the Fibonacci sequence could be represented as:

```
fibonacci[0] = 0; fibonacci[1] = 1; fibonacci[2] = 1;
fibonacci[3] = 2; fibonacci[4] = 3; fibonacci[5] = 5;
```

This representation could also be described as a one-dimensional array where each item of data is an element in the array, which can be accessed by its location, as shown on the right.

Index	0	1	2	3	4	5
Data	0	1	1	2	3	5

A dictionary is a data structure that maps a key to a value. As we have seen, we can create sets of real numbers that can then be applied over the vectors. The dictionary structure allows us to call an index, which is then used as a look-up to the real values.

```
{0: Value 1, 1: Value 2, 2: Value 3, 3: Value 4, ...}
```

The start of the Fibonacci sequence vector could be represented in a dictionary as:

```
{0:0, 1:1, 2:1, 3:2, 4:3, 5:5}
```

Representing vectors as a function

REVISED

A function is a mathematical construct that maps an input to an output. For example, the function $f(x) = x^2$, simply maps the value of x to its square. A vector can be used to represent a function. For example:

F = the function to create the vector

S = the complete set of values that the function can be applied to

R = the potential outputs of the function.

Therefore F: S → R

Note that all of the output values must be drawn from R, which is being treated as a single field from which the function takes its values.

Representing vectors as arrows

Geometrically, vectors can be represented as arrows, as shown in Figure 11.1.

The two dimensions of size (or **magnitude**) and **direction** are shown. The direction of the arrow is shown by the arrow head and v represents the size. The start of the arrow is called the tail and the top of the arrow, the head. To quantify the size and direction of the arrow, think of it plotted on x and y axes:

Figure 11.1 A vector represented as an arrow with magnitude and direction

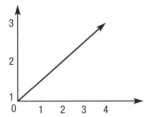

Figure 11.2 A vector visualised as an arrow with a measurement

The arrow can be represented as a vector **A** in the format **A** $= (x,y)$. x and y are called the **components** of the vector and in this case would be the distance from $(0, 0)$ on an x and y axis. Therefore, this vector is described as **A** $= (4, 3)$ often shown in the format **A** $= \binom{4}{3}$ to differentiate them from a coordinate pair used to plot points on a graph.

Already, you can see how useful vectors can be. With reference to vector graphics, for example, it would now be possible to resize an image simply by changing the component values in the vector.

> **Magnitude**: one of the two components of a vector – refers to its size.
>
> **Direction**: one of the two components of a vector.
>
> **Components**: the values within a vector.

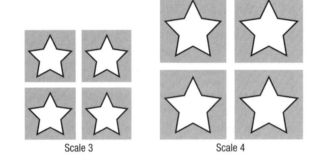

Figure 11.3 The effect of scaling a vector

Scale 2   Scale 3   Scale 4

Three-dimensional objects can be represented using the same method with the addition of a further component, the z axis.

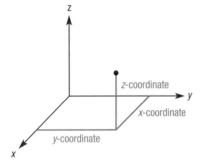

Figure 11.4 A visualisation of a vector in three dimensions

In this example, the vector could be represented as **A** $= (x, y, z)$.

Vector addition

It is possible to add vectors together, which has the effect of translating or displacing the vector. Geometrically, this could be visualised as joining the tail of one to the head of another.

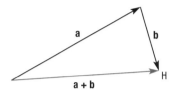

Figure 11.5 Adding vectors

Exam tip

You can read more about geometric vectors in A-level Geometry textbooks.

Notice that a new point H has been created which may be used as the head of a new vector.

The sum of two vectors **A** and **B** can be represented as follows:

A = (A1, A2, A3)

B = (B1, B2, B3)

A + **B** = (A1 + B1, A2 + B2, A3 + B3)

Note that the two vectors must have the same dimension, which in this case is three components. For example, if:

A = (2, 3, 4) and **B** = (3, 5, 10) then **A** + **B** = (5, 8, 14)

Scalar–vector multiplication

It is also possible to multiply vectors by a number, which has the effect of scaling. The number is called a **scalar** as it represents the amount by which you want change the scale of the vector. An analogy would be changing the scale of a map. If you zoom in, you are changing the scale. In the case of a vector, if you scale it by a factor of two, it will have twice the magnitude. The direction, however, will not change as a result of scaling. You can envisage this geometrically as shown in Figure 11.6.

Scalar: a real value used to multiply a vector to scale the vector.

Figure 11.6 Scaling a vector

The original vector **A** = (3, 2). Multiplying this by the scalar 2 results in vector **B** = (6, 4). Notice that the tail position and direction do not change.

Dot product

Dot product is the process of combining two vectors to calculate a single number. It is calculated in the following format (see Figure 11.7):

$$\mathbf{A} \cdot \mathbf{B} = A_x B_x + A_y B_y$$

In this example, $\mathbf{A} = (3, 5)$ and $\mathbf{B} = (7, 2)$

Therefore the dot product is $3 \times 7 + 5 \times 2 = 31$

This would also work in three dimensions by including z in the components. For example, two vectors with the coordinates $\mathbf{A} = (5, 3, 2)$ and $\mathbf{B} = (2, 7, 4)$ would result in a dot product of:

$5 \times 2 + 3 \times 7 + 2 \times 4 = 10 + 21 + 8 = 39$

> **Dot product**: multiplying two vectors together to produce a number.

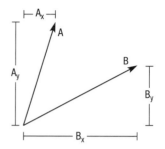

Figure 11.7 The dot product of two vectors

Convex combinations

When two vectors are combined to create a third, a relationship exists between the three vectors. In Figure 11.8 you can see that the new vector **c** has been created at right angles to the other vectors.

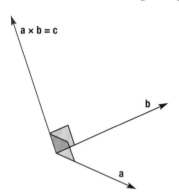

Figure 11.8 Combination of vectors

> **Convex combination**: a method of multiplying vectors that produces a resulting vector within the convex hull.
>
> **Vector space**: a collection of elements that can be formed by adding or multiplying vectors together.
>
> **Convex hull**: a spatial representation of the vector space between two vectors.

When these combinations are created, they have to be done according to certain mathematical principles. For example, a **convex combination** of vectors is one where the new vector must be within the **vector space** of the two vectors from which it is made. This could be visualised as shown in Figure 11.9.

Vector AD is created by combining vectors AC and AB. Notice an imaginary line between points B and C. The new vector must fall within the vector space defined by the points A, B and C in the diagram. This is a visual representation of what is called a **convex hull** that represents all of the points that make up the vector space. Notice point E, which represents the head for another vector. This falls outside the convex hull and is therefore not a convex combination.

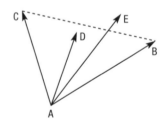

Figure 11.9 Convex combination of vectors

Mathematically, to perform a convex combination, you will be multiplying one vector either by a scalar, or by another vector. This could be represented as:

$D = \alpha AB + \beta AC$

where AB and AC are the two vectors

α and β represent the real number that each vector will be multiplied by.

α and β must both be greater than or equal to 0 and $\alpha + \beta$ must equal 1. D will then fall within the vector space.

Uses of dot product

Given two vectors **u** and **v**, it is possible to generate parity using the bitwise AND and XOR operations.

For example, where **u** = [1, 1, 1, 1] and **v** = [1, 0, 1, 1], the dot product would be **u.v** = 1. This is calculated by performing arithmetic over GF(2) where GF has two elements 0 and 1. This calculation works out the parity bit for even parity. The first vector will always be [1, 1, 1, 1] and in this example the second vector is [1, 0, 1, 1]. As you can see, we would expect the parity bit to be a 1 as the vector **v** currently has an odd number of 1s.

The calculation would work as follows:

$$\mathbf{u.v} = [1, 1, 1, 1].[1, 0, 1, 1]$$
$$= 1 \text{ AND } 1 \text{ XOR } 1 \text{ AND } 0 \text{ XOR } 1 \text{ AND } 1 \text{ XOR } 1 \text{ AND } 1$$
$$= 1 \text{ XOR } 0 \text{ XOR } 1 \text{ XOR } 1$$
$$= 1$$

Arithmetic over GF(2) can be summarised in two small tables. Multiplication can be achieved by bitwise AND operation:

×	0	1
0	0	0
1	0	1

Addition can be achieved by bitwise XOR operation:

+	0	1
0	0	1
1	1	0

Subtraction is identical to addition, −1 = 1 and −0 = 0.

Summary

- A vector can be represented as a list of numbers, as a function and as a geometric point in space.
- A vector can be created as a one-dimensional array or dictionary.
- Vectors can be combined using addition, multiplication and convex combination.
- Addition of vectors has the effect of translation or displacement.
- Multiplication of vectors by a scalar has the effect of scaling.
- Dot product can be used to generate parity.

Now test yourself

TESTED ☐

1 What is the difference between vector addition and scalar–vector multiplication? [2]
2 Two vectors are A = (2, 3) and B = (2, 1)
   (a) Draw A and B. [1]
   (b) Draw the addition of A and B. [1]
   (c) What is the dot product of A and B? [2]

Task

1 Investigate the use of vectors in Computer Science.

12 Graph and tree traversal

A-level only

Implementing a graph

REVISED

Graphs can be implemented using adjacency lists or matrices, which represent every vertex (node) and the edges (or connections) between the vertices.

Node	Adjacent nodes
A	B
B	A, C, E
C	B, D
D	C, E
E	B, D

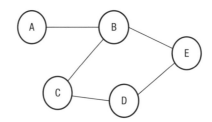

Figure 12.1 Adjacency list and corresponding graph

One possible **implementation** is to store this in an **array** showing each vertex and whether there is an **edge** between vertices. For example, the graph in Figure 12.1 could be represented by the following two-dimensional array:

Table 12.1 A two-dimensional array representing a graph

	A	B	C	D	E
A	0	1	0	0	0
B	1	0	1	0	1
C	0	1	0	1	0
D	0	0	1	0	1
E	0	1	0	1	0

A 1 represents an edge between the two vertices and a 0 means there is no edge. This approach can be used to represent any unweighted, undirected **graph**.

> **Implementation**: creating code to produce a programmed solution.
>
> **Array**: a set of data items of the same type grouped together with the same identifier.
>
> **Edge**: a connection between two nodes in a graph or tree structure.
>
> **Graph**: a data type made up of nodes and edges.

Traversing a graph

REVISED

> **Exam tip**
>
> Practise traversing graphs and trees using different methodologies. It is rare to see more than 7 nodes in exams but in real programs they can often be in the thousands or higher.

There are two ways of traversing the graph: depth first or breadth first.
- **Depth first** is a method that explores as far into a graph as possible before backtracking to visit unvisited nodes. It is often implemented using a recursive algorithm, which is explained later in the chapter.

> **Depth first**: a method for traversing a graph that starts at a chosen node and explores as far as possible along each branch away from the starting node before backtracking.

- **Breadth first** is a method that visits the nodes closest to a starting point first. A **queue** is used to keep track of the **nodes** to visit.

Using the graph in Figure 12.1 as an example, depth first works as follows:

Table 12.2 Depth first traversal

Explanation	Current node	Visited nodes
Select the node to start from (A).	A	
Mark node A as visited. Choose a node that is connected to A (B) and recursively call the search routine to explore from this node.	A	A
Mark node B as visited. Choose a node that is connected to B and has not been visited (C) and recursively call the search routine to explore from this node.	B	A B
Mark node C as visited. Choose a node that is connected to C and has not been visited (D) and recursively call the search routine to explore from this node.	C	A B C
Mark node D as visited. Choose a node that is connected to D and has not been visited (E) and recursively call the search routine to explore from this node.	D	A B C D
Mark node E as visited. All nodes connected to E have already been visited, so unwind recursion. There are no nodes left to visit during this unwinding, so the algorithm will terminate.	E	A B C D E

Using the graph in Figure 12.2 as an example, breadth first works by visiting the starting node and then all of the nodes attached to it in order. It then moves to the next closest nodes to repeat the process as follows:

Table 12.3 Breadth first traversal

Explanation	Contents of queue
Add the node to start exploring from (A) to the queue.	A
Add all nodes that are adjacent to node at front of queue (A) and not already full explored to queue (B).	A B
Remove A from queue as fully explored.	B
Add all nodes that are adjacent to B and not already fully explored to queue (C, E).	B C E
Remove B from queue as fully explored.	C E
Add all nodes that are adjacent to C and not already fully explored to queue (D).	C E D
Remove C from queue as fully explored.	E D
Add all nodes that are adjacent to E and not already fully explored to queue (none).	E D
Remove E from queue as fully explored.	D
Add all nodes that are adjacent to D and not already fully explored to queue (none).	D
Remove D from queue as fully explored. Queue empty so algorithm terminates.	

> **Breadth first**: a method for traversing a graph that explores nodes closest to the starting node first before progressively exploring nodes that are further away.
>
> **Queue**: a data structure where the first item added is the first item removed.
>
> **Node**: an element of a graph or tree.

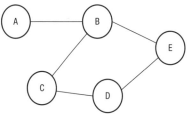

Figure 12.2 Graph for breadth first traversal

Traversing a binary tree

The process of traversing a **binary tree** extracts all the data from the tree in some sort of order. There are three ways of traversing a binary tree – **pre-order**, **in-order** and **post-order**.

To traverse a binary tree you start at the root node and move left, right or visit depending on the type of **traversal** you are using. Moving left or right entails 'looking' to see if there is a node in that direction and moving if there is. **Visit** entails extracting the data at that node.

Traversing the binary tree in Figure 12.2 gives the following results:

Table 12.4 Binary tree traversals

Pre-order	Visit, Left, Right	John, Helen, Kim
In-order	Left, Visit, Right	Helen, John, Kim
Post-order	Left, Right, Visit	Helen, Kim, John

Note that pre/in/post tells you when you do the visit stage.

An interesting feature of all this is that no matter how you set out the four nodes, an in-order traversal will always produce a sorted list, but pre-order and post-order produce a different set of data if the data are rearranged. Typical uses of each traversal are:

- Pre-order: This can be used with expression trees to evaluate the expression using prefix notation. Evaluating an expression simply means that values are to be placed into the expression to produce a result. Prefix means that the operators in the expression are evaluated before the values.
- In-order: This is the equivalent of a **binary search** of the tree, which is explained in more detail in Chapter 14.
- Post-order: This will produce Reverse Polish Notation (RPN) and this is covered in detail in Chapter 15. A post-order algorithm can also be used to empty the contents of a tree.

Binary tree: a structure where each node can only have up to two child nodes attached to it.

Pre-order: a method of traversing a tree by visiting the root, traversing the left subtree and traversing the right subtree.

In-order: a method of traversing a tree by traversing the left subtree, visiting the root and traversing the right subtree.

Post-order: a method of traversing a tree by traversing the left subtree, traversing the right subtree and then visiting the root.

Traversal: the process of reading data from a tree or graph by visiting all of the nodes.

Binary search: a technique for searching data that works by splitting datasets in half repeatedly until the search data is found.

Recursion

> **Exam tip**
>
> Recursion is simple to define but can be difficult to follow. It is worth spending time practising tracing recursive algorithms.

Recursion is the process of calling a function from within itself. The algorithm described below traverses a binary tree using recursion. Each time a call is made the current state of the procedure must be stored on the stack.

Recursion: a technique where a function can call itself in order to complete a task.

```
Define Procedure Traverse
   If there is a node to the left Then
      Go Left
      Traverse
   End If
   Visit
   If there is a node to the Right Then
      Go Right
      Traverse
   End If
End Procedure
```

After the procedure **Traverse** has been called for the first time the program will check to see if there is a node to the left. If there is, it goes left then calls the procedure **Traverse.** This means that **Traverse** has been called from inside the procedure **Traverse**, and if the next node also has a node to its left then **Traverse** will be called from inside itself again.

Recursion has a base case and general cases. The base case is also known as the terminating case and defines the point at which the recursive function will stop calling itself. In the example above, the terminating case is when there are no more nodes left to visit in the tree. The general cases are all of the inputs which require the function to call itself. In the example above, **Traverse** will continue to call itself if there is a node on either the right or the left of the current node.

Summary

- Graphs can be represented using an adjacency list or matrix.
- Traversal is the process of visiting the vertices (nodes) in different orders to generate different results.
- Graphs can be traversed depth first or breadth first.
- Breadth first traversal finds the shortest path between vertices on unweighted graphs.
- Binary trees can be traversed in-order, post-order or pre-order, to create different outputs.
- Post-order traversal of a binary tree can be used to create Reverse Polish Notation.
- Recursion is where a function calls itself.

Now test yourself

TESTED ☐

1 Starting at note F, write out the nodes of this tree, traversing it depth first. [3]
2 Starting at note F, write out the nodes of this tree, traversing it breadth first. [3]

13 Dijkstra's shortest path algorithm

Specification coverage

3.3.6 Optimisation algorithms

Dijkstra's algorithm

Dijkstra's shortest path algorithm calculates the shortest distance between two vertices (nodes) on a graph data type. The algorithm can be used to find the shortest path from one node to all other nodes in a graph.

Graphs are made up of vertices (or nodes) and edges, which are the connections between them. Some vertices are not connected and therefore have no path between them. It is also possible to have weighted graphs, where there is a value attached to each edge.

Dijkstra's algorithm works by working out the shortest path between a **single source** (the starting vertex) and every other vertex. As a result it also produces the shortest path between the starting vertex and a destination vertex. It only works on weighted graphs with positive values on the edges.

Single source: in Dijkstra's algorithm it means that the shortest path is calculated from a single starting point.

Common applications that will require a shortest path algorithm include:
- geographic information systems (GIS)
- telephone and computer network planning
- network routing/packet switching
- logistics and scheduling.

Tracing Dijkstra's algorithm

Exam tip

For more visual learners, a YouTube video may help you follow the progression through the algorithm. Search YouTube for 'Dijkstra's algorithm'.

The algorithm works as follows using Figure 13.1 as an example and assumes that we are looking for the **shortest path** between vertex A and G rather than the shortest path from A to every node.

Shortest path: the shortest distance between two vertices based on the weighting of the edges.

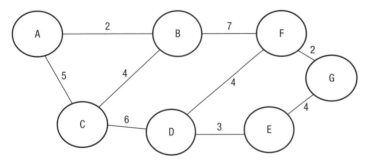

Figure 13.1 A map for tracing Dijkstra's algorithm

1 Start from the first vertex (in this case A).

2 Work out the weight (also known as the cost) for each edge between that vertex and other connected vertices, e.g. A to B is 2 and A to C is 5.

3 Move on to the next nearest vertex and repeat the process. In this case it would be B. This time you need to add the two weights together to get a total weight between two points. For example:
   ○ A to B to C would be 6.
   ○ A to B to F would be 9.

4 We now have two options for getting from A to C:
   ○ We could go from A to C direct with a weight of 5.
   ○ We could go from A to B to C with a weight of 6.

5 As we are finding the shortest path, we now know that the quickest route from A to C is to go direct from A to C. We need to retain this information and ignore other routes that are longer.

6 Now repeat the process until all vertices have been visited and you get to the destination vertex, which in this case is G.

The calculations become a little more complicated as you need to keep an accumulated total of the weights between all sets of connected vertices, and then choose the shortest one. Table 13.1 traces each stage of the algorithm and we will work through the table a step at a time.

Table 13.1 Table to trace Dijkstra's algorithm

Step	Vertex	A	B	C	D	E	F	G
1	A	0_A	2_A	5_A	∞_A	∞_A	∞_A	∞_A
2	B	0_A	2_A	5_A	∞_B	∞_B	9_B	∞_B
3	C	0_A	2_A	5_A	11_C	∞_C	9_B	∞_C
4	F	0_A	2_A	5_A	11_C	∞_F	9_B	11_F
5		0_A	2_A	5_A	11_C	∞_F	9_B	11_F

Step 1
● Place A in the first column and complete the distance between it and the other vertices.
● Notice that A to A is shown as 0. A to B is 2, A to C is 5. These are all shown with the subscript A to show clearly which vertex is being used. This becomes important later on.
● Notice that where there is no edge, the value is shown as infinite.
● We have now finished with the vertex A as there are no other edges.

Step 2
● Now move on to the next nearest vertex to A, which is B as it has the lowest value in the row above. Notice that the same value is placed in the table for B as in the row above. This is because we already know that this is the shortest path from A to B. In this case it is 2.
● The subscript A shows us clearly that the shortest path came from vertex A.
● The next path is B to C. This would be 4. However, we need to add on the 2, which is the shortest path that it took to get from A to B in the first place. This would give us a result of 6. However, this is higher than the path we already have between A and C, so we do not include it. Instead we keep the 5 from the row above. In other words, going from A to C direct is a shorter path than going from A to B to C.
● As you move through the rows you always keep the lowest value from the row above as this is the shortest path to that point.

Step 3
- Now move on to the next nearest vertex to B, which is C.
- Notice we can complete the table for the vertices that we have already visited and finished with in red. This makes it clear that the vertices have been dealt with and that we do not need to calculate them again.
- The next edge is between C and D. It has a weight of 6, but we have to add the shortest weight that it took to get to C in the first place, which you can see from the row above is 5. Therefore we put 11 in the table for the distance from C to D with a subscript C to show which vertex we came from.
- C is not connected to any other vertex that has not already been explored, so a standard way of showing this is to put the infinity sign in the table against the other vertices.
- Notice that we had a connection between A and F (via B) of only 9, so this stays in the column. This is because A to B to F is shorter than A to C to D to F.

Step 4
- Now move on to the next nearest vertex, which is F (with a weight of 9).
- Complete the table in red up to that point as before to show that we have finished with those vertices.
- Notice that we have been able to skip D and E as we already know that these will not produce the shortest path as the distance to D is equal to the shortest distance found to G so far. The algorithm will however have to calculate these distances first before it can carry out the next step.
- F connects to G in 2, but you have to add on the shortest path to this point, which is 9 making a total of 11.

Step 5
- There are no more edges to be compared so this final step simply lists the final values.
- Reading off the last row of the table you can see that the shortest path between A and G is 11 and looking at the subscript letters you can see that the route is A, B, F, G.

You can check this by looking at alternative routes and working out the total weight. The two other possible paths in this example are:
- A, C, D, E, G with a total weight of 18
- A, C, B, F, G with a total weight of 18.

Summary

- Dijkstra's shortest path algorithm calculates the shortest distance between two vertices (nodes) on a graph data type.
- Graphs are made up of vertices (or nodes) and edges, which are the connections between them.
- Dijkstra's shortest path algorithm only works on weighted graphs with positive values on the edges.
- Dijkstra's shortest path algorithm can be implemented using the values of a two-dimensional array.

Now test yourself

TESTED

1 State the purpose of Dijkstra's algorithm. [1]
2 State two requirements for Dijkstra's algorithm to be applicable. [2]
3 Trace Dijkstra's algorithm for the graph on the right. [5]

14 Search algorithms – binary, binary tree and linear search

Specification coverage

3.3.4 Searching algorithms

Search basics

REVISED ☐

Most searches are carried out on data storage systems, but they are used in other applications as well; for example, in the find and replace process on a word processor. A simple search might just look for one keyword, but most search routines allow you to construct more complex queries using logic statements such as OR, AND and NOT.

There are a number of different searching algorithms that can be used. Which one you choose depends to a large extent on the data being searched in terms of its size and complexity. The efficiency of algorithms is usually represented using Big O notation and there is more on this in Chapter 22.

Linear search

REVISED ☐

A **linear search** works by looking at every item or set of data until the details that you are searching for are found or you fail to find it altogether. The efficiency of a search can be strongly influenced by the way that the data is organised. If there is no logical or rational method in the way the data has been stored then the only option is to use a linear search. This is the simplest but also the least efficient method.

> **Linear search**: a simple search technique that looks through data one item at a time until the search term is found.

The efficiency of the search also depends on the size of the dataset being searched and where the search item is within it. The best-case scenario is that it is near the beginning in which case it could find the result quickly. However, in the worst-case scenario the search item may be near the end of the dataset in which case it could take a long time. The speed of the algorithm therefore is proportionate to the size of the dataset.

> **Exam tip**
>
> When looking at efficiency, we always consider the worst-case scenario.

Binary search

REVISED ☐

> **Exam tip**
>
> You can cultivate your knowledge of searching by developing computer programs to search through a list. By recording the time before and after the search, you can see how much of a difference it makes.

If the data you want to look through is in some sort of logical order then you might be able to use a technique called a **binary search**. This method works in the same way as the children's game where someone thinks of a number between say 1 and 100 and you have to guess what it is by being told if your guesses are higher or lower than the number.

> **Binary search**: a technique for searching data that works by splitting datasets in half repeatedly until the search item is found.

A logical person would start with 50, because they could then discount half of the numbers straight away. Guessing half way into the middle of the remaining numbers (either 25 or 75) will allow half of the remaining numbers to be discarded and so on. Each time you make a guess you halve the number of options that are left to you, and you alter the range within which the answer must be.

These 15 cells contain 15 numbers arranged in ascending order:

1	2	3	4	5	6	7	8	9	10	11	12	13	14	15

Figure 14.1

Use this method to find the number 51 which is contained in one of these cells. Start in the middle – block 8.

1	2	3	4	5	6	7	8	9	10	11	12	13	14	15
x	x	x	x	x	x	x	37							

Figure 14.2

Block 8 contains the number 37, so blocks 1 to 8 can now be discarded. Half way between 9 and 15 is 12 so look there next.

1	2	3	4	5	6	7	8	9	10	11	12	13	14	15
x	x	x	x	x	x	x	37				57	x	x	x

Figure 14.3

Block 12 contains the number 57 so blocks 12 to 15 can be discarded. Half way between blocks 9 and 11 is block 10 so look there.

1	2	3	4	5	6	7	8	9	10	11	12	13	14	15
x	x	x	x	x	x	x	37		51		57	x	x	x

Figure 14.4

Block 10 contains the number we are looking for. This has taken three 'looks' to find the missing number.

At first this seems like a very slow system, but in fact it is very efficient. If you want to search through just three records it will take a maximum of two 'looks' before you find a match and with seven records you will need three 'looks' and so on. If you have one million records you would need to take a maximum of just 20 'looks', and it would take a maximum of 33 looks to find one person in the world which currently has a population of over six billion.

Binary tree search

Binary trees are often used in programs where data is very dynamic, which means that data is constantly entering and leaving the tree. Where a binary tree has been used the process of searching it is similar to the binary search method described above except that rather than looking through a list of data items, it must traverse the tree and look at the data item stored at each node. A binary tree search is similar to the in-order tree traversal that we looked at in Chapter 12.

Summary

- There are three main search algorithms: binary, binary tree and linear.
- A linear search starts at the beginning of the data and goes through each item until it finds the search item.
- A binary search works by splitting the data in half each time until it finds the search item.
- A binary tree search traverses a binary tree until it finds the search item.
- The selection of an appropriate search method depends on how much data is being searched and how it is organised.
- Different search algorithms have different time complexities, meaning that some will be more efficient than others.

Now test yourself

TESTED

1 Describe the process of a linear search, identifying when it would be faster than a binary search and give an example of what type of data it may be applicable for. [3]
2 Describe the process of a binary search, identifying when it would be faster than a linear search and give an example of what type of data it may be applicable for. [3]
3 You have 873 records.
   (a) What is the maximum number of searches you would have to do if it is an unordered list and you use a linear search? [1]
   (b) What is the maximum number of searches you would have to do if the list is sorted and you use a binary search? [1]

15 Reverse Polish Notation

Specification coverage

3.3.3 Reverse Polish

Reverse Polish Notation (RPN)

REVISED

Reverse Polish Notation (RPN) is a way of writing mathematical expressions in a format where the operators are written after the operands. For example, the expression: 5 + 3 becomes 5 3 +. The main advantages of this method are that it eliminates the need for brackets and it puts the expression in a sequence that is more convenient for an interpreter. To get a fuller understanding of RPN you need to know how mathematical expressions are constructed and the sequence in which they are evaluated.

> **Reverse Polish Notation (RPN)**: another term for postfix notation.

Evaluating expressions

REVISED

To start with a simple example, if we have the expression 5 + 3, we know to add the 3 to the 5 to create the result. This is known as an **infix** expression because the **operator** (+) is between the operands (5 and 3).

This gets slightly more complicated where the expression is longer. For example, 3 * 2 + 5 is another infix expression, which we would evaluate by multiplying 3 and 2 and then adding 5 to the result to get 11. We evaluate it in this way according to certain rules, which tell us which part of the expression to evaluate first.

> **Infix**: expressions that are written with the operators within the operands, e.g. 2 + 3.
>
> **Operator**: the mathematical process within an expression.

> **Exam tip**
>
> Exam questions rarely run into double digits, but if they do a significant space will be left between numbers.

Brackets (or parentheses) are often used in expressions to make these rules clearer. For example, (3 * 2) + 5 makes the sequence we must use much clearer. These rules are sometimes referred to as **BODMAS**, which stands for Brackets, Order, Division, Multiplication, Addition, Subtraction. This means:

> **BODMAS**: a methodology for evaluating mathematical expressions in a particular sequence.

- Evaluate the expression inside the brackets first.
- Then evaluate any orders, which are calculations like squares or square roots.
- Carry out any division or multiplication. If both appear in the expression then they have equal importance so you work from left to right.
- Then carry out any addition or subtraction. Again, if both operators appear in an expression they have equal importance so work left to right.

If we had the infix expression: $3 + (18 / 3^2 * 3) - 4$ and evaluated it using these rules we would:

- Evaluate the expression in the brackets first:
  - Square the 3 to get 9.
  - Work out 18 / 9 to get 2.
  - Multiply 2 * 3 to get 6.
- Now we carry out the addition 3 + 6 to get 9.
- Then subtract the 4 to get an answer of 5.

Polish and Reverse Polish Notation

REVISED

Polish Notation is a way of simplifying mathematical expressions, eliminating the need for brackets completely, while still producing expressions without any ambiguity as to how they should be processed. It is a convenient format for an **interpreter** as it evaluates lines of programming code.

When code is written using a programming language, it has to be converted from that language into machine code (0s and 1s) so that it can be processed. The interpreter is a piece of software that carries out this task by parsing each line of code. This means that it analyses each line of code to check that it adheres to the rules of the language, known as the syntax. When parsing expressions, the interpreter analyses the **operands** first and then the operators. Therefore, it needs the operators to be on the right-hand side of the expression.

- Polish Notation (also known as prefix) is a method of rearranging an expression so that all of the operators are on the left and the operands are on the right. For example: 7 + 3 becomes + 7 3.
- Reverse Polish Notation rearranges an expression so that all the operators are on the right-hand side of the operands. So 7 + 3 becomes 7 3 +.

Polish Notation: another way of describing prefix notation.

Interpreter: software that translates and executes programs line by line by either converting programming statements into machine code or by calling instructions to carry out the high-level language statements.

Operand: a value within an expression.

Exam tip

Only Reverse Polish Notation is covered in the exam.

Converting expressions

REVISED

Notice that if you do change an infix notation to either **prefix** or **postfix**, you do not change the order of the operands within the expression. In the example above, the operands must appear in the order 7 followed by 3.

Where there are brackets in an expression, the same rule applies to RPN; you evaluate the expression in the brackets first. For example, the infix expression (5 + 4) / (4 − 1) would have an RPN of 5 4 + 4 1 − /.

- Notice how this is made up of two parts. The 5 + 4 is evaluated first and the RPN is created for this part of the expression: 5 4 +.
- The second part of the expression: / (4 − 1) is then evaluated and becomes 4 1 − /. Notice that the 4 − 1 is evaluated first as this is in brackets and the final operator is the divide, which will then divide the contents of the two bracketed expressions.
- Therefore, 5 + 4 = 9, 4 − 1 = 3 and 9 / 3 = 3.

Prefix: expressions that are written with the operators before the operands, e.g. + 2 3

Postfix: expressions that are written with the operators after the operands, e.g. 2 3 +

Evaluating RPN expressions

REVISED

The most common method for evaluating postfix notation is to use a stack. Consider the infix expression (2 * 3) + 5. The postfix notation would be 2 3 * 5 +. To evaluate this using a stack:

1 Push 2 onto the stack.
2 Push 3 onto the stack.
3 Push * onto the stack.

Exam tip

Don't get so caught up in the complexities of RPN that you miss the simple things. 2 + 3 still equals 5.

4 As * is an operator (multiply) we need to pop this and all of the operands currently in the stack (2 and 3) and evaluate the expression 2 3 *

5 Push the answer (6) back onto the stack.

6 Push 5 onto the stack.

7 Push + onto the stack.

8 As + is an operator (plus) we need to pop 6 5 + and evaluate the expression.

9 Push the result (11) onto the stack.

The stack could be visualised during the process as shown in Figure 15.1.

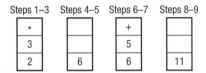

Steps 1–3   Steps 4–5   Steps 6–7   Steps 8–9

*		+	
3		5	
2	6	6	11

Figure 15.1 Representation of a stack implementing RPN

You may have noticed a similarity between the terminology used in this chapter and the terminology used to traverse a binary tree. In fact there is a direct relationship between the two:

- **In-order traversal** of a binary tree for an expression would produce an expression in infix format.
- **Post-order traversal** would produce an expression in postfix format or Reverse Polish Notation (RPN).
- **Pre-order traversal** would produce an expression in prefix format or Polish Notation.

> **In-order traversal**: a method of extracting data from a binary tree that will result in infix expressions.
>
> **Post-order traversal**: a method of extracting data from a binary tree that will result in postfix expressions.
>
> **Pre-order traversal**: a method of extracting data from a binary tree that will result in prefix expressions.

Summary

- Reverse Polish Notation (RPN) is a way of writing mathematical expressions in a format where the operators are written after the operands.
- RPN is useful as it puts expressions in a format that can be used more straightforwardly by an interpreter.
- Infix refers to expressions that are in the order that humans work with, e.g. 5 + 3.
- Postfix refers to expressions that are in RPN, e.g. 5 3 +.
- Prefix refers to expressions where the operators are first, e.g. + 5 3.
- RPN can be evaluated using a stack.

Now test yourself

TESTED ☐

1 Convert the following RPN expressions to infix.
   (a) 3 4 /   [1]
   (b) 7 2 +   [1]
   (c) 3 5 2 + *   [2]
   (d) 3 4 + 9 *   [2]
2 Convert the following infix expressions to RPN.
   (a) 4 + 2   [1]
   (b) 9 / 4   [1]
   (c) (4 + 3) * 2   [2]
   (d) (7 + 5) / (2 + 1)   [2]
3 Copy the following diagram and demonstrate how an RPN interpreter would use a stack to work out the following RPN expression: 4 2 + 1 / 2 *   [3]

16 Sorting algorithms – bubble and merge

Specification coverage

3.3.5 Sorting algorithms

Bubble sort

If the data are held in an array you can sort the data by comparing each element in the array with the following element. If the first item is bigger than the second then you swap them. If you repeat this process enough times the data will eventually be sorted in ascending order.

Element	1	2	3	4	5	6	7	8
Data	12	3	16	9	11	1	6	8

1	2	3	4	5	6	7	8
3	12	16	9	11	1	6	8

1	2	3	4	5	6	7	8
3	12	9	11	1	6	8	16

1	2	3	4	5	6	7	8
1	3	6	8	9	11	12	16

Figure 16.1

This algorithm is called a **bubble sort** because each time the algorithm carries out one pass of the array, the larger numbers are bubbling to one end of the array and the smaller ones to the opposite end.

> **Bubble sort**: a technique for putting data in order by repeatedly stepping through an array, comparing adjacent elements and swapping them if necessary until the array is in order.

Merge sort

Exam tip

Visual learners may find it easier to watch a video to aid in understanding the merge sort – while confusing at first, carrying out a practical test can embed knowledge. Search YouTube for 'merge sort'.

A **merge sort** is classified as a 'divide and conquer' algorithm, which breaks a problem down into smaller and smaller units until it gets to a level where the problem can be solved. What this means in the case of the sort routine is that if you had a list with one element it is, by definition, sorted. Therefore, if you start with a large list of elements, all you need to do is break the list down into a series of smaller lists each containing one single element. You can then compare the lists and merge them back together to produce a sorted list.

> **Merge sort**: a technique for putting data in order by splitting lists into single elements and then merging them back together again.

The merge process works as follows. Assume you have two lists that are already sorted in order:

List 1	List 2
3	2
5	6
8	9
10	12

- Compare the first element of each list. In this case 3 would be compared to 2. Put the lowest number in the new merge list. In this case we move the 2. Our lists would now look like this:

List 1	List 2
3	2
5	6
8	9
10	12
Merge list = 2	

- Repeat the process, comparing the first element in each list and placing the lowest item in the merge list. We now have 3 compared to 6, so our lists will now look like this:

List 1	List 2
3	2
5	6
8	9
10	12
Merge list = 2, 3	

- Repeat this process until there is only one element left and put this at the end of the list. You now have one list containing the sorted elements.

To sort an unordered list, you first need to break the list down. For example, if we have a list with eight elements as shown:

5	3	8	10	9	2	6	12

- Split the list in half.

5	3	8	10

9	2	6	12

- Keep splitting the list in half until each list only has one element:

5	3

8	10

9	2

6	12

| 5 | | 3 | | 8 | | 10 | | 9 | | 2 | | 6 | | 12 |

You now effectively have eight lists, all containing one element. We need to merge a pair of lists at a time until we have one complete list.

- Compare the first two lists, which are 5 and 3 and put the lowest number first. We get:

3	5

- Compare the next two lists, which are 8 and 10 and put the lowest number first. We get:

8	10

- Do this for the next two pairs of lists:

2	9

6	12

We now have four lists:

3	5

8	10

2	9

6	12

- Repeat the process merging these lists together. Start by comparing the first element in each list and putting the lowest first as shown earlier.
  For the first pair of lists:
  - Comparing 3 and 8, we would put 3 in the merge list.
  - Comparing 5 and 8, we would put 5 in the merge list.

- We then merge the 8 and the 10, which we know are already in the right order to get:

| 3 | 5 | 8 | 10 |

- Repeat this process for the other two lists and you get:

| 2 | 6 | 9 | 12 |

- Now merge these two lists together in the same way to get:

| 2 | 3 | 5 | 6 | 8 | 9 | 10 | 12 |

This is an efficient method of sorting where there are lots of elements in the original list. This is because the algorithm works by halving the lists each time. However, in terms of space, the merge sort will require more space than a bubble sort to create the intermediary lists and the final merge list.

As you have probably worked out, you can use a loop to split down the elements as many times as required to create single-element lists. Each pair of lists can then be compared and merged as many times as needed to reconstruct the list in the correct order.

Summary

- Sorting means that the data is put into a particular order, typically alphabetical or numerical in either ascending or descending order.
- There are different algorithms that can be used to sort data.
- If the data is held in an array, you can sort the data by comparing each element in the array with the data in the following element.
- A merge sort is classified as a 'divide and conquer' algorithm, which breaks a problem down into smaller and smaller units until it gets to a level where the problem can be solved.

Now test yourself

TESTED ☐

1 Create an algorithm in pseudo-code or a flowchart to implement a bubble sort. [3]
2 The following numbers are disorganised:
4, 6, 2, 9, 3, 8, 1, 7
(a) Write out the way the list changes as it is run through a bubble sort algorithm. [3]
(b) Write out the ways in which the list is split and remerged as it is run through a merge sort. [4]

17 Abstraction and automation

Specification coverage

3.4.1 Abstraction and automation

Abstraction and automation

REVISED

There are techniques that programmers can use to help with **problem solving** and in this chapter we will be looking at:

- **abstraction**, which is the concept of picking out common concepts in order to reduce the problem to its essential defining features, ignoring less significant details
- **automation**, which is the process of creating a computer model and putting it into action.

The focus of this chapter is on problems that typically require mathematical calculations to solve them, as opposed to information processing systems.

> **Problem solving**: the process of finding a solution to real-life problems.
>
> **Automation**: creating a computer model of a real-life situation and putting it into action.

Logical reasoning

REVISED

Logical reasoning is the process of using a given set of facts to determine whether new facts are true or false. More formally it is concerned with the concept of deductive reasoning, which originates from the study of mathematics and philosophy, and which identifies rules or premises and then applies these to statements to come to a conclusion.

> **Logical reasoning**: the process of using a given set of facts to determine whether new facts are true or false.

Exam tip

Using a pencil and paper to jot down what is known, what is needed, and what you can do to get them can be a great aid to logical reasoning.

Logical reasoning helps you to understand the nature of problems, to identify the facts that are relevant to the problem and to then be able to draw conclusions. It also enables you to identify new facts that you can deduce are true based on existing facts.

Problem solving

REVISED

Problem solving concerns identifying a problem and then working out the steps required to solve it. In doing this, you need to take account of any constraints that would impact on the solution. The objective is always to create the most efficient solution to any given problem and to be able to apply the solution to other, similar problems.

Developing the most efficient solution to a problem may require several iterations. One of the key aspects of computing is that solutions must be checked to ensure that they do solve the problem. Extensive testing of solutions will be undertaken in-house. Solutions will also be beta-tested by getting users to use the systems in real-life situations before releasing the technology to the general public. Feedback from customers is also used continuously in order to refine the technology.

Algorithms

An algorithm is a step-by-step procedure for carrying out a particular task. **Algorithms** are the building blocks of computer programs and ultimately all problems are solved by writing algorithms.

The start point for programmers is often to work out what algorithms are needed to solve a problem and then to write these in pseudo-code during the planning stage. This can be a time-consuming process, depending on the complexity of the solution.

Programmers use a technique called hand-tracing or dry running to work through their code. This means that they follow the code line by line to work out what is happening. This can help them to identify any problems with the code before it is implemented. Most programs are made up of multiple related procedures so it is important to identify how these link together to create the program as a whole.

When all of the procedures have been identified, the pseudo-code can be converted into proper programming code using whatever language is considered the most appropriate for solving the problem.

> **Algorithm**: a sequence of instructions to achieve a specific outcome in a finite time (independent of any programming language).

> **Exam tip**
>
> Most mistakes in trace tables and dry-running occur from trying to guess ahead – slow and steady following perfect logic and they cannot go wrong.

Abstraction

The concept of abstraction is to reduce problems to their essential features. Another way of explaining abstraction is that it is the process of finding similarities or common aspects about the problem, while ignoring differences. This is a useful concept for programmers as they can view the problem from a high level, concentrating on the key aspects of designing a solution while ignoring the detail, particularly during the initial design stages.

Once a solution has been identified for the current problem, a feature of abstraction is that the abstraction from one problem can be applied to another similar problem which shares the same common features. Broadly speaking there are two main types of abstraction: representational abstraction and abstraction by generalisation/categorisation.

> **Exam tip**
>
> Abstraction can be applied to many problems even outside Computer Science – including difficult to comprehend exam questions.

Representational abstraction

This is the process of removing unnecessary details until it is possible to represent the problem in a way that can be solved. This level of abstraction could be described as viewing the 'big picture' – working out what is relevant to solving the problem and what is unnecessary detail that can be ignored.

Abstraction by generalisation/categorisation

This is the process of placing aspects of the problem into broader categories to arrive at a hierarchical representation. This involves recognising common characteristics of representations so that more general representations can be developed. This is the same concept that is applied with object-oriented programming in Chapter 6, where subclasses are defined from the characteristics of a base class.

> **Representational abstraction**: the process of removing unnecessary details so that only information that is required to solve the problem remains.

> **Abstraction by generalisation/ categorisation**: the concept of reducing problems by putting similar aspects of a problem into hierarchical categories.

The principle of abstraction can also be applied to various elements of computing including:

- Procedural abstraction: This is the concept that all solutions can be broken down into a series of procedures or subroutines. This is the basis for **top-down design**. Other considerations include what event will trigger the procedure, how procedures will link together, including any possible side effects, and how errors will be handled.
- Functional abstraction: Similar to procedural abstraction, **functional abstraction** focuses on common functions that can be used to solve problems. Functions are a feature of procedural languages and the cornerstone of **functional programming**, where all the main processes are defined in terms of functions.
- Data abstraction: This is the process of organising and structuring data in a way that produces a particular view of the data that is useful for the programmer. Almost all data is abstracted, hence the term abstract data types. Another feature of **data abstraction** is that the data can be implemented in different ways. For example, once data is abstracted into an array, it could be used to create other abstract data types such as a stack or a binary tree. This is known as data composition where data objects are combined in order to create a compound structure.
- **Problem abstraction**: This is the process of reducing a problem down to its simplest components until the underlying processing requirements that solve the problem are identified. By doing this, these underlying processes can be applied to solve analogous problems. Therefore, the underlying principles used to solve one problem are applied to different problems with similar characteristics.

> **Top-down design**: related to the modular approach, this starts with the main system at the top and breaks it down into smaller and smaller units, a bit like a family tree.
>
> **Functional abstraction**: breaking down a complex problem into a series of reusable functions.
>
> **Functional programming**: a programming paradigm that uses functions to create programs.
>
> **Data abstraction**: hiding how data is represented so that it is easier to build a new kind of data object, e.g. building a stack from an array.
>
> **Problem abstraction**: removing unnecessary details in a problem until the underlying problem is identified to see if this is the same as a problem that has already been solved.

Information hiding

REVISED

In broad terms, **information hiding** is the process of providing a definition or interface of a system or object, while keeping the inner workings hidden. A common example of the principle is the car. All cars have a common interface in that they have a steering wheel, gearbox, pedals etc. By operating this common interface it is possible to operate the car. The actual mechanics of how the car works are hidden. An example in computing is where a common interface such as a graphical user interface (GUI) is used.

More specifically when programming, information hiding can be used to define a set of behaviours on a dataset, where the data can only be accessed through those behaviours. It is not possible for other parts of the program to access the dataset directly. This prevents unintended damage to the dataset and also means that how the dataset is stored can be changed without affecting any programs that use it, as they do not access it directly.

Information hiding is closely related to the concept of **encapsulation** where data and behaviours are stored together within a class or object. Encapsulation can be seen as a method of implementing the information-hiding principle.

> **Information hiding**: the process of hiding all details of an object that do not contribute to its essential characteristics.

Exam tip

You will practise information hiding when creating effective class diagrams.

Decomposition/Composition

> **Exam tip**
>
> Anything from writing a book to building a house can be decomposed. Try it next time you have to write an essay question.

A broad definition of **decomposition** is breaking large complex tasks or processes down into smaller, more manageable tasks. Abstraction techniques will be used in order to decompose the system requirements.

> **Decomposition**: breaking down a large task into a series of subtasks.

Procedural decomposition is the process of looking at a system as a whole and then breaking that down into procedures or subroutines needed to complete the task. Depending on the complexity of the system, subtasks may be further subdivided until the designer reaches a level of detail that is sufficient to start building the system.

Procedural **composition** is then the process of creating a working system from the abstraction. This involves:

- writing all the procedures and linking them together to create compound procedures
- creating data structures and combining them to form compound structures.

> **Composition**: building up a whole system from smaller units. The opposite of decomposition.

A satnav system could be decomposed as shown in Figure 17.1.

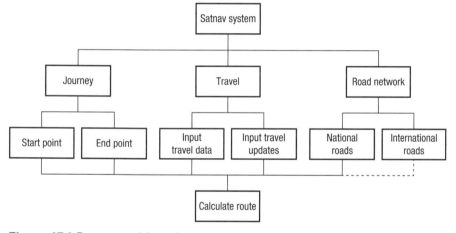

Figure 17.1 Decomposition of a satnav system

Automation

Automation in this context is the process of creating computer models of real-life situations and putting them into action. Most computer programs are created to solve real problems. One of the objectives of creating computer systems is to create elegant solutions to difficult problems. The key to this is:

- understanding the problem
- being able to create suitable algorithms
- building the algorithms up into program code
- using appropriate data in order to solve the problem.

> **Exam tip**
>
> Computer modelling is another word for automation.

Using automated models requires constant calibration of the model. This means that the designers need to see how well their modelled system works in real life. Changes either to their algorithm or to their data may be needed in order to make the model more accurate.

Summary

- Logical reasoning is the process of using a known set of facts to determine whether new facts are true or false.
- Problem solving is identifying a problem and then working out the steps required to solve it.
- Simple problems may have complex solutions.
- An algorithm is a step-by-step procedure for carrying out a particular task.
- Abstraction reduces unnecessary detail, instead focusing on the essential features that will solve the problem.

- Information hiding is the process of hiding all details of an object that do not contribute to its essential characteristics.
- Decomposition is breaking large complex tasks or processes down into smaller, more manageable tasks.
- Composition is then the process of creating a working system from the abstraction.
- Automation in this context is the process of creating computer models of real-life situations and putting them into action.

Now test yourself

TESTED ☐

1 Define abstraction. [2]
2 Define automation. [2]
3 Define decomposition. [2]
4 You have been asked to create a program to work out the area of a triangle. Decompose the problem. [4]

Now test yourself answers at www.therevisionbutton.co.uk/myrevisionnotes

18 Finite state machines

Specification coverage

3.4.2 Finite state machines

Introducing finite state machines

In general terms a **finite state machine (FSM)** is any device that can store its current status (or state) and can change state based on an input. The FSM may receive further inputs, which in turn change the state again. There are a **finite** (countable) number of transitions that may take place. Some FSMs also have outputs, one type of which is called a Mealy machine.

Finite state machines are common in everyday life and include any devices where there is a predefined set of steps and outcomes involved in the operation of the machine. In practice, finite state machines are used as a conceptual model to design and describe systems. They are particularly useful at the design stage as they force the designer to think about every possible input and how that changes the state of the machine. As a result they are commonly used to develop computer systems or design logic circuits and can also be used to check the syntax of programming languages.

There are two main ways of representing an FSM: a state transition diagram or a state transition table.

> **Finite state machine (FSM)**: any device that stores its current status and whose status can change as the result of an input. Mainly used as a conceptual model for designing and describing systems.
>
> **Finite**: countable.

State transition diagrams

State transition diagrams use circles to represent each state and arrows to represent the transitions that occur as the result of an input. For example, a ticket machine in a car park requires two inputs: money to be put in and the green button to be pressed. A double circle represents the accepting or goal state, which in this case is the state that is required in order to issue a ticket. FSMs do not necessarily need to have an **accepting state**.

> **Exam tip**
>
> While it may feel a bit childish, tracing a state transition with one finger as you move through the list of inputs can help follow the logical transitions.

Figure 18.1 A simple state transition diagram

In this case:
- S0 is the machine in its idle state, waiting for an input.
- S1 is its state after the money has been put in.
- S2 is its state after the button has been pressed. This is the accepting state.

The FSM has sequence and memory in that each transition is based on the one before. For example, the button can only be pressed after the money has been inserted. Whole systems or individual procedures can be modelled using state transition diagrams.

The example in Figure 18.2 shows an FSM that is used to check that the rules of a programming language are being followed. It is a simplified example using just the letters a, b and c, though in real life the FSM

> **State transition diagram**: a visual representation of an FSM using circles and arrows.
>
> **Accepting state**: the state that identifies whether an input has been accepted. Also known as the end or final state.

could be set up to represent all of the acceptable words and combinations of words usable in any particular programming language. Notice the addition of a start arrow.

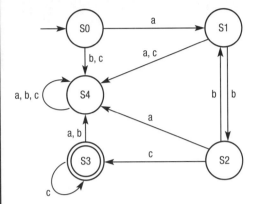

Figure 18.2 State transition diagram to show syntax rules

Looking at the diagram you can see whether certain combinations of letters are acceptable or not. For example:

- abc is an acceptable combination.
- abcc is an acceptable combination.
- acb is not acceptable. This would end in S4.
- abca is not acceptable as S3 is the accepting state so the final letter must be a 'c'. This would end in S4.

State transition tables

REVISED

The same information can also be represented as a table. These show the input and the current state, which is the state before the input. It then shows the state after the input. For example, a **state transition table** for an automated door could be:

Input	Current state	Next state
Button pressed	Door closed	Door open
Button pressed	Door open	Door closed

The table for processing the letters in Figure 18.2 would be:

Input	Current state	Next state
a	S0	S1
b	S1	S2
c	S1	S4
a	S1	S4
b	S2	S1
c	S2	S3
a	S2	S4
b	S0	S4
c	S0	S4
a	S3	S4
b	S3	S4
c	S3	S3
a	S4	S4
b	S4	S4
c	S4	S4

> **Exam tip**
>
> A table may take up more space than a diagram, but tables are easier to implement logically in software.

> **State transition table**: a tabular representation of an FSM showing inputs, current state and next state.

Some finite state machines will produce output values based on the input values. An example of this is a **Mealy machine**, named after the man who invented it. An example of an application of a Mealy machine could be a simple **cipher** where the letter input becomes transformed into another letter. Figure 18.3 shows a simple three-letter **shift cipher**, where A becomes D, B becomes E and so on.

> **Mealy machine:** a type of finite state machine with outputs.
>
> **Cipher:** an algorithm that encrypts and decrypts data, also known as code.
>
> **Shift cipher:** a simple substitution cipher where the letters are coded by moving a certain amount forwards or backwards in the alphabet.

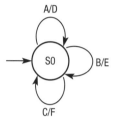

Figure 18.3 State transition diagram with outputs

This is a simple example that shows the concept of the Mealy machine where the current state is transformed to a new state with the output being shown. Mealy machines were originally devised to define electronic circuits and are commonly used to express bitwise operations.

For example, Figure 18.4 shows a right arithmetic shift on a binary value, which will have the effect of halving the value.

The state transition table for this would be:

Input	Current state	Output	Next state
0	S0	0	S2
1	S0	0	S1
0	S1	1	S2
1	S1	1	S1
0	S2	0	S2
1	S2	0	S1

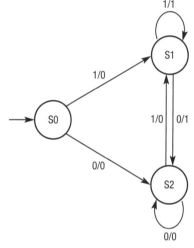

Figure 18.4 A Mealy machine performing a right shift

Summary

- A finite state machine (FSM) is a concept that shows a device that stores the current state and how the state will change as the result of an input.
- FSMs are used as a conceptual model for designing and describing computer systems.
- FSMs can be used to check the syntax of language including programming languages.
- State transition diagrams are a visual way of showing how states change as the result of an input.
- State transition tables are an alternative way of showing how states change as the result of an input.
- A special type of FSM called a Mealy machine can also produce outputs.

Now test yourself

1 The following FSM represents a saving machine that accepts £10, £20 and £50 notes. Once the total of £50 is entered the user is awarded a token.

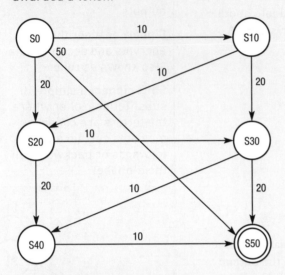

(a) What is the accepting state? [1]
(b) What are the inputs and corresponding new states from S0? [3]
(c) List three inputs that would result in the accepting state. [3]
(d) Write out a state transition table for the diagram. [4]

19 The Turing machine

Specification coverage

3.4.5 A model of computation

The Turing machine

REVISED

The **Turing machine** is a theoretical model developed by Alan Turing in 1936 as a way of trying to solve what was called 'the decision problem'. In simple terms, the problem was whether it was theoretically possible to solve any mathematical problem within a finite number of steps given particular inputs. Turing developed a theoretical machine that was able to carry out any algorithm and in doing so essentially produced a model of what is computable.

A Turing machine is a **finite state machine (FSM)** with the ability to read and write data to an unlimited tape. It can be visualised as shown in Figure 19.1.

> **Turing machine**: a theoretical model of computation.
>
> **Finite state machine (FSM)**: any device that stores its current status and whose status can change as the result of an input. Mainly used as a conceptual model for designing and describing systems.

> **Exam tip**
>
> Remember a Turing machine is a **theoretical** model.

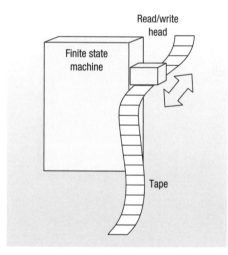

Figure 19.1 A Turing machine

The basics of its operation are:
- The tape is divided into an infinite number of cells. The tape is used as memory.
- Each cell will contain a symbol. This could be a character or number. Commonly the contents of the tape are binary digits, i.e. 0s and 1s, and the blank symbol, sometimes shown as a □. The acceptable symbols are known as the **alphabet**.
- The **read/write head** can either read what is in the cell or write into the cell. It can also erase the current contents of the cell, effectively overwriting the contents.
- The tape can move left or right one cell at a time so that every cell is accessible by the read/write head.
- The machine can halt at any point if it enters what is known as the **halting state**, or if the entire input has been processed.

> **Alphabet**: the acceptable symbols (characters, numbers) for a given Turing machine.
>
> **Read/write head**: the theoretical device that writes or reads from the current cell of a tape in a Turing machine.
>
> **Halting state**: stops the Turing machine.

Moving the tape through the read/write head will produce sequences of characters, which is analogous to a computer executing instructions in a program.

To represent programs in Turing machines you need:
- a **start state** – the state of the machine at the start of the program
- a halting state – the state that will stop the program running
- an alphabet – this is a list of the acceptable symbols that can go into each cell
- movement – the ability to move the head so that you can read/write to every cell
- a **transition function** – indicating what should be written at each cell and whether to move left or right based on the input read.

> **Start state**: the initial state of a Turing machine.
>
> **Transition function/rule**: a method of notating how a Turing machine moves from one state to another and how the data on the tape changes.

State transition diagrams

Controlling the machine is represented through state diagrams very similar to the **state transition diagrams** that we looked at for FSMs. You can visualise the tape as follows:

> **State transition diagram**: a visual representation of the transition function of a Turing machine.

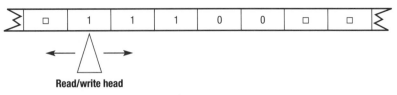

Read/write head

Figure 19.2 The tape and read/write head

At the moment the read/write head is either reading or writing a 1 in the current cell. In the examples used in this chapter the read/write head starts with the left-most non-blank location. Note that the symbols in the other cells are 0s, 1s or blanks. The arrows indicate that the head can move left or right.

Figure 19.3 shows a state transition diagram for the transition function of a Turing machine.

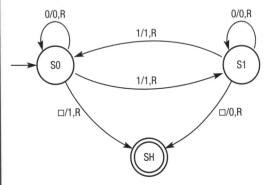

Figure 19.3 State diagram to show the operation of a Turing machine
- S0 represents the starting state.
- SH represents the halting state.
- This diagram has one other state, S1, although it would be possible to have as many states as required to represent an algorithm.
- Moving from one state to the next requires a transition function or transition rule. These are determined by the arrows in the transition diagrams. The rules are shown on the diagram in the format 1/1,R which means in this case that if the input symbol is a 1, keep the symbol on the tape as a 1 and then move the head right. Another example is □/0,R which means if the input symbol is blank, change it to a 0 and move the head right.
- Writing the transition rules effectively creates an algorithm.

Another way of notating the Turing machine is to show the transition rules in the following format:

δ (Current State, Input Symbol) = (Next State, Output Symbol, Movement)

The transition rules for the odd parity generator, for example, could be written with the following functions:

δ (S0, □) = (SH, 1, R)

δ (S0, 0) = (S0, 0, R)

δ (S0, 1) = (S1, 1, R)

δ (S1, □) = (SH, 0, R)

δ (S1, 0) = (S1, 0, R)

δ (S1, 1) = (S0, 1, R)

> **Exam tip**
>
> The δ is just a symbol. Focus on the contents of the rules – examiners are testing your comprehension, not your ability to draw.

Note the use of □ for a blank cell and the use of L and R for left and right. Other notation may be used; for example, it is common to use a B to represent a blank and left and right arrows (← →) to show movement.

Universal machine

REVISED

At a theoretical level you can use the Turing machine on any problem that is computable. The limitation of the Turing machine is that every process we need to carry out requires its own Turing machine to do it. For a large program, this could quickly become problematic. You could view this as a black box model where you define the inputs, the process carried out, and the output:

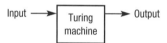

If we want to add A and B:

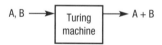

To multiply A and B:

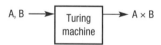

Every computation requires its own Turing machine and its own tape on which to work. However, it is inevitable that you will want to combine the results of several computations and this is why Turing developed the concept of a **universal machine**.

> **Universal machine**: a machine that can simulate a Turing machine by reading a description of the machine along with the input of its own tape.

Rather than defining each individual process within a single machine, the universal machines takes two inputs:

- a description of all the individual Turing machines required to perform the calculations
- all the inputs required for the calculations.

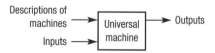

Figure 19.4 The universal machine

Perhaps the easiest way to think of it is as a series of individual Turing machines all linked together that can take any input and perform any calculation defined by any of the component machines.

This is stored on one tape (rather than lots of individual tapes) with one block of cells containing the instructions and one block of cells containing the inputs. The result of this is a machine that can simulate any number of Turing machines with their corresponding inputs and produce a range of outputs.

Summary

- The Turing machine is a theoretical machine that is able to carry out any algorithm and in doing so essentially produces a model of what is computable. It works with a tape of an infinite length split into cells.
- Each cell has a value in it, typically a 0, 1 or a blank, but could have any symbols.
- The read/write head can move in any direction along the entire length of the tape.
- The read/write head reads and writes values to the cells.
- A universal machine is a machine that can simulate any other Turing machine by processing a description of how the other Turing machine works, that is, its transition function, that is stored on the tape alongside the data that is to be processed.

Exam tip

The definitions of a Turing machine and Universal Turing Machine (UTM) have been asked for in previous exams!

Now test yourself

TESTED ☐

1 Differentiate between a Turing machine and a Universal Turing machine. [2]
2 What is the importance of a Turing machine to computation? [1]
3 A Turing machine's transition function δ is defined as:
$\delta(S1,0) = (S1,0,\rightarrow)$
$\delta(S1,1) = (S1,1,\rightarrow)$
$\delta(S1,\square) = (S2,0,\leftarrow)$
S1 is the start state and S2 is the accepting state. The read/write head is positioned under the left-most 1.
(a) Trace the computation of the Turing machine. [4]

| | | 1 | 1 | 0 | 1 | 0 | | | ... | Current State: | S1 |

↑

| | | | | | | | | | ... | Current State: | |

| | | | | | | | | | ... | Current State: | |

| | | | | | | | | | ... | Current State: | |

| | | | | | | | | | ... | Current State: | |

| | | | | | | | | | ... | Current State: | |

| | | | | | | | | | ... | Current State: | |

(b) Explain what the Turing machine does. [1]

20 Regular and context-free languages

Specification coverage

3.4.2.3 Regular expressions
3.4.2.4 Regular languages
3.4.2 Context-free languages

Regular expressions

To start with an example, the expression a|b|c is a **regular expression**, which means that the set will contain either an 'a' or a 'b' or a 'c'. A set is a collection of data that is unordered and contains each item at most once. It is written as follows, showing the name of the set and the contents within the brackets:

- alphabet = {a, b, c, d, e, f, g, ...}
- integers = {0, 1, 2, 3, 4, 5, 6, 7, 8, 9, ...}

The contents of a set are typically characters and numbers and a regular expression can be used to define and search the set. There are regular expressions for handling text strings and for handling numbers. There is also a relationship between regular expressions and finite state machines in that all regular expressions can be expressed as state transition diagrams for an FSM and vice versa, and there is more on this in this chapter.

A **regular language** is one that can be represented using regular expressions. Regular expressions contain strings of characters that can be matched to the contents of a set, allowing you to find patterns in data. They are a powerful tool for searching and handling strings. They also provide a shorthand definition of the contents of the set.

Common regular expressions are shown in Table 20.1.

> **Regular expression**: notation that contains strings of characters that can be matched to the contents of a set.

> **Regular language**: any language that can be described using regular expressions.

Table 20.1 Regular expressions with examples of outputs

Regular expression	Meaning	Strings produced
a|b|c	a or b or c	a
		b
		c
abc	a and b and c	abc
a*bc	Zero or more a followed by b and c	bc
		abc
		aabc
		aaabc
(a|b)c	a or b and c	ac
		bc

> **Exam tip**
>
> If you can't quite remember which symbol is which, it's worth having a try anyway; this is often a multi-mark question and even if you miss one mark you might get the rest.

Table 20.1 cont.

Regular expression	Meaning	Strings produced
a+bc	One or more a and b and c	abc
		aabc
		aaabc
ab?c	a and either zero or one b and c	ac
		abc

Consider the following examples:

- (a|b|c)d*e would produce the following possible strings: ade, ae, be, bde, ce and cde. There could in fact be an infinite number of the letter 'd' but it would have to end in an 'e'.
- (a⁺(b|c))d would produce abd or aabd or aaabd (and so on with the preceding 'a') or the 'b' could be replaced by a 'c' in each string.

Perhaps the easiest way to understand all the permutations is to produce a state transition diagram.

Figure 20.1 shows that 'a' can repeat any number of times and it must then be followed by 'b' and a 'c'. S2 represents the accepting state, so the last letter produced by this expression has to be a 'c'.

If you consider the expression a(bc)* it means that 'a' will be the first letter followed by any number of 'bc'. So 'a' would be one outcome as would abc or abcbc or abcbcbc. This could be represented as a state transition diagram as shown in Figure 20.2.

Here the string must start with an 'a' and end with a 'bc'. It is not possible for the outcome to be a 'c' on its own.

It is also possible to write the regular expression from the state transition diagram.

Consider the FSM in Figure 20.3; this diagram can only produce an 'a' or 'b' followed by a 'c', which would be written as (a|b)c.

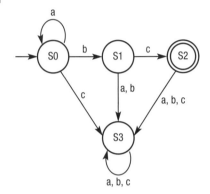

Figure 20.1 FSM to represent the regular expression a*bc

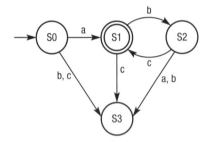

Figure 20.2 FSM to represent the regular expression a(bc)*

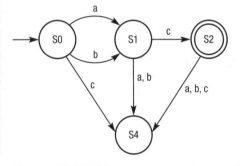

Figure 20.3 FSM to represent the regular expression (a|b)c

Searching strings

The power of regular expressions in this context is in using them to identify patterns in strings. Common uses include data validation, find and replace or searching for files with a particular file name. Most programming languages support the use of regular expressions and although the syntax and delimiters used may vary, the underlying principle remains the same. There is a standard set of expressions defined by POSIX.

Table 20.2 Standard expressions

Expression	Definition	Example
.	Effectively a wildcard and matches any character	.ole would match to mole, hole, vole etc.
[]	Matches to a single character within the brackets	[mh]ole would match to mole and hole but not vole.
[^]	Matches to any character except those in the brackets	[^ m]ole would match to hole and vole but not mole.
*	Matches the preceding characters zero or more times	m*ole would match ole, mole, mmole, mmmole, etc.
{m,n}	Matches the preceding character at least m but no more than n times	a{2,5} would match to aa, aaa, aaaa and aaaaa.

Exam tip

If you are asked to explain what an expression does and want to demonstrate an infinite number of results, include at least three and a comment that it carries on ad infinitum.

Context-free languages

A **context-free language** is a method of describing the syntax of a language used where the syntax is complex. The technique can be used to check that different components of the code are in the correct place.

Regular expressions map directly to state transition diagrams. However, there are situations where the grammar used within a language is too complex to be defined by regular expressions. The key problem with regular expressions is that they only work when matching or counting other symbols in a string where there is a finite limit.

Where the counting and matching is infinite, a context-free language is needed. Context-free languages can also support notation for recursion and are sometimes a clearer way of defining syntax even where regular expressions can be used.

Context-free language: an unambiguous way of describing the syntax of a language, useful where the syntax is complex.

Backus–Naur Form (BNF)

REVISED

The concept of context-free languages is that rules can be written that define the syntax of the language which are completely unambiguous and that can work beyond the current state. One method for doing this is to use Backus–Naur notation, known as **BNF (Backus–Naur Form)**.

In common with regular expressions, BNF produces a **set** of acceptable strings, which effectively describe the rules of the language. It uses a set of rules that define the language in the format:

```
<S> ::= <alternative1> | <alternative2> | <alternative3>
<alternative1> ::= <alternative2> | <alternative4>
<alternative4> ::= terminal
```

BNF works by replacing the symbol on the left with the symbols on the right until the string is defined. The idea is to keep going until you reach a **terminal**, which is a rule that cannot be broken down any further. In the example above:

- each symbol or element is enclosed within angle brackets <>
- the **::=** means 'is replaced with' and defines the rule for the symbol
- each symbol needs to be split down further until you reach a terminal.

To define integers, a BNF expression may look like this:

```
<integer> ::= <digit> | <digit> <integer>
<digit> ::= 0|1|2|3|4|5|6|7|8|9
```

This shows that an integer is defined as either a digit or a digit followed by another integer. A digit is defined as the numbers 0 to 9 and this is a terminal as there is no further rule needed to define digits. This expression would be recursive as integer is defined in terms of itself.

> **Backus–Naur Form (BNF):** a form of notation for describing the syntax used by a programming language.
>
> **Set:** a collection of symbols in any order that do not repeat.
>
> **Terminal:** in BNF, it is the final element that requires no further rules.

> **Exam tip**
>
> BNF has to use recursion as it has no way to loop or repeat. This is a common exam point.

Syntax diagrams

REVISED

Another way of representing BNF expressions or any kind of context-free language is a **syntax diagram**. These map directly to BNF and use the symbols shown in Figure 20.4.

> **Syntax diagram:** a method of visualising rules written in BNF or any other context-free language.

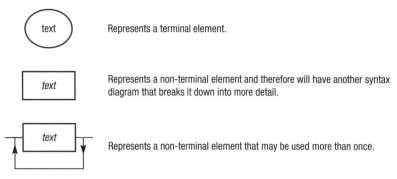

Represents a terminal element.

Represents a non-terminal element and therefore will have another syntax diagram that breaks it down into more detail.

Represents a non-terminal element that may be used more than once.

Figure 20.4 Syntax diagram symbols

Syntax diagrams are modular so there are likely to be many syntax diagrams required to represent a whole language. Each has an entry and exit point to identify the start and end of each particular part. For example, an integer would be represented as shown in Figure 20.5.

> **Exam tip**
>
> Like BNF, syntax diagrams are purely logical so as long as you follow the rules through without trying to 'guess ahead' you should arrive at the right answer.

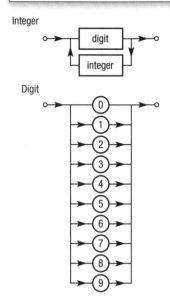

Figure 20.5 Syntax diagram to represent an integer

Figure 20.6 shows how you could break down customer details on a database into a series of syntax diagrams. This is just a partial diagram to demonstrate how to get to a terminal. In this case there are a series of non-terminal stages before you arrive at the terminal element, which are the actual characters that comprise a person's name.

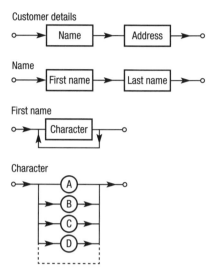

Figure 20.6 A syntax diagram for customer details

Summary

- Regular expressions are a method of defining and searching sets of data.
- Regular expressions can be used to handle text and numeric strings.
- A regular language is one that uses regular expressions.
- Context-free languages are methods that can be used to describe the syntax of programming languages.

- Backus–Naur Form (BNF) is a notation for describing the syntax of a programming language in an unambiguous way.
- Syntax diagrams are a method of visualising the syntax of a particular programming language.

Now test yourself

TESTED ☐

1 Describe the set of strings that would be matched by:
   (a) a*b [1]
   (b) c+d [1]
   (c) e?f [1]
2 Write a regular expression that matches 'a' followed by zero or one occurrences of 'bc' followed by zero or more 'e's. [2]
3 Use Backus–Naur Form (BNF) to define a two-part calculation consisting of two positive real numbers separated by an addition, subtraction, multiplication or division symbol. [4]

21 Maths for regular expressions

Specification coverage

3.4.2.2 Maths for regular expressions

Sets

REVISED

A set is a collection of unordered values where each value appears only once in the set. The values in the set are sometimes referred to as elements, objects or members. The common format for representing a set is as follows:

A = {1, 2, 3, 4, 5}

where A is the name of the set and 1 to 5 are the values or elements within it. Any value can be represented in a set. For example:

- $\mathbb{N}$ = {0, 1, 2, 3, 4, 5, 6, 7, 8, 9, ...} where $\mathbb{N}$ represents **natural numbers**
- $\mathbb{Z}$ = {..., –3, –2, –1, 0, 1, 2, 3, ...} where $\mathbb{Z}$ represents integers.

There is more on different sets of numbers in Chapter 23.

> **Natural number**: a positive whole number including zero.

> **Exam tip**
>
> There are a range of 'standard' sets in the specification that are worth remembering.

Set comprehension

REVISED

In the example for A above, the set is defined by listing the actual numbers within the set. It is also possible to define the contents or members of a set using **set comprehension**. This means that the set is defined by the properties that the members of the set must have. This is sometimes called **set building**.

For example:

A = {$x \mid x \in \mathbb{N} \wedge x \geq 1$}

where:

- A is the name of the set
- the curly brackets { } represent the contents of the set
- x represents the actual values of the set that will be defined after the pipe |
- the pipe | means 'such that', meaning that the equation after the x defines the values of x
- $\in$ means 'is a **member** of'
- $\mathbb{N}$ is all of the natural numbers, e.g. 0, 1, 2, 3 etc
- $\wedge$ means 'and'
- ≥ 1 means greater than or equal to one.

In this case we have used set comprehension to create a set of values that are the natural numbers from 1 upwards, which we could show as {1, 2, 3, 4, ...}. Note the use of the ellipsis (...) to indicate that the sequence continues.

> **Set comprehension**: see Set building.
>
> **Set building**: the process of creating sets by describing them using notation rather than listing the elements.
>
> **Member**: describes a value or element that belongs to a set.

> **Exam tip**
>
> Set comprehension can be confusing to start with so practise reading them until you are confident.

Representing sets in programming languages

REVISED

Most programming languages have set-building routines, enabling you to create sets either by entering values or using set comprehension techniques. For example:

- In Python you can write the code `a = set ([0, 1, 2, 3])` where the contents of the square brackets form the set.
- In Haskell you can write the code `[1..100]`, which makes a list containing the values 1 to 100.
- In C# you can write the code `IEnumerable<int> numbers = Enumerable.Range (0,9)` to produce the integers 0 to 9.

The empty set

REVISED

There is a special set known as the **empty set** which is represented either as {} or as Ø. The empty set has no elements. However, it is not to be confused with zero. The easiest way to think about it is as a container that could contain something, but it is empty.

> **Empty set**: the set that contains no values.

Where an operation results in no answer we can use the empty set. Consider the following operation:

$A = \{1, 3, 5, 7, 9, ...\}$

$B = \{2, 4, 6, 8, 10, ...\}$

$A \cap B = Ø$

The $\cap$ represents intersection so this equation is looking for elements that are in the first set that can also be found in the second set. As there aren't any, the answer is represented as the empty set by the Ø symbol.

Finite and infinite sets

REVISED

Sets may contain a finite number or an infinite number of elements. For example:

- $A = \{1, 2, 3, 4, 5\}$ is a **finite set** with five elements.
- $A = \{1, 2, 3, 4, 5, ...\}$ is an **infinite set** made up of natural numbers.
- $A = \{x \mid x \in \mathbb{N} \wedge x \geq 1\}$ is an infinite set of natural numbers greater than zero.

> **Finite set**: a set where the elements can be counted using natural numbers up to a particular number.
>
> **Infinite set**: a set that is not finite.
>
> **Cardinality**: the number of elements in a set.
>
> **Countable set**: a finite set where the elements can be counted using natural numbers.
>
> **Countably infinite sets**: sets where the elements can be put into a one-to-one correspondence with the set of natural numbers.

Where a set is finite it has **cardinality**, which means that it can be counted using natural numbers. It is also referred to as a **countable set**. The cardinality of a set is simply the number of elements in the set. We may also refer to this as the size of the set. For example, the first set above has a cardinality of five as it has five elements. The empty set has a cardinality of zero.

Infinite sets do not have cardinality as we do not know the total size of the set. However, for some infinite sets it is possible to go through the process of counting the elements, even though you would never reach the end. These are described as **countably infinite sets** as they can be counted off against the natural (countable) numbers.

Set operations

It is possible to join two or more sets together to create a new set. This is known as the **Cartesian product**. For example:

A = {a, b, c}

B = {1, 2, 3]

A × B would produce a set of all possible ordered pairs where:
- the first member of A is paired with the first member of B
- then the first member of A is paired with the second member of B and so on for every member of B
- then the second member of A is paired with the first member of B
- the process is repeated until every member of A has been paired with every member of B.

The resulting set or Cartesian product of the two sets would be: {(a,1), (a,2), (a,3), (b,1), (b, 2), (b,3), (c,1), (c,2), (c,3)}. This could also be written as:

A × B = {x , y | $x \in$ A $\wedge$ $y \in$ B}

When working with two or more sets there are different ways of defining the relationship between the members of the two sets. There are three main operations:
- **Union**: This means joining together two or more sets so that the new set is a combination of both sets. This can be represented as A $\cup$ B. For example, if A = {0, 1, 3, 5, 7, 9} and B = {0, 2, 4, 6, 8} then A $\cup$ B will be {0, 1, 2, 3, 4, 5, 6, 7, 8, 9}. This could be represented visually as shown in Figure 21.1.
- **Intersection**: This means when two sets are joined together, the resulting set contains those elements that are common to both. It can be represented as A $\cap$ B. For example, if A = {1, 3, 5, 7, 9} and B = {1, 3, 4, 6, 8} then A $\cap$ B would be {1, 3}. This could be represented visually as shown in Figure 21.2.
- **Difference**: This means that when two sets are joined together the resulting set contains elements that are in either set, but not in their intersection. This can be represented as A $\ominus$ B or A $\triangle$ B. For example, if A = {1, 2, 3, 4, 5, 6, 7, 8} and B = {2, 4, 6, 8, 10} then the difference would be {1, 3, 5, 7, 10}. This could be represented visually as shown in Figure 21.3.

> **Cartesian product**: combining the elements of two or more sets to create a set of ordered pairs.

> **Union:** where two sets are joined and all of the elements of both sets are included in the joined set.
>
> **Intersection:** describes which elements are common to both sets when two sets are joined.
>
> **Difference:** describes which elements differ when two sets are joined together.

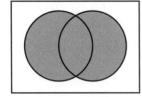

Figure 21.1 Venn diagram to represent the union of two sets

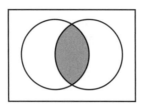

Figure 21.2 Venn diagram to represent the intersection of two sets

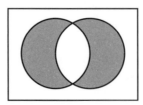

Figure 21.3 Venn diagram to represent the difference between two sets

Subsets

Where all of the elements of one set are also contained within another set, it is said to be a **subset**. For example, A = {1, 3, 5, 7, 9, ...} is a subset of B = {1, 2, 3, 4, 5, ...} as all of the elements of A are contained within B. This can be shown as A ⊂ B where the symbol means 'is a **proper subset** of'.

The definition of a proper subset is one that has fewer elements than the set. In this case, the subset A contains just the odd numbers from the other set. Similarly we could say that A ⊂ B where A = {1, 2, 3, 4, 5] and B = {1, 2, 3, 4, 5, 6} as there is at least one number in B that is not in A.

The notation of a subset (as opposed to a proper subset) is A ⊆ B and the distinction is that two sets that are the same can be said to be subsets of one another. For example, where A = {1, 2, 3, 4, 5} and B = {1, 2, 3, 4, 5} we can say that A is a subset of B because it contains everything within B.

> **Subset**: a set where the elements of one are entirely contained within the other; can include two sets that are exactly the same.
>
> **Proper subset:** where one set is wholly contained within another and the other set has additional elements.

Summary

- A set is a collection of unordered, non-repeated data items of the same type.
- Set comprehension is the process of building a set using an expression.
- Programming languages support set-building techniques.
- The empty set is a set with no values in it.
- Sets can have a finite or infinite number of elements in them.
- Sets can be combined in different ways to create new sets.

Now test yourself

1 There are two sets, A = {A, E, I, O, U} and B = {H, E, L, O}
   (a) Define the union of the two sets. [1]
   (b) Define the Cartesian product of the two sets. [1]
   (c) Define the intersection of the two sets. [1]
   (d) Define the difference of the two sets. [1]
2 Define cardinality. [1]
3 Using set comprehension, define a set that contains integers that are less than or equal to 4. [2]

21 Maths for regular expressions

22 Big O notation and classification of algorithms

Specification coverage

3.4.4 Classification of algorithms

Classifying algorithms

Faced with a problem, a programmer may come up with different **algorithms** that provide a solution. One of the objectives for writing good code is to produce an efficient solution. Efficiency is usually measured in terms of time and space:

- Time: how long the algorithm takes to run compared to other algorithms.
- Space: how much space (memory) is required by the algorithm compared to other algorithms.

The key consideration is what is called input size or problem size. Typically, this is the number of parameters or values that the algorithm will be working on. For example, a search routine written to work on a dataset with only a few values may not work as efficiently on a larger dataset with hundreds of values.

> **Algorithm**: a set of instructions required to complete a particular task in a finite time (independent of any programming language).

Functions

Comparing algorithms uses a technique called Big O notation. This uses standard mathematical functions.

A **function** simply relates an input to an output. For example, $f(x) = x^2$ is an example of a function. It means that you take the input value for the function, x, and produce an output, which in this case is the squared value of x. The set of values that can go into a function is called the **domain** and the set of values that could possibly come out of it is called the **codomain**. The set of values that are actually produced by the function is called the range. It is always the case that the range will be a subset of the codomain.

> **Function**: relates each element of a set with the element of another set.
>
> **Domain**: all the values that may be input to a mathematical function.
>
> **Codomain**: all the values that may be output from a mathematical function.

Big O notation

Big O notation is a method of describing the **time** and **space complexity** of an algorithm. It looks at the worst-case scenario by essentially asking the question: how much slower will this code run if we give it 1000 things to work on instead of 1? Big O notation provides a measure of how much the running time requirements of the code will grow as the magnitude of the inputs changes.

Big O calculates the upper bound, which is the maximum amount of time it would take an algorithm to complete. The notation refers to the order of growth, also known as the order of complexity, which is a measure of how much more time or space it takes to execute the code as the **input size** increases. The format is a capital letter O followed by a function. All of the explanations below relate specifically to **time complexity**, rather than space complexity.

> **Space complexity**: the concept of how much space an algorithm requires.
>
> **Input size**: in Big O notation the size of whatever you are asking an algorithm to work with, e.g. data, parameters.
>
> **Time complexity**: the concept of how much time an algorithm requires.

Big O notation uses five main classifications:

- O(1), known as **constant time**, means that the algorithm will always execute in exactly the same amount of time regardless of the input size. If you were to represent this as a graph, it might look like Figure 22.1. This shows that however much the input size increases, the time taken to run the algorithm remains the same.

Constant time: in Big O notation where the time taken to run an algorithm does not vary with the input size.

Exam tip

Putting a range of Big O notations in to their order of complexity is a common question and worth remembering.

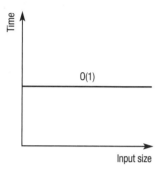

Figure 22.1 Graph to represent constant function

- O(N) represents a **linear** function and it means that the runtime of the algorithm will increase in direct proportion with the input size. This could be represented graphically as shown in Figure 22.2.

Linear time: in Big O notation where the time taken to run an algorithm increases in direct proportion to the input size.

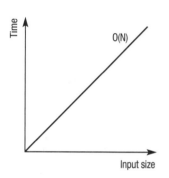

Figure 22.2 Graph to represent linear function

- O(N^2) is an example of a polynomial function and it means that the runtime of the algorithm will increase in proportion to the square of the input size. This could be represented as $y = x^2$. This could be represented graphically as shown in Figure 22.3.
- O(2^N) is an example of an **exponential** function where the runtime will double with every additional unit increase in the input size. Problems with an exponential order of growth are often referred to as intractable problems, which means that they can't be solved with a computer in a reasonable time.

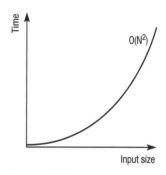

Figure 22.3 Graph to represent polynomial function

Exponential time: in Big O notation where the time taken to run an algorithm increases as an exponential function of the number of inputs. For example, for each additional input the time taken might double.

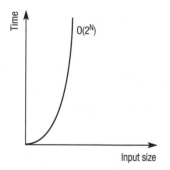

Figure 22.4 Graph to represent exponential function

- O(log$N$) represents a **logarithmic** function which uses an exponent to raise the value of a base number in order to produce the desired number. This could be represented graphically as shown in Figure 22.5.

The value of using Big O notation is that you can find the most efficient solution for your problem. As a broad rule of thumb:

- An O(1) algorithm scales the best as it never takes any longer to run.
- An O(log$N$) algorithm is the next most efficient.
- An O(N) algorithm is the next most efficient.
- An O(N^2) algorithm is a polynomial and is considered to be the point beyond which algorithms start to become intractable. Note that the superscript number could be any value.
- An O(2^N) algorithm is the least efficient and considered intractable.

> **Logarithmic time**: in Big O notation where the time taken to run an algorithm increased or decreases in line with a logarithm.

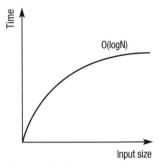

Figure 22.5 Graph to represent logarithmic function

Deriving the complexity of an algorithm

It is possible to derive the time complexity of an algorithm by looking at the contents of the code. For example:

- An algorithm that requires no data and contains no loops or recursion, such as a simple assignment statement or comparison statement, will have a time complexity of O(1).
- An algorithm that loops through an array accessing each data item once will have a time complexity of O(N).
- An algorithm with inner and outer loops will be polynomial with runtime increasing depending on the depth of the nesting and the number of loops. In this case it will be O(N^2).
- The addition of a loop within the inner loop would alter the **polynomial time** to O(N^3).
- An algorithm that uses recursion to call itself could have a time complexity of O(a^N).

With Big O notation, to describe the complexity of a problem, the usual practice is to quote the worst-case scenario for the most efficient algorithm. However, in choosing a suitable algorithm it is possible to make a comparison between the worst, best and average cases based on time complexity. Some common algorithms are known to have certain time complexities as shown in Table 22.1.

> **Polynomial time**: in Big O notation where the time taken to run the algorithm is a polynomial function of the input size, e.g. the square of the input size.

Table 22.1 Common algorithms with time complexity in Big O notation

Complexity	Algorithms
O(1)	Indexing an array
O(log$N$)	Binary search
O(N)	Linear search of an array
O(N^2)	Bubble sort
	Selection sort
	Insertion sort
O(2^N)	Intractable problems

Tractable and intractable problems

REVISED

A **tractable problem** is one that is said to be solvable in polynomial time. In simple terms this means that the algorithm that solves the problem runs quickly enough for it to be practical to solve the problem on a computer.

Intractable problems are those which are theoretically possible to solve, but cannot be solved within polynomial time. The problem may be solvable if the input size is small, but as soon as the input size increases it is considered impractical to try to solve it on a computer.

Faced with intractable problems, programmers often produce **heuristic** algorithms. Having accepted that the perfect solution is not possible, a solution that provides an incomplete or approximate solution is seen as being preferable to no solution at all. Often this will involve ignoring certain complex elements of the problem, or accepting a solution that is not optimal.

Heuristics often use 'rules of thumb' and therefore cannot guarantee accurate results for every possible set of inputs. Instead they produce results that may be accurate for common uses of the program, but less accurate where the program is being used with less likely inputs. The objective with a heuristic algorithm is to produce an acceptable solution in an acceptable time frame, where the optimum solution would simply take too long.

> **Tractable problem**: a problem that can be solved in an acceptable amount of time.
>
> **Intractable problem**: a problem that cannot be solved within an acceptable time frame.
>
> **Heuristic**: with algorithms it is a method for producing a 'rule of thumb' to produce an acceptable solution to intractable problems.

> **Exam tip**
>
> Programmers can be said to make a guess or approximation based on experience – they do not just guess.

Unsolvable problems

REVISED

Unsolvable problems are those which will never be solved regardless of how much computing power is available either now or in the future and regardless of how much time is given to solve them. The 'halting problem' is an example of a problem that is proven to be unsolvable. In simple terms, the halting problem is whether it is possible to make a program to determine if a program will finish running for a particular set of inputs.

The question, devised by Alan Turing in the 1930s, asks whether it would be possible to write a computer program to solve the halting problem. The conclusion is that the problem is unsolvable, as it is proven that it cannot be done.

The halting problem is considered to be one of the first unsolvable problems ever identified and has led to the discovery of many other unsolvable problems. This area of computing has led to a general acceptance that there are some problems which:
- simply cannot be solved by computers (unsolvable problems)
- can theoretically be solved by computers but it is not possible within a reasonable time frame (intractable problems).

> **Unsolvable problem**: a problem that it has been proven cannot be solved on a computer.
>
> **Halting problem**: an example of an unsolvable problem where it is impossible to write a program that can work out whether another problem will halt given a particular input.

Summary

- Some algorithms are more efficient than others in terms of their time and space complexity.
- Time complexity is the amount of time an algorithm takes to solve a problem and is the main focus of study for A level.
- Space complexity is the amount of memory an algorithm takes to solve a problem.
- Big O notation is a method of comparing algorithms in terms of their time and space complexity.
- Big O notation uses standard mathematical functions to classify algorithms.

Now test yourself

TESTED ☐

1 Explain the difference between an unsolvable problem and an intractable problem. [2]
2 Explain the importance of the halting problem. [1]
3 Describe what a programmer might do when faced with an intractable problem. [2]
4 Put the following notations in order of efficiency from most to least efficient. [2]
   - $O(N^2)$
   - $O(2^N)$
   - $O(N)$
   - $O(N \log N)$

23 Number systems

Natural numbers

REVISED

These are the most recognisable type of number as they are the numbers that we use every day for counting and ordering. Typically these are numbers made up of the decimal digits 0, 1, 2, 3, 4, 5, 6, 7, 8, 9. This is known as decimal or base 10 as there are ten different digits that we use. Using a single-digit number we can represent a maximum value of 9. We simply add a new digit to create the numbers 10–99. We then continue adding digits to create hundreds, thousands and so on. Each extra digit we add is worth ten times as much as the previous digit, as it is base 10.

The mathematical symbol for **natural numbers** is $\mathbf{N}$ or $\mathbb{N}$ so you might represent them as follows:

$\mathbb{N} = \{0, 1, 2, 3, 4, 5, 6, 7, 8, 9, \ldots\}$

> **Natural number**: a positive whole number including zero.

Integer numbers

REVISED

An **integer** is a whole number whose value can be positive or negative. Zero is also classed as an integer. A whole number is one that does not contain a fractional part, which means there can be no fractions after the number and no decimal place values.

Negative values are indicated by the minus sign (–). The relationship between the negative and positive integers is that if you add the two you get back to zero. For example $-3 + 3 = 0$ or $3 + (-3) = 0$.

The mathematical symbol for integer numbers is $\mathbf{Z}$ or $\mathbb{Z}$ so you might represent them as follows:

$\mathbb{Z} = \{\ldots, -3, -2, -1, 0, 1, 2, 3, \ldots\}$

> **Integer**: any whole positive or negative number including zero.

> **Exam tip**
>
> Some students choose to remember that $\mathbb{N}$ and $\mathbb{Z}$ are similar, only $\mathbb{Z}$ is bigger (further down the alphabet) so has room to include negatives.

Rational numbers

REVISED

A **rational number** is one that can be expressed as a fraction, also known as a quotient. Fractions are made up of two integers with the value being the ratio between the two. The ratio can be expressed as a fraction or as its decimal equivalent. For example we know ½ as half, and it can also be represented as a decimal as 0.5.

> **Rational number**: any number that can be expressed as a fraction or ratio of integers.

The top integer is called the numerator and the bottom integer is called the denominator. The numerator can be any integer, which means that it can be any positive or negative whole number. The value of the fraction therefore can be negative or positive and it can be greater or less than one, or zero. Fractions can also result in the value of one. The only rule is that the denominator can be any integer apart from zero, as dividing by zero creates an undefined result. The mathematical symbol for rational numbers is **Q** or $\mathbb{Q}$.

Irrational numbers

REVISED

An **irrational number** is any number that cannot be represented as a ratio of integers because the decimal equivalent would go on forever without repeating. A classic example of an irrational number is π. As a fraction, a widely used approximation is $\frac{22}{7}$. In decimal form, the number is infinite so it has to be truncated (cut off) to a set number of decimal places, for example to 3.14 or if more accuracy is required, to 3.1415926535. Some square roots and cube roots are irrational numbers.

A feature of an irrational number is that the values after the decimal place do not repeat in a pattern. For example, there is no pattern to the decimal places in π. Recurring decimals do have a pattern and therefore are classed as rational numbers. For example, one-third = 0.333... recurring.

Irrational number: a number that cannot be represented as a fraction or ratio as the decimal form will contain infinite repeating values.

Real numbers

REVISED

Exam tip

Some languages refer to 'reals' and some to 'floats'. This is largely down to how they are stored, and to all intents and purposes they mean the same thing.

A **real number** is any positive or negative value and can include a fractional part. Integers, rational numbers and irrational numbers are all real numbers. The defining feature of a real number is that the fractional part can be any length, allowing the number to represent a measurement to any level of precision and accuracy required.

Real number: any positive or negative number with or without a fractional part.

Ordinal numbers

REVISED

Exam tip

ASCII characters are the most common ordinal numbers you will come across.

Ordinal numbers are those that identify the position of something within a list. For example: first, second and third. They are often used with **cardinal numbers**, which identify the size of the list. For example, you might say you were third out of 20.

In computing, ordinal numbers are used to identify the position (location) of data within an ordered set. Consider the following set:

S = {'Anne', 'Asif', 'John', 'Mary', 'Wanda', ...}

Ordinal number: a number used to identify position relative to other numbers.

Cardinal number: a number that identifies the size of something.

This set is said to be **well-ordered** as it has an internal structure that defines the relationship between the data items. In this case, the data is made up of names in ascending alphabetical order. The ordinal number is one that shows the order of the data so in this case the first item S(1) = Anne, the second item S(2) = Asif, the third item S(3) is John and so on.

> **Well-ordered set**: a group of related numbers with a defined order.

Counting and measurement

REVISED

As we have seen, the basic use of numbers is to count and measure. We use different types of numbers in different ways depending on the task. For example, we:

- count using natural numbers as we only need to use positive whole numbers
- measure using real numbers as the range of numbers may be positive or negative and may require a fractional part.

The use of natural numbers to count is common in programming. For example:

- a counter may be used to keep track of how many times a loop statement is repeated
- the program counter in the processor keeps track of which instruction needs to be processed next
- a natural number is used to identify the location of data within a data structure
- a variable may be set up to keep count, for example, of the number of items in a stock control system, or the score in a computer game.

The use of real numbers to measure is common in programming. For example:

- CNC machines handle measurements that vary from millimetres to metres and must work to a high degree of accuracy
- microwave cookers control and measure both time and temperature
- power stations use data control systems to optimise the production of electricity
- robotics engineers use real-time measurements of the environment in which the robot is working.

Summary

- It is important to understand that there are different types of numbers.
- We use the word decimal to refer to numbers that are base 10; that is, made up of the numbers 0 to 9.
- Numbers are used to count and to measure (or quantify).

- Numbers used to count are called ordinals and are an important concept in computing; for example, when identifying the location of items within a list.
- As a programmer, you need to choose the right number type when working with data, e.g. whether to work with a number as an integer or a real number.

Now test yourself

TESTED

1 What are the symbols used to designate:
   (a) rational numbers   (b) integers   (c) natural numbers?   [3]
2 Identify one example of the following:
   (a) a rational number   (b) an irrational number   (c) an integer.   [3]
3 ASCII is a character set that has ordinal numbers designating the characters. What does this mean?   [2]
4 What makes a set well-ordered?   [1]

24 Number bases

Specification coverage

3.5.2.1 Number base
3.5.3.1 Bits and bytes
3.5.3.2 Units

The bit

REVISED

Computers process data in digital form. Essentially this means that they use microprocessors, also referred to as chips or silicon chips, to control them. A chip is a small piece of silicon implanted with millions of electronic circuits. The chip receives pulses of electricity that are passed around these microscopic circuits in a way that allows computers to represent text, numbers, sounds and graphics.

A **bit** is a **bi**nary digi**t**. The processor can only handle electricity in a relatively simple way – either electricity is flowing or it is not. This is often referred to as two states. The processor can recognise whether it is receiving an off signal or an on signal. This is handled as a zero (0) for off and a one (1) for on. Each binary digit therefore is either a 0 (no signal) or a 1 (a signal).

> **Bit**: a single binary digit from a binary number – either a zero or a one.

The processor now needs to convert these 0s and 1s into something useful for the user. Everything you use your computer for is represented internally by a series of 0s and 1s. Computers string zeros and ones together to represent text, numbers, sound, video and everything else we use our computers for.

The clock speed of your computer indicates the speed at which the signals are sent around the processor. In simple terms, a clock speed of 2 GHz means that it will receive 2 billion of these on/off pulses per second.

The byte

REVISED

A single **byte** is a string of eight bits. Eight is a useful number of bits as it creates enough permutations (or combinations) of zeros and ones to represent every character on your keyboard:

> **Byte**: a group of bits, typically 8, used to represent a single character.

- With one bit we have two permutations: 0 and 1.
- With two bits we have four permutations: 00, 01, 10 and 11. This could be represented as 2^2 or 2×2. As we increase the number of bits, we increase the number of permutations by the power of two.
- Three bits would give us 2^3 which is $2 \times 2 \times 2 = 8$ permutations.
- Four bits would give us 2^4 permutations which is $2 \times 2 \times 2 \times 2 = 16$ permutations.

The basic point here is that the more bits you use, the greater the range of numbers, characters, sounds or colours that can be created. Taking numbers as an example, as we have seen, 8 bits would be enough to represent 256 different numbers (0–255). As the number of bits increases, the range of numbers increases rapidly. For example 2^{16} would give 65 536 permutations, 2^{24} would give approximately 1.6 million and 2^{32} would give over 4 billion permutations.

Units

REVISED

Larger combinations of bytes are used to measure the capacity of memory and storage devices. The size of the **units** can be referred to either using binary or decimal prefixes. For example, in decimal, the term kilo is commonly used to indicate a unit that is 1000 times larger than a single unit. So the correct term would be kilobyte (KB). In binary, the correct term is actually kibibyte (Ki) with 1024 bytes being the nearest binary equivalent to 1000.

> **Unit**: the grouping together of bits or bytes to form larger blocks of measurement, e.g. GB, MB.

Common units are shown in Table 24.1 using both binary and decimal prefixes.

Table 24.1 Common binary and decimal units

Binary			Decimal		
kibibyte	Ki	2^{10}	kilobyte	KB	10^3
mebibyte	Mi	2^{20}	megabyte	MB	10^6
gibibyte	Gi	2^{30}	gigabyte	GB	10^9
tebibyte	Ti	2^{40}	terabyte	TB	10^{12}

Number bases

REVISED

A **number base** indicates how many different digits are available when using a particular number system. For example, decimal is number base 10 which means that it uses ten digits: 0, 1, 2, 3, 4, 5, 6, 7, 8 and 9 and binary is number base 2 which means that it uses two digits: 0 and 1. Different number bases are needed for different purposes. Humans use number base 10 whereas computers use binary which is a form of digital data.

> **Number base**: the number of digits available within a particular number system, e.g. base 10 for decimal, base 2 for binary.

The number base determines how many digits are needed to represent a number. For example, the number 98 in decimal (base 10) requires two digits. The binary (base 2) equivalent is 1100010 which requires seven digits. As a consequence of this there are many occasions in computing when very long binary codes are needed. To solve this problem, other number bases can be used, which require fewer digits to represent numbers. For example, some aspects of computing involve number base 16 which is referred to as hexadecimal.

The accepted method for representing different number bases (in textbooks and exam questions) is to show the number with the base in subscript. For example:

- 43_{10} is decimal
- 1011_2 is binary
- $2A7_{16}$ is hexadecimal.

Hexadecimal

REVISED

Hexadecimal or hex is particularly useful for representing large numbers. Hex is used in a number of ways. Memory addresses are shown in hex format as are colour codes. The main advantage of hex is that two hex digits represent one byte.

> **Exam tip**
>
> It is important to remember that hexadecimal saves space when **displaying** data but it is still stored as binary. It is also easier for recognising patterns and avoiding human error.

Consider the number 11010011_2. This is an 8-bit code which when converted to decimal equals 211_{10}. The same number in hex is $D3_{16}$. This basic example shows that an 8-bit code in binary can be represented as a two-digit code in hex. Consequently hex is often referred to as 'shorthand' for binary as it requires fewer digits.

As it is number base 16, hex uses 16 different digits: 0 to 9 and A to F.

Working with number bases

When performing any calculations, humans use number base 10, probably because we have ten digits on our hands. When we get to 9 we add an extra digit to the left and start again. When we get to 99, we add a further digit to the left and so on. Each digit we add is worth ten times the previous digit.

Binary is number base 2 and works on exactly the same principle. This time we only have two digits, 0 and 1. It has to be binary because computers only work by receiving a zero or one (off and on). So, 1 is the biggest number we can have with one bit. To increase the size of the number, we add more bits. Each bit is worth two times the previous bit because we are using number base 2. The table below shows an 8-bit binary number 10000111. Notice the value of each new bit is doubling each time, as binary is base 2.

128	64	32	16	8	4	2	1
1	0	0	0	0	1	1	1

Using the same principle as with decimal to work out the number we have:

$(1 \times 128) + (1 \times 4) + (1 \times 2) + (1 \times 1)$. This adds up to 135.

Therefore 10000111 in binary = 135 in decimal.

Binary to decimal conversions

Binary numbers are converted to decimal integers as follows:

- Write down a binary number (e.g. 10000111).
- Above the number, starting from the least significant bit (LSB), write the number 1.
- As you move left from the LSB to the most significant bit (MSB), double the value of the previous number:

MSB							LSB
128	64	32	16	8	4	2	1
1	0	0	0	0	1	1	1

> **Exam tip**
>
> The LSB is the right-most bit, it has the 'least significance' in the number overall.

- Wherever there is a 1, add the decimal value: the above example represents one 128, one 4, one 2 and a 1 giving a total value of 135 (128 + 4 + 2 + 1 = 135). Therefore 10000111 in binary equals 135 as a decimal integer.

Decimal to binary conversions

To convert a decimal integer to a binary number, use the same method as above, but working the other way. For example, to convert the number 98:
- Write down the power of 2 sequence. (Eight bits are used here but you will notice that you only need seven for this example.)

MSB							LSB
128	64	32	16	8	4	2	1

 Now test yourself answers at www.therevisionbutton.co.uk/myrevisionnotes

- Starting from the MSB, put a 1 or 0 in each column as necessary to ensure that it adds up to 98 as follows:
  - ○ 0 under 128
  - ○ 1 under 64
  - ○ 1 under 32
  - ○ 0 under 16
  - ○ 0 under 8
  - ○ 0 under 4
  - ○ 1 under 2
  - ○ 0 under 1
  Therefore 01100010 = 98.

> **Exam tip**
>
> It may help to write down the number you're looking for. Then as you work left to right, ask is (the binary heading number) in the number I am looking for? If not write a 0, if it is write a 1 and subtract from the number you're looking for. When the number written down is 0, you have your binary number.

Another way of carrying out this calculation is to carry out repeated divisions on the decimal number as follows:

- 98 divide by 2 = 49 with a remainder of 0
- 49 divide by 2 = 24 with a remainder of 1
- 24 divide by 2 = 12 with a remainder of 0
- 12 divide by 2 = 6 with a remainder of 0
- 6 divide by 2 = 3 with a remainder of 0
- 3 divide by 2 = 1 with a remainder of 1
- 1 divide by 2 = 0 with a remainder of 1

Notice that you keep dividing by 2 until there is nothing left to divide. Reading from the bottom this gives us 1100010 which equals 98. (Note that the leading zero is omitted.)

Check your answer by working it back the other way:

MSB							LSB
128	64	32	16	8	4	2	1
0	1	1	0	0	0	1	0

$64 + 32 + 2 = 98$

Decimal to hex conversions

REVISED

A common approach to convert decimal integers to hex is to first convert the decimal to binary and then convert the binary to hex. Taking the decimal number 211 as an example:

- Work out the binary equivalent.

128	64	32	16	8	4	2	1
1	1	0	1	0	0	1	1

> **Exam tip**
>
> Taking a two-step approach is perfectly acceptable in an exam.

- Split the binary number into two groups of four bits and convert each into the hex equivalent.

8	4	2	1	8	4	2	1
1	1	0	1	0	0	1	1

Therefore $11010001_2 = 211_{10}$

$8 + 4 + 1 = D$ (the hex equivalent of 13) and $2 + 1 = 3$

Therefore $211_{10} = 11010011_2 = D3_{16}$

Hex to decimal conversions

The process here is to convert the hex to binary, and then the binary into decimal. Hex to binary conversions are the reverse of the above process. Take the hex number, and then convert each digit in turn into its binary equivalent using groups of four bits. Take $2A3_{16}$ as an example:

	2				A				3		
8	4	2	1	8	4	2	1	8	4	2	1
0	0	1	0	1	0	1	0	0	0	1	1

2 = 0010, A = 1010, 3 = 0011

Therefore 1010100011_2 is the binary equivalent of $2A3_{16}$

This binary code can then be converted into decimal in the usual way:

512	256	128	64	32	16	8	4	2	1
1	0	1	0	1	0	0	0	1	1

$512 + 128 + 32 + 2 + 1 = 675_{10}$

When carrying out a conversion, it is useful to remember the binary equivalent of the 16 digits used in hex.

Summary

- Computers process data in digital form; that is, as series of discrete values.
- 0s and 1s are called binary digits or bits.
- Bits are grouped together to create bytes.
- Bytes are grouped together to create kilobytes, megabytes, gigabytes and terabytes.
- Computing uses three main number bases: binary (base 2), decimal (base 10) and hexadecimal (base 16).
- You need to be able to convert between the three number bases.

Now test yourself

1 Which is biggest, a Mi, a Ki or a Gi? [1]
2 Convert 112 to binary. [1]
3 Convert 11011010 to decimal. [1]
4 Convert F4 to decimal. [1]
5 Convert 119 to hexadecimal. [1]
6 Give two reasons why a programmer might utilise hexadecimal. [2]

25 The binary number system

Adding unsigned binary integers

REVISED

To add two numbers together in binary, first line up the numbers in the same way as you would do column addition in decimal:

```
  00110010+
  10110101
 ──────────
  11100111
    11
```

Now add the columns starting from the right-hand side, remembering that you can only use 0s and 1s:

- 0 + 0 will equal 0 so put 0 on the answer line
- 0 + 1 or 1 + 0 will both equal 1 so put 1 in the answer line
- 1 + 1 will equal 10 (one, zero) so put 0 in the answer line and carry the 1
- 1 + 1 + 1 will equal 11 (one, one) so put 1 in the answer line and carry the 1.

You can check your answer by converting all the numbers to decimal, carrying out the addition and then converting the answer back to binary. In this case, the first number is 50, the second number is 181, so the answer should be 231.

> **Unsigned binary:** binary that represents positive numbers only.

> **Exam tip**
>
> Many binary arithmetic questions have multiple marks. In some cases you not only should, but must, show your working!

Multiplying unsigned binary integers

REVISED

To multiply in binary, you multiply the first number by each of the digits of the second number in turn starting from the right-hand side (in the same way that you would do multiplication in decimal). This means you are either multiplying each digit by 0 or by 1, which will give you either a 0 or 1 as the answer. You then do the same for the next digit, shifting your answers to the left as you would in decimal multiplication.

> **Exam tip**
>
> This can often be easier understood when you watch someone do it. YouTube has a multitude of videos on the subject.

You then carry out a binary addition to find the final answer. For example, to multiply 11011 by 11:

```
   11011×
      11
   11011
  110110
 1010001
    1111
```

Note the zero on the LSB as the numbers have been shifted to the left.

Again you can work this out by converting the binary to decimal to check your answer. In this case the first number is 27 (twenty-seven), the second number is 3 (three), so the answer is 81 (eighty-one).

Two's complement

Two's complement is a method used to represent signed integers in binary form. This means that it can be used to represent positive and negative integers. This section shows how two's complement can represent negative integers.

> **Two's complement:** a method of working with signed binary values.

Assume we want to convert the binary code 10011100 into decimal using two's complement:

- Write out the denary equivalents as shown:

MSB							LSB
−128	64	32	16	8	4	2	1

- You will notice that with two's complement, the most significant bit becomes negative. Using an 8-bit code, this means that the MSB represents a value of −128
- Now write in the binary code:

MSB							LSB
−128	64	32	16	8	4	2	1
1	0	0	1	1	1	0	0

- Now add up the values:
  $-128 + 16 + 8 + 4 = -100$

Converting from denary to binary using two's complement can be slightly more difficult for negative numbers as you will be starting from a negative number and working forward. Remember that with two's complement, when the MSB is 1 it means that the number must be negative. You may find it easier to use the following method:

- To convert −102 into binary, first write out the binary equivalent of +102 as shown:

MSB							LSB
128	64	32	16	8	4	2	1
0	1	1	0	0	1	1	0

- Starting at the LSB, write out the number again until you come to the first 1.
- Then reverse all the remaining bits, that is, 0 becomes 1 and 1 becomes 0.

- The number becomes 10011010.
- The number is now in two's complement.

MSB							LSB
−128	64	32	16	8	4	2	1
1	0	0	1	1	0	1	0

To check, add these up: −128 + 16 + 8 + 2 = −102

Adding and subtracting using two's complement

Adding numbers together using two's complement is the same as adding numbers together in decimal: you add up the total and carry values across to the next column. For example, in decimal to add 48 to 83:

```
  48
  83+
 131
  11
```

Binary addition is the same. To add 01101100 to 10001000:

```
 01101100
 10001000+
 11110100
        1
```

Remember that in binary 1 + 1 = 10 and that 1 + 1 + 1 = 11

In order to carry out subtractions, the method used is to convert the number to be subtracted to a negative number, and then to add the negative number. For example 20 − 13 in denary would actually be performed by adding 20 to −13 giving the answer of 7. To do this in binary:
- Calculate the binary equivalent of 20 which equals 00010100
- Calculate the binary equivalent of −13 which equals 11110011
- Add 20 to −13 in binary form:

```
 00010100
 11110011+
 00000111
      111
```

- Check your answer by converting it to denary and the answer is 7 which is correct.
- You may notice that this calculation would have a final 1 to be carried. This is called an 'overflow bit' and is handled separately to the calculation. There is more on this later in the chapter.

Fixed point numbers

REVISED

In order to represent real decimal numbers, that is, numbers with decimal places or a fractional part, **fixed point** representation can be used. In the same way that decimal has a decimal point, binary has a binary point. The numbers after the binary point represent fractions. For example, if you had an 8-bit binary code, you may place the binary point after the fourth bit as shown:

1	0	0	0	1	1	0	0

The binary point is not actually stored in the 8-bit code, its position is fixed by the programmer. It is shown here purely to aid understanding.

To convert this to a decimal number is a similar process to the other conversions we have done. This time, the digits after the binary point become fractions as follows:

8	4	2	1	$\frac{1}{2}$	$\frac{1}{4}$	$\frac{1}{8}$	$\frac{1}{16}$
0	1	1	0	0	1	1	0

The conversion of the bits before the binary point are handled in the same way as before with each value doubling as you move from right to left. The numbers after the binary point halve each time as you move from left to right as shown.

Therefore the number above is

$$4 + 2 + \frac{1}{4} + \frac{1}{8}$$

giving a total of $6\frac{3}{8}$ or 6.375.

Floating point numbers

A-level only REVISED

In **floating point**, the binary point can be moved depending on the number that you are trying to represent. It 'floats' from left to right rather than being in a fixed position. A floating point number is made up of two parts – the mantissa and the exponent.

The mantissa and/or the exponent may be negative as the two's complement method is also used on each part. Consider the following 12-bit code: 000011000011.

The code can be broken down as follows:
- the first eight bits are the mantissa which can be broken down further as:
  - the MSB is 0 which means that the number is positive
  - the next seven bits are the rest of the mantissa: 0001100
- the remaining four bits are the exponent: 0011.

Floating point: where the decimal/binary point can move within a number.

It is common to show the mantissa and exponent more clearly as follows:

Mantissa

0	0	0	0	1	1	0	0

Exponent

0	0	1	1

- First, work out the exponent in the usual way, remembering that two's complement is being used.
  Therefore the exponent is +3.

−8	4	2	1
0	0	1	1

This means that the binary point will 'float' three places to the right.
- Now calculate the mantissa. The binary point is always placed after the most significant bit as follows:

−1	$\frac{1}{2}$	$\frac{1}{4}$	$\frac{1}{8}$	$\frac{1}{16}$	$\frac{1}{32}$	$\frac{1}{64}$	$\frac{1}{128}$
0	0	0	0	1	1	0	0

- The point now floats three places to the right. The values for the conversion have changed because the binary point has now moved.

8	4	2	1	$\frac{1}{2}$	$\frac{1}{4}$	$\frac{1}{8}$	$\frac{1}{16}$
0	0	0	0	1	1	0	0

- Therefore, $0000 1100 0011 = 0.75$

Two's complement can also be used on the mantissa or exponent to represent negative values. The process of converting negatives is similar. A negative exponent would move the binary point to the left rather than the right.

For the value −10.5:
- First calculate the fixed point representation of the positive value, that is 10.5:

−16	8	4	2	1	$\frac{1}{2}$	$\frac{1}{4}$	$\frac{1}{8}$
0	1	0	1	0	1	0	0

- Starting at the LSB, write out the number again until you come to the first 1.
- Then reverse all the remaining bits, that is, 0 becomes 1 and 1 becomes 0.

−16	8	4	2	1	$\frac{1}{2}$	$\frac{1}{4}$	$\frac{1}{8}$
1	0	1	0	1	1	0	0

- The number is now in two's complement.
- Normalise the number, which for a negative value means you need to position the binary point so that the first bit of the mantissa after the binary point is the first 0 in the number. This means floating (moving) it four places to the left:

1	0	1	0	1	1	0	0

Exam tip

In a properly normalised number, the bits either side of the point will be different.

- We now need to use the exponent to indicate that the floating point needs to be moved four places to the right:

Mantissa

1	0	1	0	1	1	0	0

Exponent

1	0	0

- In this case therefore we have used an 8-bit mantissa and a 3-bit exponent to represent the value.

Fixed point compared to floating point **A-level only**   REVISED ☐

As you have seen, fixed point and floating point are two methods for representing values. Both systems have their advantages. The advantages of using floating point are:
- a much wider range of numbers can be produced with the same number of bits as the fixed point system
- consequently, floating point lends itself to applications where a wide range of values may need to be represented.

The advantages of using fixed point are:
- The values are handled in the same way as decimal values, so any hardware configured to work with integers can be used on reals.
- The absolute error will always be the same, whereas with floating point numbers the absolute error could vary.
- It is suited to applications where speed is more important that precision.
- It is suited to applications where an absolute level of precision is required.

Underflow and overflow

A-level only   REVISED ☐

It is possible when using **signed binary** that you will generate a number that is either too large or too small to be represented by the number of bits that are available to store it. When the number is too large, we get an **overflow** and when it is too small we get an **underflow**.

An underflow or overflow could cause serious errors in a program. It could generate erroneous results or even cause the program to crash. There are various methods for dealing with overflows and underflows. A common method is the use of a flag to indicate where an overflow or underflow has occurred and to 'carry' the additional bits in the same way that you carry digits when adding up in decimal. Overflow can also be represented as ∞.

Signed binary: binary with a positive or negative sign.

Overflow: when a number is too large to be represented with the number of bits allocated.

Underflow: when a number is too small to be represented with the number of bits allocated.

Normalisation and precision

A-level only   REVISED ☐

Normalisation is a technique used to ensure that when numbers are represented they are as precise as possible in relation to how many bits are being used.

With a fixed number of bits that can be used to represent the mantissa, the **precision** of the number can be affected by where the binary point is positioned. The exponent is used to ensure that the floating point is placed to optimise the precision of the number.

Normalisation: a process for adjusting numbers onto a common scale.

Precision: how accurate a number is.

For example 234 000 can be represented as:
- 23400×10^1
- 2.34×10^5
- $0.00000234 \times 10^{11}$

The second option is the best way to represent the number as it uses the least number of digits yet provides a precise result. This number is referred to as being in 'normal form' or 'normalised'.

With binary codes, in order to be 'normalised' the first bit of the mantissa, after the binary point, should always be a 1 for positive numbers, or a 0 for negative numbers and the bit before the binary point should be the opposite. So a normalised positive floating point number must start 0.1 and a normalised negative floating point number must start 1.0. For example, the binary equivalent of 108 in decimal using an 8-bit code would be 01101100:
- The normalised mantissa would be 0.1101100
- The binary point will have to be moved seven places to the right in order to convert it back to the original number
- Therefore the exponent must be 7
- Two's complement for 7 is 0111
- Therefore the normalised representation of 108 is 0.11011000111

Exam tip

Facts such as the first bit after the point being 1 for positive and 0 for negative allow you to see at a glance that there might be an error in your working.

Rounding errors

A-level only

When working with decimal numbers, we are used to the idea of rounding numbers up or down. As a consequence, we will get rounding errors. A similar phenomenon occurs with binary representation. For example, if you try to convert 0.1 in decimal into binary you will find that you get a recurring number, so it is not possible to exactly represent it. If we try to represent 1.95 with 8-bits and a fixed point:

1.1111010 would give us 1.953125:

1	$\frac{1}{2}$	$\frac{1}{4}$	$\frac{1}{8}$	$\frac{1}{16}$	$\frac{1}{32}$	$\frac{1}{64}$	$\frac{1}{128}$
1	1	1	1	1	0	1	0

1.1111001 would give us 1.9453125:

1	$\frac{1}{2}$	$\frac{1}{4}$	$\frac{1}{8}$	$\frac{1}{16}$	$\frac{1}{32}$	$\frac{1}{64}$	$\frac{1}{128}$
1	1	1	1	1	0	0	1

With 8 bits the nearest we can get is 0.003125 out. We could extend the number of bits that we use to try and get an answer that is closer to 1.95.

Absolute and relative errors

A-level only

There are two main methods for calculating the degree of error in numbers that we use within a program. The absolute error is the actual mathematical difference between the answer and the approximation of it that you can store. For example, if a calculation requires 8 decimal places, but we only allocate 8 digits, we would have to either round or truncate the number. So the number 1.65746552 would become 1.6574655. In this case, to work out the absolute error we would subtract the two values and that would give us an absolute error of 0.00000002. Note that the absolute error is always a positive number.

With relative error, rather than applying a rigid margin of error, you would look at the value that was being stored and then decide on a relative margin of error. In this way you are comparing the actual result to the expected result. For example, you might decide that ±5% would be sufficient.

Relative error can be calculated using the formula:

$$\text{Relative error} = \frac{\text{Absolute error}}{\text{Numver intended ot be stored}}$$

For example, if trying to represent the value 6.95 using floating point with an 8-bit **mantissa** and a 3-bit **exponent**, it could be shown as 0.1101111011. This works out to be 6.9375. Therefore:

Absolute error = 6.95 − 6.9375 = 0.0125

$$\text{Relative error} = \frac{0.0125}{6.95} = 0.001798561151$$

> **Mantissa:** the significant digits that make up a number.
>
> **Exponent:** the 'power of' part of a number indicating how far a binary point should be shifted left or right.

Summary

- Binary addition and multiplication of positive integers use the same methodology as decimal addition and multiplication.
- Two's complement is a method used to represent signed integers in binary form.
- Fixed point binary numbers are used to represent fractions. The binary point is in a fixed position.
- Floating point binary numbers are used to represent fractions. The binary point can move position.
- A floating point number is made up of two parts – the mantissa and the exponent.
- It is possible that when using signed binary you will generate a number that is either too large or too small to be represented by the number of bits that are available to store it.
- Normalisation is a technique used to ensure that when numbers are represented they are as precise as possible in relation to how many bits are being used.
- When working with decimal numbers, we are used to the idea of rounding numbers up or down. As a consequence, we will get rounding errors, which can be quantified as absolute or relative.
- Precision refers to how accurate the number needs to be in the context that it is being used.

Now test yourself

TESTED ☐

1 Add the following numbers of unsigned binary.
   (a) 10010110
       00110110 [1]
   (b) 11001111
       00011101 [1]
2 Convert the following numbers to 2's complement.
   (a) 45 [1]
   (b) −75 [1]
   (c) −117 [1]
3 Subtract 45 from 94 using 2's complement binary. [2]
4 Represent the following numbers as fixed point binary with 5 digits and 3 digits after the point.
   (a) 4.75 [2]
   (b) 19.25 [2]
   (c) 6.375 [2]
5 Represent the following fixed point binary numbers as denary.
   (a) 11011.101 [2]
   (b) 10110.001 [2]
   (c) 1110.1111 [2]
6 Represent the following normalised floating point numbers as denary.
   (a) 1.0011100 (mantissa) 0011 (exponent) [2]
   (b) 0.1100000 (mantissa) 1111 (exponent) [2]
7 Write the normalised floating point representation of −117. Include your working. [3]
8 (a) Write the normalised floating point representation of 7.9 using 8 bits for the mantissa and 4 bits for the exponent. Include your working. [3]
   (b) Calculate the absolute error that has occurred. [1]
   (c) Calculate the relative error that has occurred. [1]

26 Coding systems

ASCII and Unicode

REVISED

A standard method for the representation of all the keyboard characters, including the numbers, and other commonly used functions is **ASCII** or the American Standard Code for Information Interchange. The most recent version is an 8-bit code allowing for 256 characters.

The limitations of ASCII are:

- 256 characters are not sufficient to represent all of the possible characters, numbers and symbols.
- It was initially developed in English and therefore did not represent all of the other languages and scripts in the world.
- Widespread use of the web made it more important to have a universal international coding system.
- The range of platforms and programs has increased dramatically with more developers from around the world using a much wider range of characters.

As a result, a new standard called **Unicode** has emerged which follows the same basic principles as ASCII in that in one of its forms it has a unique 8-bit code for every keyboard character on a standard English keyboard. ASCII codes have been subsumed within Unicode meaning that the ASCII code for a capital letter A is 65 and so is the Unicode code for the same character. Unicode also includes international characters for over 20 countries and even includes conversions of classical and ancient characters.

To represent these extra characters it is obviously necessary to use more than 8 bits per character and there are two common encodings of Unicode in use today (UTF-8 and UTF-16). As the name suggests the latter is a 16-bit code.

> **Character code:** a binary representation of a particular letter, number or special character.
>
> **ASCII:** a standard binary coding system for characters and numbers.

> **Unicode:** a standard binary coding system that has superseded ASCII.

Error checking and correction

REVISED

A **parity bit** is a method of detecting errors in data during transmission. When you send data, it is being sent as a series of 0s and 1s. In Figure 26.1, a Unicode character is transmitted as the binary code 01101111. It is quite possible that this code could get corrupted as it is passed around either inside the computer or across a network.

> **Parity bit:** a method of checking binary codes by counting the number of 0s and 1s in the code.

Exam tip

Parity can only detect odd numbers of errors and cannot repair the damaged bits.

In the top example the parity bit is set to 0 to maintain an even number of ones. The bottom example shows another binary code where the parity bit is set to 1 in order to ensure an even number of ones.

One method for detecting errors is to count the number of ones in each byte before the data is sent to see whether there is an even or odd number. At the receiving end, the code can be checked to see whether the number is still odd or even.

> **Exam tip**
>
> We have to remember to count 1s not 0s and the parity bit is normally put as the MSB.

Majority voting

Majority voting is another method of identifying errors in transmitted data. In this case, each bit is sent three times. So the binary code 1001 would be sent as:

111000000111

When the data is checked, you would expect to see patterns of three bits. In this case, it is 111 for the first bit, then 000 and so on. Where there is a discrepancy, you can use majority voting to see which bit occurs the most frequently. For example, if the same code 1001 was received as:

101010000111

you could assume that the first bit should be 1 as two out of three of the three bits are 1. You would assume that the second bit is 0 as two of the three bits are 0. The last two bits are 0 and 1 as there appears to be no errors in this part of the code.

Check digits

Like a parity bit, a **check digit** is a value that is added to the end of a number to try and ensure that the number is not corrupted in any way. The check digit is created by taking the digits that make up the number itself and processing them in some way to create a single digit. The simplest but most error-prone method is to add the digits of the number together, and keep on adding the digits until you have only a single digit remaining. So the digits of 123456 add up to 21 and 2 and 1 in turn add up to 3, so the number with its check digit becomes 1234563. When the data is being processed the check digit is recalculated and compared with the digit that has been transmitted. Where the check digit is the same then it is assumed that the data is correct. Where there is a discrepancy, an error message is generated.

Bit-mapped graphics

REVISED

All computer graphics are represented using sequences of binary digits (bits).

The display on a monitor is made up of thousands of tiny dots or picture elements called **pixels**. A typical monitor might have a grid of 1366 by 768 pixels. This is known as the **resolution**. This term is also used on individual picture files. So the formula for the resolution of a file in pixels is:

resolution = width × height

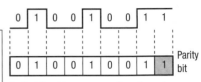

Parity bit = 0 to ensure number of ones is even

Parity bit = 1 to ensure number of ones is even

Figure 26.1 Even parity (note: odd parity is the opposite of even parity)

> **Majority voting:** a method of checking for errors by producing the same data several times and checking it is the same each time.

> **Exam tip**
>
> Majority vote can repair errors but if two errors are made on the same bit then it will not be detected. And of course three times as much data must be transmitted.

> **Check digit:** a digit added to the end of binary data to check the data is accurate.

> **Exam tip**
>
> Check digits identify one or more errors have occurred but need more processing than parity and don't repair like majority vote.

> **Bit-mapped graphic:** an image made up of individual pixels.
>
> **Pixel:** an individual picture element.
>
> **Resolution:** width × height or pixels per inch.

You can also define resolution in terms of the number of pixels per inch (PPI). For example, a monitor that is 12 × 9 inches, which is 1366 by 768, will have 1366 divided by 12 pixels per inch, or around 114 PPI on the horizontal axis and 768 divided by 9, which is around 85 PPI on the vertical axis.

Each of these pixels can be controlled to display different colours. By combining the pixels, a picture is created on the screen. At a very simple level, each pixel could be controlled by one bit. This means that each pixel is mapped to one bit in memory. The bit could be set to either 0 or 1 representing off or on which in this case would be black or white.

To create colour graphics, each pixel is mapped to more than one bit. For example, a pixel might be represented by a byte (8 bits) in memory. This means that each pixel could be any one of 2^8 or 256 different colours. The amount of memory allocated to each pixel is referred to as the **colour depth**. Your computer will contain a graphics card for controlling graphics. The amount of memory allocated for bit-mapping depends on the amount of memory on this card:

$$\text{storage} = \text{resolution} \times \text{colour depth}$$

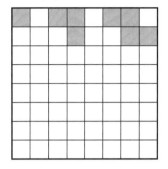

Data stored in memory

| 0 | 1 | 0 | 0 | 1 | 0 | 0 | 1 |

| 1 | 1 | 1 | 0 | 1 | 1 | 0 | 0 |

Data displayed on screen

Figure 26.2 Bit-mapped display

> **Colour depth:** the number of bits or bytes allocated to represent the colour of a pixel in a bit-mapped graphic.

Vector graphics
A-level only   REVISED ☐

> **Exam tip**
>
> Objects in a vector graphic need to store all of the relevant data to recreate the image – sizes, positions, colours, styles etc.

Vector graphics are created using objects and coordinates. A vector is a measure of quantity and direction. It is easier to think of vector graphics as geometric shapes. To rescale the object requires an adjustment of the coordinates. Therefore, the graphics are being controlled mathematically rather than being completely regenerated as with a bit map. An image created on the screen will be made up of lines and the scale and position of the lines will be adjusted as the screen display changes to create an image.

Vector images are made up of primitives, which are the basic pieces of data needed to create an image. Typically this will be points, lines, curves and polygons. This includes common shapes and will also include letters. The colour gradient may also be contained as a primitive.

> **Vector graphic:** an image made up of objects and coordinates.

● Start coordinate

Figure 26.3 Scaled vector graphic

Analogue and digital signals
REVISED ☐

All the processing carried out by a computer is digital, yet there are occasions when either the input or output required is analogue. Analogue data are data that are infinitely variable and are often represented in the form of a wave. Figure 26.4 shows a typical sound wave.

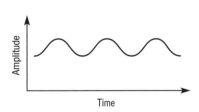

Figure 26.4 An analogue wave

Digital data are often represented as discrete values, shown in Figure 26.5 with the ons and offs shown as set peaks and troughs. As we have seen in this section, digital data are often represented as a sequence of 0s and 1s.

Figure 26.5 A digital signal

Analogue to digital conversions

A problem arises when we need to input analogue data into the computer or when we want to output digital data from the computer in analogue form. In order to do this, a converter is needed, which could be either an analogue to digital converter (ADC) or a digital to analogue converter (DAC).

One example is a MIDI device for an acoustic guitar. This device fits beneath the strings on the guitar and when the strings are played they generate an analogue sound wave. The sound waves are picked up and converted to digital form.

MIDI uses event messages to control various properties of the sound. These messages are typically encoded in binary and provide communication between MIDI devices or between a MIDI device and the processor. For example, on a MIDI keyboard, an event message may contain data on:

Figure 26.6 A MIDI keyboard

- when to play a note
- when to stop playing the note
- timing a note to play with other notes or sounds
- timing a note to play with other MIDI-enabled devices
- what pitch a note is
- how loud to play it
- what effect to use when playing it.

The advantages of using MIDI files over other digital audio formats are:

- MIDI files tend to be much smaller. This means they require less memory and also load faster, which is particularly advantageous if the MIDI file is embedded in a web page.
- MIDI files are completely editable as individual instruments can be selected and modified.
- MIDI supports a very wide range of instruments providing more choices for music production.
- MIDI files can produce very high quality and authentic reproduction of the instrument.

Sound sampling and synthesis

REVISED

Sampling is the process of converting analogue sound waves into digital form to create what is commonly known as digitised or digital sound. This is sometimes referred to as analogue to digital (ADC) conversion. An analogue sound wave is infinitely variable so in order to store this digitally, a series of readings at fixed intervals are taken from the wave in order to create the discrete data values that are a defining feature of binary data. These readings are then stored as binary codes. It is called sampling because you do not record every single change in amplitude of the waveform. Instead, you choose set points at which a reading (or sample) will be taken. Figure 26.7 shows the points at which the sample readings are taken.

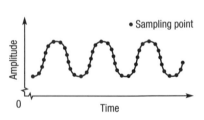

Figure 26.7 Sampling an analogue wave

To calculate how large the file size will become, you can use the following calculation:

sample rate (Hz) × length of recording (seconds) × sampling resolution (bits)

Sample rate represents the number of samples that will be taken per second. The length of the recording is simply measured in seconds and the sampling resolution refers to the number of bits allocated to representing the sound.

For example the following three samples are recorded at a resolution of 16 bits (two bytes).

0011 1100 0000 0011
1111 0101 0110 0101
0110 0110 0011 1110

Assuming a sample rate of 44 000 Hz, with a recording lasting 60 seconds, the file size would be:

$$44\,000 \times 60 \times 16 = 42\,240\,000 \text{ bits} = 5\,280\,000 \text{ bytes or } 5.28 \text{ MB}$$

When deciding on the optimum sampling rate, many programmers refer to Nyquist's Theorem, which states that to faithfully recreate the analogue signal, you should sample at least twice the highest frequency. For example, if the human ear can cope with frequencies of 20 Hz – 20 000 Hz, then the analogue frequency must be sampled at at least 40 000 Hz. The reason for doubling the frequency is to ensure that the sample covers the complete range of peaks and troughs in the analogue signal, which then allows a faithful reproduction of the sound.

Sound synthesis is another term that is used to refer to sound that is produced digitally rather than in analogue format. It means that the sound is synthesised or manufactured rather than being in its original analogue format. By definition, all sounds created by a computer are digital.

After sound has been digitally recorded, in order to hear it, the user will use either earphones or speakers. These devices are driven by analogue signals yet the data is stored as digital signals. In order to convert it so that it can be amplified and played, a digital to analogue converter (DAC) is required. Typically, the DAC is embedded in the device that plays the audio data and the signal is passed in analogue form to the loudspeakers or headphones.

Data compression

REVISED

Compression is the process of encoding information with fewer bits, so that the files take up less memory. There are several methods for doing it, depending on the type of data being encoded. Any type of data can be compressed and different techniques are used depending on the data type. These techniques lead to either lossless or lossy compression.

- Lossless means that the compressed file is as accurate as it was before compression, i.e. no data is lost.
- Lossy means that there will be some degradation in the data, for example, a grainier image might be produced.

> **Compression:** the process of reducing the number of bits required to represent data.

Lossless compression

Imagine a picture made up of millions of pixels. The picture file will contain data about each pixel, for example its colour. So part of the file might simply read: blue, blue, blue, dozens of times where there is a run of blue pixels. Rather than storing this same data over and over, you can use **run-length encoding**, which states that the next *x* pixels will be blue. So B,B,B,B,B,B,B,B becomes 8B. This is a simple example but you can see that only two encoded digits are needed to represent eight uncompressed ones, and there is no loss of data accuracy.

When compressing text files, **dictionary-based** compression techniques can be used. These work on the basis that within the text, there will be common strings of characters. Rather than rewriting these same strings, they can be coded in some way.

For example, the characters 'tion' are commonly found at the end of many words, such as 'station', 'nation' and 'creation'. Rather than storing the words individually, 'tion' can be encoded to the dictionary and then used in combination with other prefixes to form words. At the same time, 'sta', 'na' and 'crea' can be encoded to the dictionary as they too can be made into other words. Now when you need to encode any words that contain those strings of text, you can use the dictionary entry rather than writing the whole strings out again in the file.

> **Run-length encoding:** a method of compressing data by eliminating repeated data.
>
> **Dictionary-based encoding:** a method of compressing text files.

Lossy compression

There are cases where lossless compression still results in a large file as there is a limit to how small it can get while still maintaining accuracy. In some cases where the amount of memory is an issue, or where data is being transmitted across a network and the speed of transmission is vital, it might be necessary to make these files even smaller.

Figure 26.8 Lower resolution images resulting in pixellation

This is often the case with streaming audio or video. In these cases, a compression technique that leads to some degradation in data quality may be acceptable.

Lossy compression techniques work by identifying data that can be removed, while still creating an acceptable representation. In the case of audio, graphics and video, the user will have some control over the level of compression and therefore the quality of the compressed file. For example, a low resolution JPEG file will have more of the original data removed and therefore produce a pixellated image.

Summary

- Binary codes can be used to represent text, characters, numbers, graphics, video and audio.
- ASCII and Unicode are systems for representing characters.
- It is possible that the data can get corrupted at any point when it is being either processed or transmitted.
- Error detection and correction methods include check digits and majority voting.
- Bit-mapped graphics are made up of individual pixels (picture elements).

- Vector graphics are composed of objects.
- Resolution is the measure of the height and width of an image.
- Analogue signals such as sound waves need to be converted into digital form so they can be processed by the computer by sampling.
- Data is compressed to make file sizes more manageable.
- Compression can either be lossless, which means no degradation of the data after compression, or lossy, which means there will be degradation of the data.

Now test yourself

TESTED ☐

1 Describe the differences between ASCII and Unicode. [2]
2 Describe the similarities between ASCII and Unicode. [2]
3 Compare the usefulness of parity checking, check digits and majority voting. [3]
4 Calculate the resolution in pixels and storage space needed for a bitmap image 1000 × 600 pixels of 12-bit colour depth. [2]
5 Identify three things other than size and position that may need to be stored about a vector graphic image. [3]
6 Compare and contrast bitmap and vector images. [4]
7 (a) A 2½-minute song is sampled at 44 000 Hz in 16-bit samples. What size is required on disk? [2]
   (b) What difference would it make if the song was stereo instead of mono? [1]
   (c) According to Nyquist's Theorem, what should the highest frequency of the song be? [1]
8 Explain the difference between lossy and lossless compression. [2]
9 Describe how the following work:
   (a) run-length encoding [3]
   (b) dictionary-based encoding. [3]
10 Identify whether lossy or lossless compression is suitable for:
   (a) jpeg images [1]
   (b) an email [1]
   (c) a document. [1]

27 Encryption

Specification coverage

3.5.6.8 Encryption in AS Level
3.5.6.10 Encryption in A Level

Encryption basics

REVISED

Encryption is the process of scrambling data so that it cannot be understood by another person unless they know the encryption method and key used. **Decryption** is the process of turning the scrambled data back into data that can be understood. Data is encrypted before it is transmitted and decrypted when it is received. Therefore, encryption keeps data secure during transmission.

Encryption: the process of turning plaintext into scrambled ciphertext, which can only be understood if it is decrypted.

Decryption: the process of deciphering encrypted data or messages.

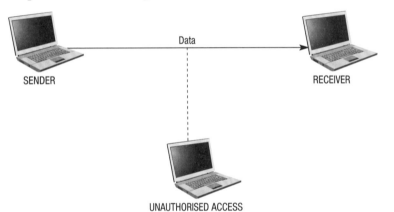

Figure 27.1 Unauthorised interception of data

All encryption works on the basis of turning **plaintext** into **ciphertext** as shown in Figure 27.2.

Plaintext: data in human-readable form.

Ciphertext: data that has been encrypted.

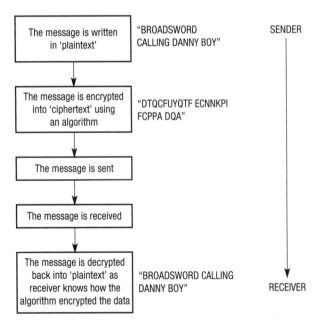

Figure 27.2 The encryption–decryption process

Plaintext is the original data in a format that can be understood. The data are then encrypted or encoded using an algorithm that turns the data into ciphertext. The message can then be sent. Encryption does not prevent the data from being intercepted, it just makes them meaningless to the person who intercepted them unless they know how the data have been encrypted.

The Caesar cipher

The **Caesar cipher** is an example of a shift or **substitution cipher**. This method substitutes each letter of the alphabet for another character by simply shifting the letters forwards or backwards. A variation on this would be to shift letters on a random basis.

A random substitution might look like this:

A	B	C	D	E	F	G	H	I	J	K	L	M	N	O	P	Q	R	S	T	U	V	W	X	Y	Z
O	Z	P	C	Y	D	B	Q	X	K	L	A	V	W	R	I	S	M	J	E	G	N	F	T	U	H

Our message when encrypted with this random substitution becomes: 'ZMROCJFRMC POAAXWB COWWU ZAU'.

Both of these methods would be fairly easy to work out, even without the key. A **key** is a piece of data used in encryption that defines the way in which plaintext is turned into ciphertext.

It could be made more secure by adding a keyword; for example, you might select the word 'BEESWAX'. First, you need to delete any repeated letters in the word, leaving you with 'BESWAX'. Then add this word to the start of the alphabet. In other words, the first seven letters of the alphabet are substituted for the keyword. Then add the remaining letters in alphabetical order:

A	B	C	D	E	F	G	H	I	J	K	L	M	N	O	P	Q	R	S	T	U	V	W	X	Y	Z
B	E	S	W	A	X	C	D	F	G	H	I	J	K	L	M	N	O	P	Q	R	T	U	V	Y	Z

A further level of complexity can be added to a substitution cipher with the use of more than one alphabet. This is known as a **polyalphabetic** cipher and rather than having one set of substitutions it could have any number of alphabets or look-up tables to work with.

This concept goes back to the fifteen century and is known as the Alberti cipher. This is also one of the underlying principles used in the Enigma machine, where several randomised alphabets were used to encrypt a message.

> **Caesar cipher:** a substitution cipher where one character of plaintext is substituted for another, which becomes the ciphertext.
>
> **Substitution cipher:** a method of encryption where one character is substituted for another to create ciphertext.
>
> **Key:** in cryptography it is the data that is used to encrypt and decrypt the data.

> **Polyalphabetic:** using more than one alphabet.

Exam tip

Although only two types of cipher are mentioned by name in the specification, you may be assessed on your understanding of general principles at a similar level.

Frequency analysis

The Caesar cipher is one of the easiest to crack because of the nature of language. In English, for example, certain letters are used more frequently than others and certain combinations of letters are also common. By examining ciphertext for frequently used letters and patterns of letters, it is possible to work out what letter has been substituted for which other letter.

> **Frequency analysis:** in cryptography it is the study of how often different letters or phrases are used.

Transposition cipher

With this type of cipher, the letters of the message are transposed or rearranged to form an anagram. You must rearrange the letters according to a set pattern to make it possible to decrypt the message. One way of doing this is called the **railfence** method where the message is split across several lines. For example:

B		O		D		W		R		C		L		I		G
	R		A		S		O		D		A		L		N	

If you now read the message off line by line it becomes: 'BODWRCLIGRASODALN'. If you were decrypting this message you would need to know that the key is that it has been split over two lines.

B	W	L
R	O	L
O	R	I
A	D	N
D	C	G
S	A	A

A variation is to put the message into a grid. This is called a **route cipher**. For example, the same message is placed into a 6 × 3 grid.

Reading down in columns from left to right will decrypt the message. Notice that you can add null or meaningless values if you have spare cells in your grid. In this case, the letter 'A' has been added to the bottom right-hand cell.

As with Caesar ciphers, complexity can be added to the key with the addition of a keyword before the main message. It is also common practice to combine then apply a substitution cipher to the transposed message so that there are two codes to crack to decipher the original message as shown in Figure 27.3.

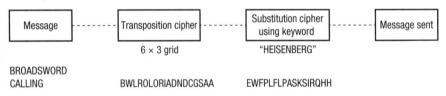

BROADSWORD
CALLING   BWLROLORIADNDCGSAA   EWFPLFLPASKSIRQHH

Figure 27.3 A substitution cipher

Vernam cipher

The **Vernam cipher** is an example of a class of encryption techniques known as **one-time pad** techniques. The key that is used is a sequence of letters that should be as long as the plaintext that is being encoded. The key can be recorded on a pad, although in the Vernam case the key was written on a punched tape for input into the telex device. For maximum security, a particular key should only be used to encrypt one message, hence the name one-time pad.

To encrypt a message, each character in the plaintext is combined with the character at the corresponding position in the key by converting the corresponding plaintext and key characters into a binary code (originally a 5-bit **Baudot code**) and using a logical XOR on these binary representations to produce a new binary code, which in turn maps back to a character. Once the ciphertext is created the key is never used again for encryption, although it will be used once more to decrypt the ciphertext.

A message is encrypted and decrypted as follows:

- The key is created, which is a completely random sequence of characters. For example, each letter in the plaintext message 'BROADSWORD' is combined with the letter at the corresponding position in the key that is written on the pad or tape:

Plaintext message	B	R	O	A	D	S	W	O	R	D
Key	H	E	L	K	K	J	V	T	U	I

- For each character in the plaintext and the key, the 5-bit Baudot representation is identified. For example, B = 11001, H = 10100. A logical XOR is then performed on the two values, which is a bitwise operation that results in a 1 only if the two bits being compared are different. In this case:

Baudot code for plaintext B	1	1	0	0	1
Baudot code for one-time pad H	1	0	1	0	0
XOR the two codes to produce ciphertext	0	1	1	0	1

- The Baudot table is then used to find the corresponding character that is represented by 01101, which is F. Therefore, the first character in the ciphertext becomes F. This process is repeated for each letter in the plaintext.

- On receipt of the ciphertext, assuming the receiver has access to the key, an XOR can be performed on the ciphertext with the key to find the original plaintext:

Baudot code for ciphertext F	0	1	1	0	1
Baudot code for key H	1	0	1	0	0
XOR the two codes to reproduce plaintext	1	1	0	0	1

- You can see that the result of the XOR operation is 11001, which is the original plaintext character of B. This process is repeated on every character in the ciphertext.

Once the entire message has been encrypted and decrypted the key is destroyed and a new random key is created. As long as the key is completely random, and is kept secret and only used once, then it is mathematically impossible to crack the code.

Computational security

The Vernam or one-time pad cipher is the only cipher that is considered to be 100% mathematically secure. All other ciphers can be cracked given enough time and enough ciphertext to work on. This leads to the concept of **computational security** or **computational hardness**. A cipher that is computationally secure is theoretically breakable but not when using current technology in a time frame that would be useful. This recognises the fact that although most encryption can theoretically be cracked, in practice it will be secure enough to withstand most threats.

Computational security: a concept of how secure data encryption is.

Computational hardness: the degree of difficulty in cracking a cipher.

Exam tip

Although mathematically secure, the Vernam cipher is dependent on the encoder having the pad with them, which makes it insecure in other ways.

When devising encryption algorithms, programmers need to be aware that some levels of encryption are harder to crack than others and that the level of security they use needs to be commensurate with the level of risk of the data being intercepted.

Computational security means that cryptographers need to be aware of the ways in which their encryption could be cracked. In addition to frequency analysis discussed earlier, there are several different methods for cracking codes:

- Identifying commonly used techniques: Many ciphers are based on substitution or transposition.
- Reverse engineering: This is the process of going back step by step until you work out how something has been put together.
- Dictionary attacks: This is the process of using a dictionary that contains common words and phrases.
- Brute force: This is similar to a dictionary attack but takes much longer as rather than looking at common words and phrases it looks at every single permutation of characters that can be created.

Summary

- Data are vulnerable to interception whenever they are being transmitted.
- Encryption is the process of scrambling data so that they can only be understood if they are decrypted.
- Decryption is the process of turning encrypted data back into meaningful data.
- A cipher is a code or key applied to plaintext to turn it into ciphertext.
- There are three main types of cipher you need to be aware of: Caesar, Vernam and transposition.
- As a programmer you need to be conscious of security issues relating to your own programs and data.

Now test yourself

TESTED

1 Define computational security. [2]
2 Compare and contrast the Caesar cipher with the Vernam cipher. [4]
3 Apply a 3-letter right-shift to the text 'Computer Science is great'. [1]

Task

1 Visit the Bletchley Park website and research the history of encryption and code breaking.

28 Hardware and software

Specification coverage

3.6.1 Hardware and software

Hardware

Computer **hardware** is the physical components of the computer. It is important to distinguish between the internal components, which are the processing and storage devices, and external components, normally referred to as peripherals.

- **External components (peripherals):** The external components of hardware are the parts that you can touch, for example the monitor, mouse, keyboard and printer. The external components are used either to get data into or out of the system. Consequently, they are referred to as input and output (I/O) devices.
- **Internal components (processing and storage):** the internal hardware components are housed within the casing of the computer and include the processor, the hard disk, memory chips, sound cards, graphics cards and the circuitry required to connect all of these devices to each other and to the I/O devices.

> **Hardware:** a generic term for the physical parts of the computer, both internal and external.

> **Exam tip**
>
> Although input/output devices as peripherals are no longer on the specification, an understanding will allow you to access wider reading and deepen your knowledge.

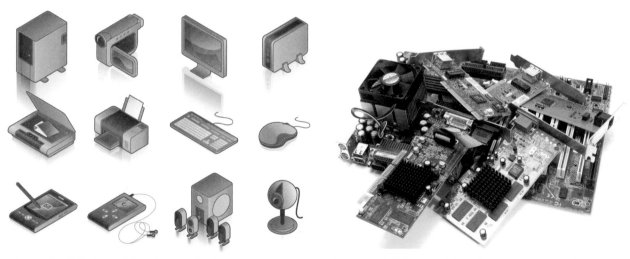

Figure 28.1 External hardware devices   **Figure 28.2 Internal hardware components**

Software

Software is the general term used to describe all of the programs that we run on our computers. These programs contain instructions that the processor will carry out in order to complete various tasks. This covers an enormous range of possibilities from standard applications, such as word processors, spreadsheets and databases, to more specific applications, such as web-authoring software and games. It also includes programs that the computer needs in order to manage all of its resources, such as file management and virus-checking software.

> **Software:** a generic term for any program that can be run on a computer.

Application software refers to all of the programs that the user uses in order to complete a particular task. In effect, it is what users use their computers for. **System software** covers a range of programs that are concerned with the more technical aspects of setting up and running the computer. There are four main types: utility programs; library programs; compilers, assemblers and interpreters; and operating system software.

Utility programs covers software that is written to carry out certain housekeeping tasks on your computer. **Utility programs** are often made available as free downloads and are designed to enhance the use of your computer and programs though your computer will still work without them. A common example of a utility program is compression software.

Library programs are similar to utility programs in that they are written to carry out common tasks. The word library indicates that there will be a number of software tools available to the users of the system. Whereas some utility programs are non-essential, library programs tend to be critical for the applications for which they were built, for example Dynamically Linked Library (DLL) files, which contain code, data and resources.

> **Application software:** programs that perform specific tasks that would need doing even if computers didn't exist, e.g. editing text, carrying out calculations.
>
> **Utility programs:** programs that perform specific common task related to running the computer, e.g. zipping files.
>
> **Library programs:** code, data and resources that can be called by other programs.

Translators: compilers, assemblers and interpreters

Translators are software used by programmers to convert programs from one language to another. There are three types: **compilers**, **assemblers** and **interpreters**. At some point, every piece of software, whether it is application software or system software, has to be written by a programmer. In order to write software, programmers use programming languages which allow them to write code in a way that is user-friendly for the programmer. However, the processor will not understand the programmers' code, so it has to be translated into machine code, that is, 0s and 1s. Compilers, assemblers and interpreters are used to carry out this translation process.

> **Translators:** software that converts programming language instructions into 0s and 1s (machine code). There are three types – compilers, assemblers and interpreters.
>
> **Compiler:** a program that translates a high-level language into machine code by translating all of the code.
>
> **Assembler:** a program that translates a program written in assembly language into machine code.
>
> **Interpreter:** a program for translating a high-level language by reading each statement in the source code and immediately performing the action.

> **Exam tip**
>
> The clue is often in the name; compilers compile source code into object code (programs), assemblers assemble assembly code, while interpreters, much like their human counterparts, interpret one line at a time.

Operating system software

An **operating system** is a collection of software designed to act as an interface between the user and the computer and manages the overall operation of the computer. It links together the hardware, the applications and the user, but hides the true complexity of the computer from the user and other software – a so-called **virtual machine**.

> **Operating system:** a suite of programs designed to control the operations of the computer.
>
> **Virtual machine:** the concept that all of the complexities of using a computer are hidden from the user and other software by the operating system.

> **Exam tip**
>
> The definition of an operating system as a virtual machine is one of the most important facts, but you may also need to be able to identify the differences in functionality between general and specific types of operating system in some detail. Wording is important (e.g. the difference between a 'reasonable' amount of time and a 'specific' amount of time for real-time operating systems).

Common tasks carried out by the operating system (OS) include:

- controlling the start-up configuration of your computer
- recognising when you have pressed a mouse button and then deciding what action to take
- sending signals to the hard disk controller, telling it what program to transfer to memory
- managing memory
- handling errors as and when they occur
- shutting down properly when you have finished
- controlling print queues
- managing the users on a network.

Resource management

In a computer with only one **processor**, only one program can be live at any one moment in time. In order to allow more than one program to appear to run simultaneously, the operating system has to allocate access to the processor and other resources such as peripherals and memory.

One of the main tasks that an operating system has to do is to make sure that all these allocations make the best possible use of the available resources. Usually the most heavily used resource in a computer is the processor. The process of allocating access to the processor and other resources is called **scheduling**.

The simplest way that an operating system can schedule access to the processor is to allocate each task a time slice. This means that each task is given an equal amount of processor time. This process of passing access to the processor from one task to the next is also known as 'round-robin' scheduling.

Accessing some devices is a relatively slow process compared to the speed at which the processor can handle requests. Rather than wait for each process to end before it can continue, the OS can effectively create a queue of commands that are waiting for the device and then handle each request in sequence or based on priority.

Every input/output device has a device driver, which is a piece of software that enables the device to communicate with the OS. Device drivers are often built in to the OS or installed when new devices are attached. When the OS starts up it loads the various drivers for all of the input/output devices it detects.

> **Resource management:** how an operating system manages hardware and software to optimise the performance of the computer.
>
> **Processor:** a device that carries out computation on data by following instructions, in order to produce an output.
>
> **Scheduling:** a technique to ensure that different users or different programs are able to work on the same computer system at the same time.

Memory management

In the same way that the operating system of a computer controls the way files are stored on a secondary storage system, such as a hard disk, the OS also controls how the primary memory or RAM is used.

The OS stores details of all the unallocated locations in a section of memory known as the heap. When an application needs some memory, this is allocated from the heap, and once an application has finished with a memory location or perhaps an application is closed, the now unneeded memory locations are returned to the heap.

The OS controls the use of main memory by creating a memory map, which shows which blocks of memory have been allocated to each task. In this way an operating system can control more than one task in the RAM at any one time.

> **Memory management:** how the operating system uses RAM to optimise the performance of the computer.

Virtual memory and paging

In some cases, the application or file you are trying to work with will be too big to fit in the available RAM. In this case a process called virtual memory can be used. This involves using secondary storage such as a hard disk to store code or files that would normally be held in RAM. The operating system then treats that part of the hard disk as if it is part of the RAM, hence the name virtual memory.

An alternative method is to hold a kernel or central block of the code in RAM. Other sections of code known as 'pages' are loaded from the secondary storage as and when they are needed. Using this method allows very large applications to run in a small section of RAM. This in turn frees up memory for other applications to use.

File management

One of the many tasks the operating system has to deal with is managing files – this includes controlling the structures that are used to store the files. The OS on a home computer uses folders or directories. These allow the user to group similar files together.

Each file has a filename but because of the folder structure it is possible to use the same filename for different files.

As hard disks get larger and larger, it is becoming increasingly common to split up or partition a hard disk. This means that although you actually only have one hard disk in your computer, the operating system splits it up into a number of partitions or logical drives. This means your computer seems to be fitted with more than one hard drive. You might use this system to store your applications on one logical drive and your data on another.

> **File management:** how an operating system stores and retrieves files.

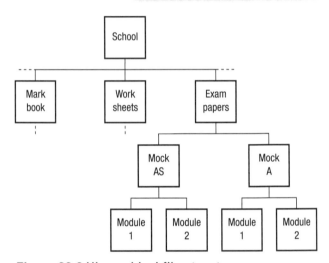

Figure 28.3 Hierarchical file structure

Summary

- A computer system is made up of hardware and software.
- Hardware is usually classified in terms of internal and external components.
- System software includes the operating system, library and utility programs.

- Compilers, interpreters and assemblers are programs that convert high-level programming languages into executable instructions.
- The operating system plays a critical role in managing resources.

Now test yourself

TESTED ☐

1 Discuss the differences between an interpreter, a compiler and an assembler. [3]
2 Identify three pieces of hardware external to the CPU. [3]
3 Define an operating system and explain three responsibilities it has to perform. [7]

29 Classification of programming languages and translation

Specification coverage

3.6.2 Classification of programming languages
3.6.3 Types of translator

Types of programming languages

REVISED

There are three main types of languages:
- machine code
- assembly language
- high-level language.

The processor of a computer can only work with binary digits (bits). This means that all the instructions given to a computer must, ultimately, be a pattern of 0s and 1s. Programs written in this format are said to be written in **machine code**.

The need to make programs more programmer-friendly led to the development of **assembly languages**. Rather than using sequences of 0s and 1s, an assembly language allows programmers to write code using words. There is a very strong connection between machine code and assembly language. This is because assembly language is basically machine code with words. The number of words that can be used in an assembly language is generally small. Each of these commands translates directly into one command in machine code. This is called a one-to-one relationship.

Most, but not all, assembly codes use a system of abbreviated words called **mnemonics**. For example, the mnemonic **LDR** stands for **Load Register** and **STR** means **Store Register**. **ADD** and **SUB** should be more obvious.

Although assembly language uses words, some of which you might recognise, the code is not particularly easy to understand. Before any code written in assembly language can be executed it has to be converted into machine code. This conversion process is carried out by an assembler.

The assembler will be able to identify some, but not all, of the errors that are likely to be hidden somewhere in the code. The code that the programmer creates is known as the **source code**. The **assembler** takes this source code and translates it into a machine code version that is known as the **object code**. As with machine code, assembly languages are based on one processor so they are generally not very portable.

Assembly language is still used in certain situations today as it has a number of advantages over high-level languages:

- Programs are executed quickly as a compiler does not optimise the machine code that it produces as effectively as a programmer who codes in an assembly language that maps directly to machine code.
- Program code is relatively compact for the same reason.
- Assembly language allows direct manipulation of the registers on the processor, giving high levels of control.

Machine code: the lowest level of code made up of 0s and 1s.

Assembly language: a way of programming that involves writing mnemonics.

Mnemonics: short codes that are used as instructions when programming, e.g. LDR, ADD.

Exam tip

Practising your assembly code will enable you to learn the foibles and save time in the exam.

Exam tip

The version of assembly language AQA will expect you to know is based on the ARM processor in the Raspberry Pi.

Source code: programming code that has not yet been compiled into an executable file.

Assembler: a program that translates a program written in assembly language into machine code.

Object code: compiled code that can be run as an executable on any computer with the same CPU architecture.

High-level languages

Machine code and assembly languages are known collectively as **low-level languages**. The increasingly complex demands made on computers meant that writing programs in assembly code was too slow and cumbersome. **High-level languages** were developed to overcome this problem.

Whereas low-level languages are machine-oriented, high-level languages are problem-oriented. This means that the commands and the way the program is structured are based on what the program will have to do rather than the components of the computer it will be used with. This means that a program written in a high-level language will be portable. It can be written on one type of computer and then executed on other types of computer.

High-level languages are often classified into three groups based on the programming paradigm. A paradigm is a concept for the way something works:

- **Imperative languages**: Also known as procedural languages, these work by typing in lists of instructions (known as subroutines or procedures) that the computer has to follow.
- **Object-oriented languages**: These work by creating objects where the instructions and data required to run the program are contained within a single object. Objects can be further grouped into classes.
- **Declarative languages**: These work by describing what the program should accomplish rather than how it should accomplish it. One type of declarative language is logic programming, which is used widely in the fields of artificial intelligence and works by programming in facts and rules, rather than instructions. Another type of declarative language is a **functional language**, which works by treating procedures more like mathematical functions. The building blocks of the program therefore are functions rather than lists of instructions. SQL is another type of declarative language which you will become familiar with.

The main characteristics of a high-level language are:

- It is easier for a programmer to identify what a command does as the keywords are more like natural language.
- Like assembly languages, high-level languages need to be translated.
- Unlike assembly code, one command in a high-level language might be represented by a whole sequence of machine-code instructions. This is called a one-to-many relationship.
- They are portable.
- They make use of a wide variety of program structures to make the process of program writing more straightforward. As a result, they are also easier to maintain.

> **Low-level language:** machine code and assembly language.
>
> **High-level language:** a programming language that allows programs to be written using English keywords and that is platform independent.
>
> **Imperative language:** a language based on giving the computer commands or procedures to follow.
>
> **Object-oriented language:** a programming paradigm that encapsulates instructions and data together into objects.
>
> **Declarative languages:** languages that declare or specify what properties a result should have, e.g. results will be based on functions.
>
> **Functional language:** a programming paradigm that uses mathematical functions.

Translating high-level languages

REVISED

One of the main features of high-level languages is that they are programmer-friendly. Unfortunately, this means the computer will not understand any of the high-level language source code, so it will have to be translated in some way. This process is called translation and in order to carry it out a special piece of systems software called a **translator** is needed.

The assembler is the translator used for low-level languages and there are two types of translator for high-level languages: an interpreter and a compiler.

> **Translator:** the general name for any program that translates code from one language to another, for example translating source code into machine code.

Interpreters

An **interpreter** works by reading a statement of the source code and immediately performing the required action. It may do this by interpreting the syntax of each statement, or by calling predefined routines.

Benefits of using an interpreter:
- You do not need to compile the whole program in order to run sections of code. You can execute the code one statement at a time.
- As the code is translated each time it is executed, program code can be run on processors with different instruction sets.
- Because of this, an interpreter is most likely to be used while a program is being developed.

Drawbacks of using an interpreter:
- No matter how many times a section of code is revisited in a program it will need translating every time. This means that the overall time needed to execute a program can be very long.
- The source code can only be translated and therefore executed on a computer that has the same interpreter installed.
- The source code must be distributed to users, whereas with a compiled program, only the executable code is needed.

Compilers

A **compiler** converts the whole source code into object code before the program can be executed. The good thing about this is that once you have carried out this process you will have some object code that can be executed immediately every time, so the execution time will be quick. This is ideal once you have sorted out all the bugs in your program.

Benefits of using a compiler:
- Once the source code has been compiled you no longer need the compiler or the source code.
- If you want to pass your object code on to someone else to use they will find it difficult to work out what the original source code was. This process of working out what the source code was is known as reverse engineering.

Drawbacks of using a compiler:
- Because the whole program has to be converted from source code to object code every time you make even the slightest alteration to your code, it can take a long time to debug.
- The object code will only run on a computer that has the same platform.

Bytecode

Some programming languages use **bytecode**, which is an instruction set that can be executed using a virtual machine. The virtual machine can emulate the architecture of a computer, meaning that the source code written using bytecode can be translated into a format that can be executed on any platform using a virtual machine. One example of this is Java.

> **Interpreter:** a program for translating a high-level language by reading each statement in the source code and immediately performing the action.
>
> **IDE:** Integrated Development Environment, for example IDLE in Python.

> **Exam tip**
>
> Interpreted languages such as Python may not pick up even minor errors until the code is run. Use the IDE helpers such as error highlighting to save you debugging time during Paper 1.

> **Compiler:** a program that translates a high-level language into machine code by translating all of the code.

> **Bytecode:** an instruction set used for programming that can be executed on any computer using a virtual machine.

> **Exam tip**
>
> Bytecode tends to be closer to machine code so is faster to execute than an interpreted language, but slower than a natively compiled language.

Summary

- There are three main types of programming languages: machine code, assembly language and high-level languages.
- Machine code and assembly language are known as low-level languages.
- Machine code uses 0s and 1s.
- Assembly languages use mnemonics.
- High-level languages use natural language keywords.
- Assembly language needs to be converted to machine code using an assembler.

- High-level languages need to be converted to machine code using an interpreter or a compiler.
- There are three main programming paradigms: imperative (procedural), declarative and object-oriented.
- Bytecode is an instruction set that can be implemented using a virtual machine and is therefore platform independent.

Now test yourself

TESTED ☐

1 Identify and justify a solution where the following would be suitable:
  (a) high-level imperative language [2]
  (b) high-level functional language [2]
  (c) high-level declarative language [2]
  (d) low-level assembly language [2]
  (e) low-level machine code. [2]
2 Describe the difference between an interpreter and a compiler. [4]
3 Explain when a developer may want to use a bytecode-based language such as Java. [2]

30 Boolean algebra

Specification coverage

3.6.4 Logic gates
3.6.5 Boolean algebra

Introducing Boolean algebra

REVISED

Boolean algebra is a form of algebra named after George Boole who originally developed it in the mid–1800s. The study of Boolean algebra is closely linked to logic gates. The basic principle is that logical expressions can be evaluated that will result in one of two results/outcomes – either TRUE or FALSE.

For example, the following are examples of **Boolean expressions**:

```
The button has been pressed
5 < 10
Age > 17 and hold a driving licence
```

As there is one input there are two possible results, 0 and 1. Boolean logic can be used to evaluate statements with any number of inputs to return a TRUE or FALSE value. The statement about the driving licence above has two inputs. To evaluate it:

```
At least 17 = 1
Under 17 = 0
```

and

```
Hold a licence = 1
No licence = 0
```

In this case there are four possible inputs: 00, 01, 10, 11.

> **Boolean expression:** an equation made up of Boolean operations.

Truth tables

REVISED

We can use a **truth table** to combine the permutations of 0s and 1s and work out which shows whether the answer is TRUE or FALSE. Table 30.1 shows all the possible inputs and the output of each combination as follows.

In this example: A = `at least 17` and B = `Holds a licence`.

> **Truth table:** a method of representing/calculating the result of every possible combination of inputs in a Boolean expression.

Exam tip

Truth tables are common 1-mark questions and memorising them can be a good way to 'bank' time within an exam.

Table 30.1 A truth table

Inputs		Output
A	B	Q
0	0	0
0	1	0
1	0	0
1	1	1

Exam tip

Much like ordinary algebra, the letters for inputs can be anything; starting from A is common practice for inputs and Q is common for the output.

Q shows the possible results. The two inputs need to be ANDed together to generate the final result. In this case there is only one combination of A and B that will lead to a TRUE statement being returned, which is where A and B are both 1.

When creating Boolean statements, it is possible to use the relational operators in Table 30.2.

Table 30.2 **Relational operators**

Operator	Name of operator
<	less than
<=	less than or equal to
==	equal to
!=	not equal to
>=	greater than or equal to
>	greater than

Statements can be combined to form more complex expressions and this is done using six main **Boolean operations**: AND, OR, NOT, NAND, NOR and XOR. We will look at each of these in turn.

Boolean operation: a single Boolean function.

AND operation

REVISED

As we saw in the first example, in an **AND** statement, all conditions (inputs) must be TRUE to generate a TRUE output. Q = A AND B, which can also be notated as Q = A.B

AND gate: result is true if both inputs are true.

Table 30.3 **Truth table for AND**

Inputs		Output
A	B	Q
0	0	0
0	1	0
1	0	0
1	1	1

The expression therefore is only TRUE when A and B are both 1. You could also say that the expression is TRUE when Q = 1.

OR operation

REVISED

An **OR** expression can return a TRUE result when any of the inputs are true. This is written as Q = A OR B or Q = A+B with the + representing the OR expression.

OR: Boolean operation that outputs true if either of its inputs are true.

Table 30.4 **Truth table for OR**

Inputs		Output
A	B	Q
0	0	0
0	1	1
1	0	1
1	1	1

Exam tip

Confusing the + symbol and the AND operation is a common mistake.

NOT operation

The **NOT** statement inverts the input so that TRUE becomes FALSE and FALSE becomes TRUE.

This is written as Q = NOT A or $Q = \bar{A}$. Notice the overbar above the A, which is standard notation for NOT.

NOT: Boolean operation that inverts the result so true becomes false and false becomes true.

Table 30.5 Truth table for NOT

A	Q
0	1
1	0

Notice that the results are inverted so FALSE becomes TRUE and TRUE becomes FALSE.

The NOT statement can be used in combination with other Boolean expressions to create more complex selections.

NAND operation

NAND is a combination of NOT and AND and produces a TRUE result if any of the inputs are false. It is commonly used to create **NAND gates** on integrated circuits.

NAND: Boolean operation that outputs true if any of the inputs are false.

NAND gate: result is true if any of the inputs are false.

Table 30.6 Truth table for NAND

Inputs		Output
A	B	Q
0	0	1
0	1	1
1	0	1
1	1	0

This is written as $Q = \overline{A.B}$, which means Q = NOT A.B. This could be described as the inverted form of A.B.

NOR operation

The **NOR** or NOT OR expression results in a TRUE value only if all inputs are FALSE. It means that the answer is TRUE if it is neither A nor B. It is used to create **NOR gates** on integrated circuits, which can be used, for example, to make CMOS devices (see Chapter 35).

NOR: Boolean operation that outputs true if all of its inputs are false.

NOR gate: result is true if both inputs are false.

Table 30.7 Truth table for NOR

Inputs		Output
A	B	Q
0	0	1
0	1	0
1	0	0
1	1	0

This is written as $Q = \overline{A+B}$, which means it is Q = NOT A+B. This could be described as the inverted form of A+B.

XOR operation

The exclusive OR expression produces a TRUE result only when one of the inputs is TRUE and the other is FALSE. If they are both TRUE it returns a FALSE result. It can be used to carry out bitwise operations and to create an adder in logic circuits.

XOR: Boolean operation that is true if either input is true but not if both inputs are true.

Table 30.8 Truth table for XOR

Inputs		Output
A	B	Q
0	0	0
0	1	1
1	0	1
1	1	0

Exam tip

The XOR is sometimes written as GOR or EXOR but they all mean the same thing.

This is written as Q = A⊕B, which means Q is true when either A or B are true, but not when both are true. Note that A⊕B is the same as $A.\overline{B}+\overline{A}.B$.

Simplifying Boolean expressions

When using Boolean expressions, it is good practice to reduce the expression into its simplest form. As Boolean algebra is used to create logic gates, simplifying the expressions also simplifies the actual circuit that will be built, reducing the number of components needed, which in turn will make the circuit cheaper to make, more efficient in operation and more reliable as fewer gates are being used.

To help visualise the process for ensuring that Boolean expressions are in their simplest form you can run it through a truth table. For example, take the expression A.B+A. The values of A can be 0 or 1 and the values of B can be 0 or 1 leading to four possible inputs: 00, 01, 10, 11.

The first part of the statement is A.B so the result is true when A and B = 1.

Exam tip

Unless otherwise specified in the question, you can simplify Boolean expressions using either truth tables or Boolean algebra. While you need skills in either, truth tables can be faster and are less prone to errors.

Table 30.9 Truth table for A AND B

A	B	A.B
0	0	0
0	1	0
1	0	0
1	1	1

Next we look at the +A part of the expression, which means OR A in Boolean expressions. This means that (A.B)+A will be true when A and B is 1 or A is 1.

Table 30.10 Truth table for (A.B)+A

A	B	A.B	(A.B)+A
0	0	0	0
1	0	0	1
0	1	0	0
1	1	1	1

 Now test yourself answers at www.therevisionbutton.co.uk/myrevisionnotes

Looking at the final column of Table 3.10 you can see that (A.B)+A is only true when A is true. Therefore the expression can be reduced to A:

$$(A.B)+A = A$$

Rules have been developed as a method of simplifying expressions. Table 30.11 shows the common rules associated with what are known as Boolean identities.

Exam tip

Being familiar with the truth tables for the standard gates can help you spot patterns when simplifying.

Exam tip

The expressions factorise the same way as normal mathematical expressions, e.g. A.B+A≡A(B+1). This often makes it easier to simplify expressions. In the example above B+1 is just 1 so the expression simplifies to A.

Table 30.11 Common rules associated with Boolean identities

Identity name	AND form	OR form
Identity	A.1 = A	A+0 = A
Null (or Dominance) Law	A.0 = 0	A+1 = 1
Idempotence Law	A.A = A	A+A = A
Inverse Law	A.Ā = 0	A+Ā = 1
Commutative Law	A.B = B.A	A+B = B+A
Associative Law	(A.B).C = A.(B.C)	(A+B)+C = A+(B+C)
Distributive Law	A+B.C = (A+B).(A+C)	A.(B+C) = A.B+A.C
Absorption Law	A.(A+B) = A	A+A.B = A
De Morgan's Law	$\overline{(A.B)} = \overline{A}+\overline{B}$	$\overline{(A+B)} = \overline{A}.\overline{B}$
Double Complement Law		$\overline{\overline{A}} = A$

Table 30.12 Explanations of the main identities and rules

A.B = B.A	The order in which two variables are ANDed makes no difference
A+B = B+A	The order in which two variables are ORed makes no difference
A.0 = 0	A variable ANDed with 0 equals 0
A+1 = 1	A variable ORed with 1 equals 1
A+0 = A	A variable ORed with 0 equals the variable
A.1 = A	A variable ANDed with 1 equals the variable
A.A = A	A variable ANDed with itself equals the variable
A+A = A	A variable ORed with itself equals the variable
A.Ā = 0	A variable ANDed with its inverse equals 0
A+Ā = 1	A variable ORed with its inverse equals 1
$\overline{\overline{A}}$ = A	A variable that is double inversed equals the variable
(A.B).C = A.(B.C)	It makes no difference how the variables are grouped together when ANDed
(A+B)+C = A+(B+C)	It makes no difference how the variables are grouped together when ORed
A.(B+C) = A.B+A.C	The expression can be distributed or factored out, meaning that variables can be moved in and out of brackets either side of the expression. In English this expression would be A AND (B OR C) = (A AND B) OR (A AND C)

De Morgan's Law

De Morgan's Law is another way of simplifying Boolean statements by inverting all the variables, changing ANDs to ORs and ORs to ANDs and then inverting the whole expression. One application is to simplify statements so that only NAND or NOR gates are used. This makes it much simpler to create logic gates and circuits, which in turn makes it easier to design and build microprocessors. For example, solid state drives are made up of NAND gates.

In simple terms this means that ANDs can replace ORs and ORs can replace ANDs. This works as long as the rest of the expression is changed or negated to take account of this.

The basic principles are:
- Rule 1: NOT (A AND B) is the same as (NOT A) OR (NOT B)
- Rule 2: NOT (A OR B) is the same as (NOT A) AND (NOT B)

In algebraic notation:
- Rule 1: $\overline{A.B}$ is the same as $\overline{A}+\overline{B}$
- Rule 2: $\overline{A+B}$ is the same as $\overline{A}.\overline{B}$

The Venn diagram in Figure 30.1 shows the concept. The area outside the Venn diagram is X. We can define X as being:
- NOT in A+B and
- NOT in A and also NOT in B.

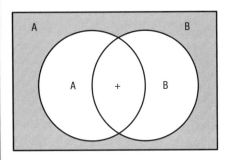

Figure 30.1 Venn diagram representing NOT (A and B)

This could be written as follows:

$$X = \overline{A+B}$$

$$X = \overline{A}.\overline{B}$$

$$\overline{A.B} = \overline{A}+\overline{B}$$

When using De Morgan's Law to write Boolean expressions, the following steps must be taken:
- You can only apply De Morgan's Law to one operator at a time.
- If the operator is an OR, change it to an AND, and vice versa.
- Invert the terms on either side of the operator.
- Invert the entire expression.

> **De Morgan's Law**: a process for simplifying Boolean expressions.

> **Exam tip**
>
> If you need to use De Morgan's Law in the exam when simplifying expressions, writing 'DML' is sufficient to identify it to the examiner.

> **Exam tip**
>
> An easy way to remember this is to remember that everything changes, i.e. if you have a bar over the whole expression it will be split into two, if an input has a single bar it will lose it or if it doesn't have a bar it will gain one. Plus it changes to OR and vice-versa, e.g. $\overline{A}.\overline{B} \equiv A+B$ in the most extreme case.

For example, Figure 30.2 shows two ways to simplify the expression: $A + \overline{A} . \overline{B}$.

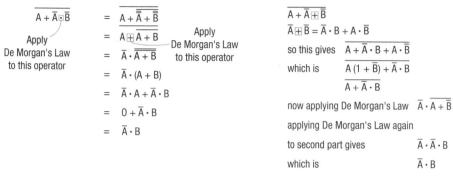

$$\overline{A + \overline{A} \oplus \overline{B}} = \overline{A + \overline{A} + \overline{\overline{B}}}$$

Apply De Morgan's Law to this operator

$$= \overline{A \oplus \overline{A} + B}$$

Apply De Morgan's Law to this operator

$$= \overline{A} \cdot \overline{\overline{A} + B}$$

$$= \overline{A} \cdot (A + B)$$

$$= \overline{A} \cdot A + \overline{A} \cdot B$$

$$= 0 + \overline{A} \cdot B$$

$$= \overline{A} \cdot B$$

$$\overline{A + \overline{A} \oplus \overline{B}}$$

$$\overline{A} \oplus \overline{B} = \overline{A} \cdot B + A \cdot \overline{B}$$

so this gives $\overline{A + \overline{A} \cdot B + A \cdot \overline{B}}$

which is $\overline{A(1 + \overline{B}) + \overline{A} \cdot B}$

$$\overline{A + \overline{A} \cdot B}$$

now applying De Morgan's Law $\overline{A} \cdot \overline{\overline{A} + \overline{B}}$

applying De Morgan's Law again

to second part gives $\overline{A} \cdot \overline{A} \cdot B$

which is $\overline{A} \cdot B$

Figure 30.2 **Applying De Morgan's Law**

Summary

- Boolean algebra returns a value that is either TRUE or FALSE.
- Truth tables are a visual method of showing the results of a Boolean expression.
- You need to know how to construct AND, OR, NOT, NAND, NOR and XOR statements

and combine them to create more complex expressions.
- You should always try to create Boolean expressions in their simplest form.
- De Morgan's Law is a method that can be used to simplify Boolean algebra expressions.

Now test yourself

TESTED ☐

1 Draw truth tables for:
   (a) AND [1]
   (b) OR [1]
   (c) NOT [1]
   (d) XOR [1]
   (e) NAND [1]
   (f) NOR [1]
2 Describe De Morgan's Laws. [3]
3 Simply the following Boolean expressions without the use of truth tables
   (a) $\overline{(A.B)} + (A.\overline{B})$ [3]
   (b) $(C + D) + C$ [2]
4 Simply the following Boolean expressions using truth tables
   (a) $(\overline{A}.B) + \overline{(A.B)}$ [3]
   (b) $C.D + C + \overline{D}$ [3]
5 Prove that $\overline{A.B} = \overline{A} + \overline{B}$ [3]

31 Logic gates

Logic gates

Logic gates are electronic components used in registers, memory chips and processors to evaluate **Boolean expressions**. There is a one-to-one relationship between Boolean expressions and logic gates. Logic gates are represented as logic diagrams and also have a corresponding truth table. Consequently, there is a logic diagram for each of the main Boolean expressions that we looked at in the previous chapter.

The logic gates for each of the six basic Boolean expressions are shown in Figure 31.1.

> **Logic gate:** an electronic component used to perform Boolean algorithms.
>
> **Boolean expressions:** an equation made up of Boolean operations.

Gate	Symbol	Operator
and	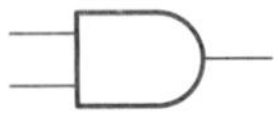	$A{\cdot}B$
or	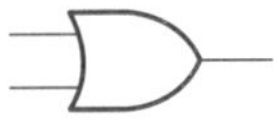	$A{+}B$
not	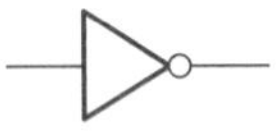	$\overline{A}$
nand	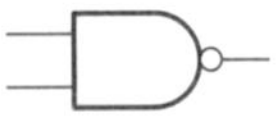	$\overline{A{\cdot}B}$
nor	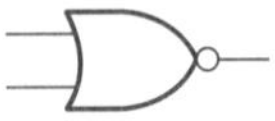	$\overline{A{+}B}$
xor	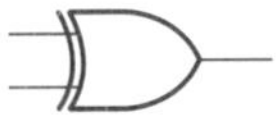	$A{\oplus}B$

Figure 31.1 Logic gate symbols and corresponding Boolean expressions

Logic gates take inputs and produce a single output. In the electronic circuit, the inputs are voltages with a high voltage representing a 1 and a low voltage representing a 0. For example, the logic gate for an AND expression is shown in Figure 31.2.

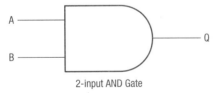

2-input AND Gate

Figure 31.2 The AND gate

A and B are the inputs and Q is the output so this diagram is the equivalent of A.B = Q

The standard ANSI/IEEE standard 91–1984 diagram for each logic gate is shown below along with its truth table and Boolean notation for ease of reference.

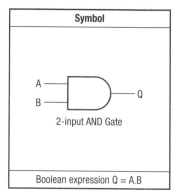

Symbol	Truth table		
	A	B	Q
	0	0	0
	0	1	0
2-input AND Gate	1	0	0
	1	1	1
Boolean expression Q = A.B	A AND B = Q		

Figure 31.3 The AND gate with truth table

AND gate: result is true if both inputs are true.

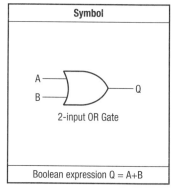

Symbol	Truth table		
	A	B	Q
	0	0	0
	0	1	1
2-input OR Gate	1	0	1
	1	1	1
Boolean expression Q = A+B	A OR B = Q		

Figure 31.4 The OR gate with truth table

OR gate: result is true if either input is true.

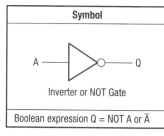

Symbol	Truth table	
	A	Q
	0	1
Inverter or NOT Gate	1	0
Boolean expression Q = NOT A or $\overline{A}$	The inversion of A = Q	

Figure 31.5 The NOT gate with truth table

NOT gate: inverts the result so true becomes false and false becomes true.

Symbol	Truth table		
	A	B	Q
	0	0	1
	0	1	1
A	1	0	1
B	1	1	0
2-input NAND Gate			
Boolean expression Q = $\overline{A.B}$	A AND B = NOT Q		

Figure 31.6 The NAND gate with truth table

NAND gate: result is true if any of the inputs are false.

Symbol	Truth table		
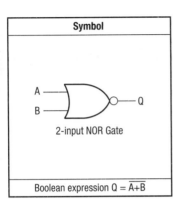	A	B	Q
	0	0	1
	0	1	0
	1	0	0
	1	1	0
Boolean expression Q = $\overline{A+B}$	A OR B = NOT Q		

2-input NOR Gate

Figure 31.7 The NOR gate with truth table

> **NOR gate**: result is true if both inputs are false.

> **Exam tip**
>
> Compare the truth table of this to $\overline{A}.\overline{B}$ and you will see that they are identical

Symbol	Truth table		
2-input Ex-OR Gate	A	B	Q
	0	0	0
	0	1	1
	1	0	1
	1	1	0
Boolean expression Q = A⊕B			

Figure 31.8 The XOR gate with truth table

> **XOR gate**: result is true if either input is true but not if both inputs are true.

> **Exam tip**
>
> Compare the truth table of this to $A.\overline{B}+\overline{A}.B$ and you will see that they are identical.

Combining logic gates

REVISED

> **Exam tip**
>
> To create a logic gate diagram from a Boolean expression, apply decomposition; break the problem down into manageable parts and deal with them a bit at a time.

Logic circuits are made up of a series of logic gates to create full systems. These can get very complex as there may be thousands of gates connected together. The output from the first gate becomes the input for the second gate and so on. Therefore, there will be various values generated until a final value of Q is arrived at. Two examples of combining logic gates together are to create the half and full adder.

> **Logic circuit**: a combination of logic gates.

> **Exam tip**
>
> In some exam questions you may be limited to certain gates only. Using the same input signal in both inputs of a gate can alter how the gate behaves.

Full and half adder

Adders are commonly found in the **Arithmetic Logic Unit (ALU)** in the CPU and are used to add binary values. There are two main types, the **half adder** and the **full adder**.

> **Arithmetic Logic Unit (ALU)**: part of the processor that processes and manipulates data.
>
> **Half adder**: a circuit that performs addition using inputs from A and B only.
>
> **Full adder**: a circuit that performs addition using inputs from A and B plus a carry bit.

Adders take in two bits A and B and add them to create a sum, S. So A + B = S. There is a further bit required called a **carry bit**, for when the result of the sum requires a further digit. For example, binary addition of 1 + 1 results in 10 (i.e. 0 carry 1), so the carry bit is needed to store this additional bit.

A half adder calculates the sum and stores the value of the carry bit C as well as the result S. The logic diagram to represent this is shown in Figure 31.9.

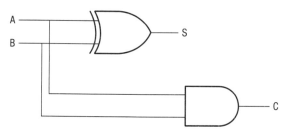

Figure 31.9 A logic circuit for a half adder

The XOR gate is used to look at inputs A and B:
- If A = 0 and B = 1 or if A = 1 and B = 0 then the value for S will be 1.
- Where A and B are both 0, the sum will be 0.
- Where A and B are both 1, then the answer is 10 in binary, which means that 0 is the result for S with the 1 put into the carry bit.

The truth table shows the values of C and S for every possible input of A and B.

Inputs		Outputs	
A	B	C	S
0	0	0	0
1	0	0	1
0	1	0	1
1	1	1	0

Half adders can be added/chained together to create a full adder. Full adders take three inputs, which are the two binary digits to be added, plus the carry bit from the previous addition. The output is the sum (S) plus the carry bit. Notice in Figure 31.10 that C_{in} represents the value of the carry bit at the start of the addition and C_{out} is the value of the carry bit at the end. C_{out} from the first addition becomes C_{in} on the second addition and so on.

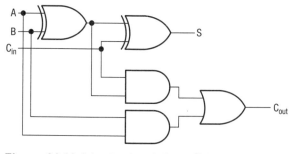

Figure 31.10 A logic circuit for a full adder

- The XOR gate works in the same way as a half adder to identify where the values of A and B are different. Where they are different the result is 1; where they are the same the result is 0.
- A second XOR gate is used to perform the same function on the result of A and B with the value of C_{in} to generate S.

> **Carry bit:** used to store a 0 or 1 depending on the result of binary addition.

- A and B are ANDed together.
- C_{in} is ANDed with the result A XOR B.
- These two are ORed together to calculate C_{out}.

The truth table shows the values of C_{in} and C_{out} and S for every possible input of A and B.

Inputs			Outputs	
A	B	C_{in}	C_{out}	S
0	0	0	0	0
1	0	0	0	1
0	1	0	0	1
1	1	0	1	0
0	0	1	0	1
1	0	1	1	0
0	1	1	1	0
1	1	1	1	1

Edge-triggered D-type flip-flop

Logic gates and logic circuits show how 0s and 1s can be manipulated to evaluate Boolean expressions. Data is passed around these gates and circuits at very high speed. However, as soon as the next set of inputs are fed in, the previous inputs are lost. Therefore some form of memory is needed and this is provided by a **flip-flop**, which is capable of storing one bit.

> **Flip-flop:** a memory unit that can store one bit.

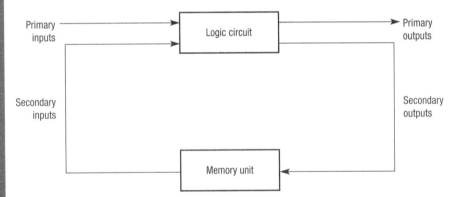

Figure 31.11 An edge-triggered D-type flip-flop

This means that the logic circuit is now receiving two sets of inputs, primary and secondary. It uses the system **clock** to synchronise these requests. Each pulse of the system clock has a rising edge and a falling edge, which represents each pulse of the clock.

> **Clock:** a device that generates a signal used to synchronise the components of a computer.

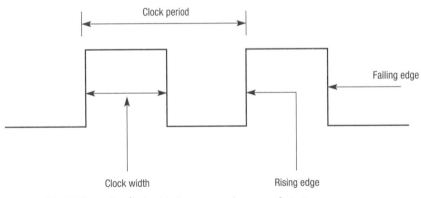

Figure 31.12 How the 'edge' triggers a change of state

In the case of an **edge-triggered D-type flip-flop** this means that on each pulse of the clock, the flip-flop will change state. This means that for each pulse of the clock, data coming from the input will be stored in the flip-flop and continue to be output until the next trigger pulse is received.

> **Edge-triggered D-type flip-flop:** a memory unit that changes state with each pulse of the clock.

Summary

- Logic gates are a way of designing and describing the way in which electronic components within registers and processors are constructed.
- Logic gates evaluate Boolean expressions.
- There are six main symbols that relate directly to the six main Boolean expressions.

- Logic gates can be combined to represent more complex systems.
- Logic gates effectively show how 0s and 1s are manipulated and binary addition takes place within them using either a half or a full adder.
- An edge-triggered D-type flip-flop is a memory unit that temporarily stores the result of an operation.

Exam tip

Although not required, writing the operator in the middle of your logic gate symbols can aid clarity.

Now test yourself

TESTED ☐

1 Draw a diagram using AND and XOR symbols only to represent the following Boolean expressions.
  (a) Q = A ⊕ (B.B)   [2]
  (b) Q = A ⊕ (B.C)   [2]
2 Draw diagrams for the following Boolean expressions.
  (a) Q = $\overline{(A + B)}$. $\overline{(A.C)}$ [5]
  (b) Q = (A + B) . (C + A)   [3]
3 Draw a Boolean expression and a truth table for the following circuit diagram.   [6]

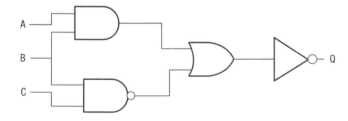

Task

1 Research and draw a half-adder and full-adder diagram.

32 Internal hardware of a computer

Processor

REVISED ☐

The **processor** is a device that carries out computation on data by following instructions. It handles all of the instructions that it receives from the user and from the hardware and software.

Physically, the processor is made up of a thin slice of silicon approximately 2 cm square. Using microscopic manufacturing techniques, the silicon is implanted with millions of transistors. Microscopic wires called buses connect groups of transistors together. The transistors are used to control the flow of electrical pulses that are timed via the computer's clock. The pulses of electricity represent different parts of the instruction that the processor is carrying out. Each of these pulses is routed around the circuitry of these transistors at very high speeds. In theory a 3 GHz processor could process 3000 million instructions per second.

> **Processor**: a device that carries out computation on data by following instructions, in order to produce an output.

Figure 32.1 A modern processor

Main memory

REVISED ☐

Memory is used to store data and instructions. It is connected to the processor which will fetch the data and instructions it needs from memory, decode the instructions and then execute them. This is commonly known as the **fetch–execute cycle** and is a key principle in modern computing. Any new data created will be stored back into memory. Put simply, memory is a medium of storage. There are two main types: RAM and ROM.

> **Main memory**: stores data and instructions that will be used by the processor.
>
> **Fetch–execute cycle**: the continuous process carried out by the processor when running programs.
>
> **Random Access Memory (RAM)**: stores data and can be read to and written from.
>
> **Chip**: an electronic component contained within a thin slice of silicon.

RAM – Random Access Memory

RAM is temporary storage space that can be accessed very quickly. This means that applications such as word processors and spreadsheets will run at high speed. Physically, RAM is a chip or series of **chips** on which the data is stored electronically. It is made up of millions of cells, each of which has its own unique address. Each cell can contain either an instruction or some data.

The cells can be accessed as they are needed by the processor, by referencing the address. That is, they can be accessed randomly, hence the name. Because they are electronic they are able to be accessed quickly. However, RAM is volatile, which means that when you turn your computer off, all of the contents of RAM are lost.

Figure 32.2 RAM chips

ROM – Read Only Memory

ROM is also a method of storing data and instructions. However, it is not volatile which means that the contents of ROM are not lost when you switch off. Unlike RAM, the user cannot alter the contents of ROM as it is read-only. It is important to note that it is possible to have programmable ROM, which is used in memory sticks and other devices. The definition here is of traditional ROM used within a PC.

In this case, ROM is used to store a limited number of instructions relating to the set-up of the computer. These settings are stored in the BIOS which stands for Basic Input/Output System.

When you switch on your computer it carries out a number of instructions. For example, it checks the hardware devices are plugged in and it loads parts of the operating system. All of these instructions are stored in ROM. The instructions are programmed into ROM by the manufacturer of the PC.

> **Read Only Memory (ROM):** stores data and can be read from, but not written to (unless programmable ROM).

> **Exam tip**
>
> Although RAM normally refers to the RAM chip memory discussed on the previous page, there are other instances not covered by this specification. Don't think RAM and ROM are mutually exclusive and fall into the trap of comparing and contrasting them.

Addressable memory

REVISED

Memory is made up of millions of addressable cells and the various instructions and data that make up a program will be stored across a number of these cells. Each address can be uniquely identified. It is the job of the processor to retrieve each instruction and data item and to carry out instructions in a sequential manner.

Memory is organised in a systematic way. Using the addresses, different programs can be stored in different parts of memory. In this way the processor is able to find the data and instructions it needs much more quickly than if the programs were stored completely randomly. A memory map can be produced which shows which programs are stored at which addresses. You will see that memory addresses are normally shown in hexadecimal format rather than binary as the hex version is shorter.

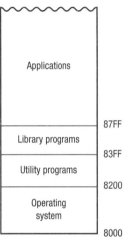

Figure 32.3 A basic memory map

Buses

REVISED

Buses are groups of parallel microscopic wires that connect the processor to the various input and output controllers being used by the computer. They are also used to connect the internal components of a microprocessor, known as registers, and to connect the microprocessor to memory. There are three types of **bus**: data, address and control.

Data bus

The instructions and data that comprise a computer program pass back and forth between the processor and memory as the program is run. The **data bus** carries the data both to and from memory and to and from the **I/O controllers**, that is, the bus is bidirectional or two-way. The instructions and data held in memory will vary in size. Each memory cell will have a width measured in bits. For example, it may have a width of 32 bits.

> **Bus:** microscopic parallel wires that transmit data between internal components.
>
> **Data bus:** transfers data between the processor and memory.
>
> **Input/Output (I/O) controller:** controls the flow of information between the processor and the input and output devices.

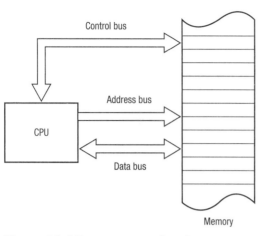

Figure 32.4 **Buses connecting the processor to memory**

The data bus connects the registers to each other and to memory. The amount of data that can be passed along the bus depends on how many wires are in the bus. An 8-bit data bus has eight wires. There are only two things that can pass down each wire, that is a 0 or a 1. Therefore, by using eight wires on the data bus, we can transmit any item of data that can be represented using 2^8 combinations which is 256.

The greater the width of the data bus, in terms of wires, the more data can be transmitted in one pulse of the clock. Consequently, the size of the data bus is a key factor in determining the overall speed and performance of the computer. 32-bit and 64-bit buses are the norm at the time of writing. The data bus width is usually the same as the **word length** of the processor and the same as the memory word length.

Address bus

The **address bus** only goes in one direction – from the processor into memory. All the instructions and data that a processor needs to carry out a task are stored in memory. Every memory location has an address. The processor carries out the instructions one after the other. The address bus is used by the processor and carries the memory address of the next instruction or data item. The address bus therefore is used to access anything that is stored in memory, not just instructions.

The size of the address bus is also measured in bits and represents the amount of memory that is addressable. An 8-bit bus would only give 256 directly **addressable memory** cells. 24 lines on the address bus would give 2^{24} combinations, which means it can access 16 MB of memory. A 32-bit address bus, which is common for most PCs, would provide 4 GB of addressable memory. A 64-bit address bus would provide, in theory, addressable memory of 16.8 million terabytes.

Control bus

The **control bus** is a bidirectional bus which sends control signals to the registers, the data and address buses. There is a lot of data flowing around the processor, between the processor and memory, and between the processor and the input and output controllers. Data buses are sending data to and from memory while address buses send only to memory.

The job of the control bus therefore is to ensure that the correct data is travelling to the right place at the right time. This involves the synchronisation of signals and the control of access to the data and address buses which are being shared by a number of devices.

Input/Output (I/O) controllers

In addition to the direct link between the processor and main memory, the processor will also receive and send instructions and data to the various input and output devices connected to the computer. Basic I/O devices would be the keyboard, monitor, mouse and printer, though modern computer systems would typically include several other devices.

Figure 32.5 Physical ports on a standard PC

Inside the computer, the data buses carry the signals to and from the processor. In order to do this the processor works in the same way as if it were sending data to or from memory. The difference, however, is that the processor does not communicate directly with the I/O devices. Instead, there is an interface called an I/O controller.

Controllers consist of their own circuitry that handles the data flowing between the processor and the device. Every device will have its own controller which allows new devices to be connected to the processor at any time. A key feature of an I/O controller is that it will translate signals from the device into the format required by the processor. There are many different devices and many different types of processor and it is the I/O controller that provides the flexibility to add new devices without having to redesign the processor.

Another important feature is that the I/O devices themselves respond relatively slowly compared to the speed at which a processor can work. Therefore the I/O controller is used to buffer data being sent between the processor and the device, so that the processor does not have to wait for the individual device to respond.

Von Neumann and Harvard architectures

The word 'architecture' is widely used in computing and usually refers to the way that something is built. For example, a microprocessor has an architecture that refers to the way that the chip is built. The von Neumann method of building computers therefore is often referred to as **von Neumann architecture**, see Figure 32.6.

An alternative method of building chips is the **Harvard architecture**. The key difference between this and von Neumann is that separate buses are used for data and instructions, both of which address different parts of memory. So rather than storing data and instructions in the same memory and then passing them through the same bus, there are two separate buses addressing two different memories.

> **Von Neumann architecture:** a technique for building a processor where data and instructions are stored in the same memory and accessed via buses.
>
> **Harvard architecture:** a technique for building a processor that uses separate buses and memory for data and instructions.

The advantage of this is that the instructions and data are handled more quickly as they do not have to share the same bus. Therefore, a program running on Harvard architecture can be executed faster and more efficiently. Harvard architecture is widely used on embedded computer systems such as mobile phones, burglar alarms etc. where there is a specific use, rather than being used within general purpose PCs.

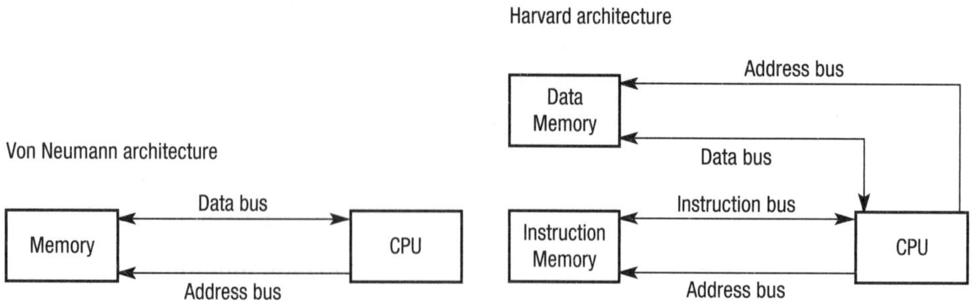

Harvard architecture

Figure 32.6 The von Neumann and Harvard architectures

Summary

- The processor handles and processes instructions from the hardware and software.
- Processors can handle millions of instructions every second.
- Memory is made up of millions of addressable cells.
- Data and instructions are fetched, decoded and executed.

- There are two main types of main memory, RAM and ROM.
- The processor is connected to main memory and data and instructions are passed around circuitry known as buses.
- In von Neumann architecture, instructions and data are stored together in memory.
- In Harvard architecture, separate memory is used for data and instructions.

Now test yourself

TESTED ☐

1 What would happen if you:
   (a) increased the clock speed   [1]
   (b) increased the width of the address bus?   [1]
2 What is meant by the term **bus**?   [2]
3 Which of the following diagrams correctly demonstrates data
   flow between the address bus and the listed components?   [1]

(a)

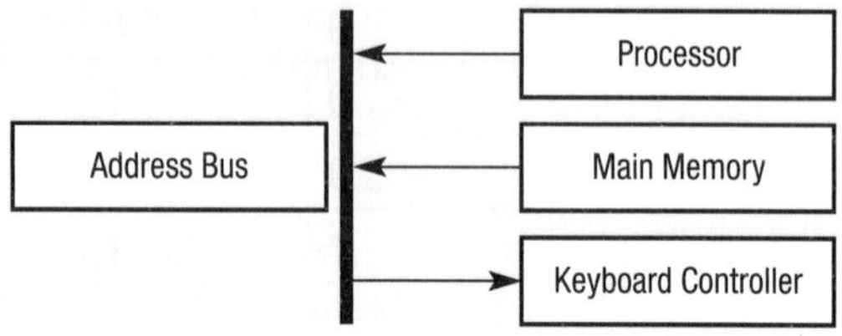

(b)

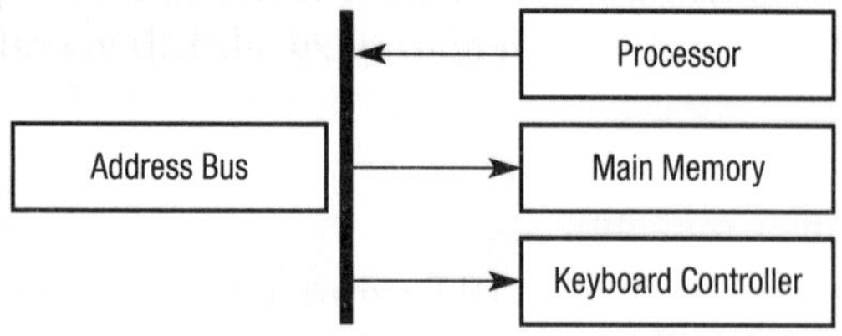

(c)

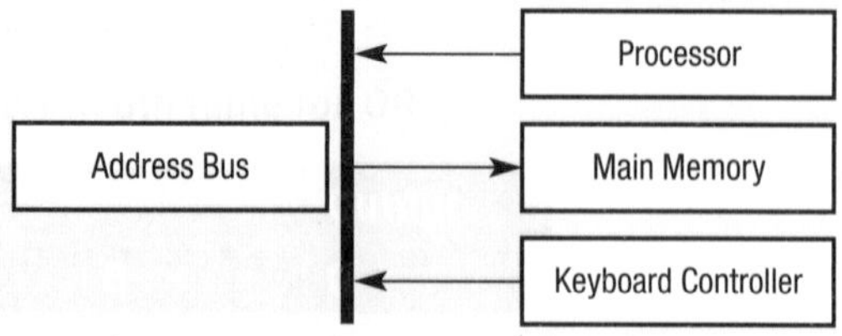

33 The stored program concept and processor components

The stored program concept

REVISED

The von Neumann concept was to store instructions and data in the same memory unit. Each instruction or data item is fetched from memory, decoded and then executed, with any new data created being placed back into memory. Every time a program is run, the processor runs through this **fetch–execute cycle**.

Therefore, all the processor is doing is running through this cycle over and over again, millions of times every second. The computer's clock times the electrical pulses into the processor.

- Fetch – the processor fetches the program's next instruction from memory. The instruction will be stored at a memory address and will contain the instruction in binary code.
- Decode – the processor works out what the binary code at that address means.
- Execute – the processor carries out the instruction which may involve reading an item of data from memory, performing a calculation or writing data back into memory.

> **Stored program concept:** the idea that instructions and data are stored together in memory.
>
> **Fetch–execute cycle:** the continuous process carried out by the processor when running programs.

> **Exam tip**
>
> Looking at the process as three separate stages can help you remember the cycle more easily than going through it all in one go.

The control unit

The **control unit** is the part of the processor that supervises the fetch–execute cycle. The control unit also makes sure that all the data that is being processed is routed correctly – it is put in the correct register or section of memory.

> **Control unit:** part of the processor that manages the execution of instructions.

The arithmetic logic unit (ALU)

The **ALU** carries out two types of operation – arithmetic and logic. The ALU can be used to carry out the normal mathematical functions such as add, subtract, multiply and divide, and some other less familiar processes such as shifting. The ALU is also used to compare two values and decide if one is less than, greater than or the same as another. Some comparisons will result in either TRUE or FALSE being recorded.

The ALU is sent an operation code (opcode) and the operands (the data to be processed). The ALU then uses logical operations such as OR, AND and NOT to carry out the appropriate process. In some computers, a separate arithmetic unit (AU) is used to cope with floating point operations.

> **Arithmetic Logic Unit (ALU):** part of the processor that processes and manipulates data.

The clock

All computers have an internal **clock**. The clock generates a signal that is used to synchronise the operation of the processor and the movement of data around the other components of the computer.

The speed of a clock is measured in either megahertz (MHz – millions of cycles per second) or gigahertz (GHz – 1000 million cycles per second). In 1990 a clock speed of between 4 and 5 MHz was the norm. In 2000, 1 GHz clock speeds were common. The typical clock speed at the time of writing is 2–3 GHz.

> **Clock:** a device that generates a signal used to synchronise the components of a computer.

Registers

> **Exam tip**
>
> Registers are specialised, very fast (and relatively expensive) memory locations, located inside the CPU rather than in main memory.

The control unit needs somewhere to store details of the operations being dealt with by the fetch–execute cycle and the ALU needs somewhere to put the results of any operations it carries out. There are a number of storage locations within the processor that are used to store this sort of data. They are called **registers** and although they have a very limited storage capacity they play a vital role in the operation of the computer.

A register must be large enough to hold an instruction – for example, in a 32-bit instruction computer, a register must be 32 bits in length. Some of these registers are general purpose but a number are used for a specific purpose:

- The **status register** keeps track of the status of various parts of the computer – for example, if an overflow error has occurred during an arithmetic operation.
- The **interrupt register** is a type of status register. It stores details of any signals that have been received by the processor from other components attached to it; for example, the I/O controller for the printer.

There are four registers that are used by the processor as part of the fetch–execute cycle:

- The **Current Instruction Register (CIR)** stores the instruction that is currently being executed by the processor.
- The **Program Counter (PC)** stores the memory location of the next instruction that will be needed by the processor.
- The **Memory Buffer Register (MBR)**, also known as the **Memory Data Register (MDR)**, holds the data that has just been read from or is about to be written to main memory.
- The **Memory Address Register (MAR)** stores the memory location where data in the MBR is about to be written to or read from.

> **Exam tip**
>
> Don't rely on the acronyms, some exam questions require you to use full names.

> **Register:** a small section of temporary storage that is part of the processor. Stores data or control instructions during the fetch–decode–execute cycle.
>
> **Status register:** keeps track of the various functions of the computer such as if the result of the last calculation was positive or negative.
>
> **Interrupt register:** stores details of incoming interrupts.
>
> **Current Instruction Register (CIR):** register that stores the instructions that the CPU is currently decoding/executing.
>
> **Program counter (PC):** register that stores the address of the next instruction to be taken from main memory into the processor.
>
> **Memory Buffer Register (MBR):** register that holds data that is either written to or copied from the CPU.
>
> **Memory Data Register (MDR):** another name for the MBR.
>
> **Memory Address Register (MAR):** register that stores the location of the address that data is either written to or copied from by the processor.

How the cycle works

- Fetch: The PC holds the address of the next instruction. The processor sends this address along the address bus to the main memory. The contents of the memory location at that address are sent via the data bus to the CIR and the PC is incremented. The details of addresses are initially loaded into the MAR and the data initially goes to the MBR.
- Execute: The processor then takes the instruction from the CIR and decides what to do with it. It does this by referring to the instruction set. These instruction sets are either classed as a RISC (reduced instruction set) or a CISC (complex instruction set). An instruction set is a library of all the things the processor can be asked to do. Each instruction in the instruction set is accompanied by details of what the processor should do when it receives that particular instruction. This might be to send the contents of the MBR to the ALU.
- Once the instruction that has just been taken from the memory has been decoded, the processor now carries out the instruction. It then goes back to the top of the cycle and fetches the next instruction. A simple instruction will require only a single clock cycle, whereas a complex instruction may need three or four. The results of any calculations are written to either a register or a memory location.

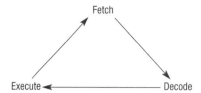

Figure 33.1 The fetch–execute cycle

Factors affecting processor performance

- Clock speed: As we saw earlier, clock speed is one measure of the performance of the computer. It indicates how fast each instruction will be executed. In theory therefore, increasing the clock speed will increase the speed at which the processor executes instructions.
- Bus width: The processor needs to optimise the use of the clock pulse. One way of doing this is to increase the **bus width**. Increasing the width of the data bus means that more bits and therefore more data can be passed down it with each pulse of the clock, which in turn means more data can be processed within a given time interval. Increasing the width of the address bus will increase the amount of memory that can be addressed and therefore allows more memory to be installed on the computer.
- Word length: Related to the data bus width is the **word length**. A word is a collection of bits that can be addressed and manipulated as a single unit. Computer systems may have a word length of 32 or 64 bits, indicating that 64 bits of data can be handled in one pulse of the clock. Word length and bus width are closely related in that a system with a 64-bit word length will need 64-bit buses.
- Multiple cores: Most computer systems have one processor. One way of increasing system performance is to use several processors. For convenience, multiple processors can be incorporated onto one single chip; this is known as a **multi-core** processor. A dual-core processor therefore has two processors on the one chip and will run much faster than a single-core system, which only has one processor. The term 'core' is used to define the components that enable instructions to be fetched and executed.

> **Bus width:** the number of bits that can be sent down a bus in one go.
>
> **Word length:** the number of bits that can be addressed, transferred or manipulated as one unit.
>
> **Multi-core:** a chip with more than one processor.

- **Cache** memory: Caching is a technique where instructions and data that are needed frequently are placed into a temporary area of memory that is separate from main memory.

Cache: a high-speed temporary area of memory.

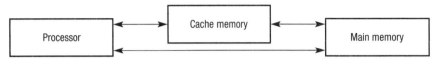

Figure 33.2 Cache memory

Interrupts

A-level only ~~REVISED~~

The processor in a computer is always working, irrespective of whether there is an application active or not. This is because the operating system, which is itself a large collection of programs, is always active. This means that the fetch–execute cycle is always in use. If an error occurs or a device wants the computer to start doing something else then we need some way to grab the processor's attention. The way to do this is to send an **interrupt**. An interrupt is a signal sent to the processor by a program or an external source such as a hard disk, printer or keyboard.

Interrupt: a signal sent by a device or program to the processor requesting its attention.

There are a number of different sources of an interrupt. These are some typical examples:

- a printer sends a request for more data to be sent to it
- the user presses a key or clicks a mouse button
- an error occurs during the execution of a program; for example, if the program tries to divide by zero or tries to access a file that does not exist
- an item of hardware develops a fault
- the user sends a signal to the computer asking for a program to be terminated
- the power supply detects that the power is about to go off
- the operating system wants to pass control to another user in a multitasking environment.

How an interrupt works

What happens is that an additional step is added to the fetch–execute cycle. This extra step fits between the completion of one execution and the start of the next. After each execution the processor checks to see if an interrupt has been sent by looking at the contents of the interrupt register.

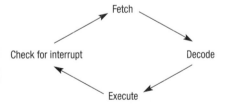

Figure 33.3 The fetch–execute cycle with interrupts

If an interrupt has occurred, the processor will stop whatever it is doing in order to service the interrupt. It does this using the **Interrupt Service Routine (ISR)** which calls the routine required to handle the interrupt. Most interrupts are only temporary so the processor needs to be able to put aside the current task before it can start on the interrupt. It does this by placing the contents of the registers, such as the PC and CIR, on to the system stack. Once the interrupt has been processed the CPU will retrieve the values from the stack, put them back in the appropriate registers and carry on.

Interrupt Service Routine (ISR): calls the routine required to handle an interrupt.

Priorities

Sometimes the program that has interrupted the running of the processor is itself stopped by another interrupt. In this case the processor will either place details of its current task on the stack or it will assess the priority of the interrupts and decide which one needs to be serviced first. Assigning different interrupts different priority levels means that the really important signals, such as a signal indicating that the power supply is about to be lost, get dealt with first.

Vectored interrupt mechanism

Once the values of the registers have been pushed to the stack, the processor is then free to handle the interrupt. This can be done using a technique called a **vectored interrupt mechanism**.

Each interrupt has an associated section of code that tells the processor how to deal with that particular interrupt. When the processor receives an interrupt it needs to know how to find that code. Every type of interrupt has an associated memory address known as a vector. This vector points to the starting address of the code associated with each interrupt.

So when an interrupt occurs, the processor identifies what kind of interrupt it is, then finds its associated interrupt vector. It then uses this to jump to the address specified by the vector, from where it runs the Interrupt Service Routine (ISR).

> **Priorities**: a method for assigning importance to interrupts in order to process them in the right order.

> **Exam tip**
>
> The interrupt priority system is an example of a priority queue.

> **Vectored interrupt mechanism**: a method of handling interrupts by pointing to the first memory address of the instructions needed.

Summary

- The stored program concept is the idea of instructions and data being stored together in memory.
- The fetch–execute cycle explains how an instruction is fetched from memory, and executed to produce a result and place this back into memory.
- There are a number of key components of the processor including: the clock, the control unit, the arithmetic logic unit and various registers.

- You need to know how an instruction passes through all of these components.
- There is a combination of factors that affect the performance of a processor including clock speed, bus width, word length and caching.
- An interrupt is a signal (e.g. from a hardware device) that stops the processor from carrying out its current instruction in order to deal with another task.

Now test yourself

TESTED ☐

1. Identify and describe the purpose of three different registers. [6]
2. Describe the effect of increasing the clock speed. [2]
3. Describe the fetch–decode–execute cycle in full. [6]

34 The processor instruction set and addressing modes

Specification coverage

3.7.3.3 The processor instruction set
3.7.3.4 Addressing modes
3.7.3.5 Machine-code/assembly language operations

Instruction set

In order to write assembly code, you need to be familiar with the mnemonics that can be used and this will depend on what processor is being used. Each processor will have its own **instruction set**. These instruction sets are either classed as RISC (reduced instruction set) or CISC (complex instruction set). An instruction set is the patterns of 0s and 1s that a particular processor recognises as commands, along with their associated meanings.

> **Instruction set:** the patterns of 0s and 1s that a particular processor recognises as commands, along with their associated meanings.

A typical assembly language statement consists of four parts as shown in Figure 34.1.

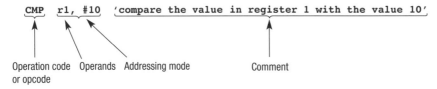

Figure 34.1 A typical assembly language statement

- Operation code: The operation code, or **opcode** as it is more commonly called, is shown as a mnemonic consisting of one to four characters.
- Operands: The number of **operands** following an operation code and the way they are interpreted depends on the sort of code it is. For example, the command **CMP** must be followed by two operands – the first identifies the memory address or register that is to be accessed and the second the data that is to be compared with. Note that with the ARM6 architecture, the first operand always refers to a register.
- The use of # indicates the **addressing mode**. In this case the # refers to immediate addressing, which means that the value that follows it is the actual data item.
- Comments: The comment part of the statement is optional. **Assembly language** programs can be hard to follow and tend to be very long, so being able to add comments makes them easier to understand.

> **Opcode**: an operation code or instruction used in assembly language.
>
> **Operand**: a value or memory address that forms part of an assembly language instruction.
>
> **Addressing mode**: the way in which the operand is interpreted.
>
> **Assembly language**: a way of programming using mnemonics.

In machine code, the instruction will operate using a fixed number of bits. Within that, the operator, operand and addressing mode will be assigned a certain number of bits. For example, a 32-bit system means that the whole instruction is 32-bits. It might assign 12 bits for the opcode, 4 bits for the addressing mode and 16 bits for the operand.

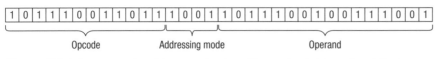

Figure 34.2 An example of how an instruction set might assign bits to instructions

Immediate and direct addressing

In order to access anything that is held in memory you need to know its address. The address is a number that tells the computer where in memory to go to find a specific item of data. Data is put into or copied out of memory in different ways using addressing modes. Two of the main addressing modes are:

- Direct addressing: Using a **direct address** mode tells the CPU which address contains the data you want to access. So LDR r1, 100 would copy the data held in memory location 100 into register 1.
- Immediate addressing: Rather than loading the contents of a memory address, the **immediate address** method loads the data directly. Therefore, the operand would have to be the actual number that you wish to use. A command such as MOV r1, #10 would move the value 10 into register 1.

> **Exam tip**
>
> There are a range of addressing modes not on the specification. Be careful when reading around the subject.

> **Direct address**: the operand is the datum.
>
> **Immediate address**: the operand is the memory address or register number.

Types of operation codes

The operation codes of an assembly language can be placed in one of four groups: data transfer operations, arithmetic operations, logical operations and branch operations.

Data transfer operations include commands that move data between the registers and main memory. Typical instructions include move (MOV), store (STR) and load (LDR).

Arithmetic operations include the four normal arithmetic functions – add, subtract, multiply and divide. Other arithmetic operations include the increment (increase by one), decrement (reduce by one), negate (reverse the sign), compare (two values) and shift instructions.

The status register is used to record certain features of a calculation. These include whether the calculation has generated an overflow error or whether the result is zero or negative. **Shift instructions** are used to move the bits within a register. Shifts can move bits either left or right.

A logical shift can be used to extract the content of just one bit. This is achieved by repeatedly shifting until the bit you want is put in the carry bit. If this bit pattern:

1	0	1	1	1	0	0	1

is operated on with a shift right then it becomes:

| 0 | 1 | 0 | 1 | 1 | 1 | 0 | 0 | → | 1 | (Carry bit)
|---|---|---|---|---|---|---|---|---|---|

The least significant bit (the right-hand most) is placed in a carry bit; in this case it is a 1, and a 0 is placed in the most significant bit (left-hand most).

Logical operations include the logical bitwise functions AND, OR, NOT and XOR. Bitwise means that each bit within a bit string is compared to a corresponding bit in another bit string of the same length. The results of these operations can be used to compare and calculate values. They can also be used to mask out or ignore the contents of some of the bits in a byte.

AND will compare each bit in the string. Where they are both 1, the answer is 1. Otherwise the result is 0. This effectively produces a mask allowing just parts of the bit string to be used. This would be useful, for example, if identifying a parity bit.

> **Data transfer operations**: operations within an instruction set that move data around between the registers and memory.
>
> **Arithmetic operations**: operations within an instruction set that perform basic maths, such as add and subtract.
>
> **Shift instructions**: operations within an instruction set that move bits within a register.

> **Logical operations**: operations within an instruction set that move the bits around within the operand.

```
      0 0 1 1
AND   0 0 1 0
=     0 0 1 0
```

OR will compare each bit in the string. If either or both bits are 1 then the result is 1. Otherwise the result is 0. This could be used to set up a mask where if any of the bits are 1, the flag is TRUE.

```
  0011
OR 0010
= 0011
```

NOT will negate each value so that a 0 becomes a 1 and 1 becomes a 0. The result is the equivalent of the two's complement value −1. In this case, +3 becomes −4.

```
NOT 0011
=  1100
```

XOR will compare each bit and return a 0 if both bits are 0 or both bits are 1. If one bit is 0 and the other is 1 then it will return a 1. This is commonly used to set a register to 0 as if you perform an XOR operation of a number on itself, it will always return a zero.

```
   0011
XOR 0011
=  0000
```

Branch operations

Without the ability to branch or jump, all assembly programs, and by extension all high-level languages, would have to be linear. There are a number of ways you can create a branch.

Conditional branches take the form:
- BNE – branch if not equal
- BEQ – branch if equal
- BGT – branch if greater than
- BLT – branch if less than.

The result of the last comparison will determine whether the jump is executed or not. This is where the labels come in.

> **Branch operations:** operations within an instruction set that allow you to move from one part of the program to another.

> **Exam tip**
>
> AQA use a restricted instruction set based on the ARM processor in the Raspberry Pi.

Table 34.1 The ARM processor set codes

LDR Rd, <memory ref>	Load the value stored in the memory location specified by <memory ref> into register d.
STR Rd, <memory ref>	Store the value that is in register d into the memory location specified by <memory ref>.
ADD Rd, Rn, <operand2>	Add the value specified in <operand2> to the value in register n and store the result in register d.
SUB Rd, Rn, <operand2>	Subtract the value specified by <operand2> from the value in register n and store the result in register d.
MOV Rd, <operand2>	Copy the value specified by <operand2> into register d.
CMP Rn, <operand2>	Compare the value stored in register n with the value specified by <operand2>.
B <label>	Always branch to the instruction at position <label> in the program.
B <condition> <label>	Conditionally branch to the instruction at position <label> in the program if the last comparison met the criteria specified by the <condition>. Possible values for <condition> and their meaning are: • EQ: equal to • NE: not equal to • GT: greater than • LT: less than.
AND Rd, Rn, <operand2>	Perform a bitwise logical AND operation between the value in register n and the value specified by <operand2> and store the result in register d.
ORR Rd, Rn, <operand2>	Perform a bitwise logical OR operation between the value in register n and the value specified by <operand2> and store the result in register d.

Table 34.1 cont.

EOR Rd, Rn, <operand2>	Perform a bitwise logical exclusive or (XOR) operation between the value in register n and the value specified by <operand2> and store the result in register d.
MVN Rd, <operand2>	Perform a bitwise logical NOT operation on the value specified by <operand2> and store the result in register d.
LSL Rd, Rn, <operand2>	Logically shift left the value stored in register n by the number of bits specified by <operand2> and store the result in register d.
LSR Rd, Rn, <operand2>	Logically shift right the value stored in register n by the number of bits specified by <operand2> and store the result in register d.
HALT	Stops the execution of the program.

<operand2> can be interpreted in two different ways, depending upon whether the first symbol is a # or an R:

- # – Use the decimal value specified after the #, e.g. **#25** means use the decimal value 25.
- Rm – Use the value stored in register **m**, e.g. **R6** means use the value stored in register 6.

Summary

- In order to write assembly code you need to be familiar with the mnemonics that can be used and this will depend on what processor is being used.
- Instructions are made up of opcode and operand.
- Direct addressing tells the CPU which memory or register address contains the data you want to access.
- Immediate addressing loads the data directly from the operand.
- Logical operations include the logical bitwise functions AND, OR, NOT and XOR.
- Transfer operations move data between the registers and main memory.
- Arithmetic operations include add, subtract, multiply, divide, increment, decrement, negate, compare and shift instructions.

Now test yourself

TESTED ☐

1 Describe the difference between immediate and direct memory addressing. [2]
2 State the differences between the opcode and the operand. [2]
3 Write an assembly language program based on the ARM processor to:
    read two memory locations
    IF location 1 is more than location 2
    THEN store the value '1' in register 1
    ELSE IF the location 2 is more than location 1
        THEN store the value '2' in register 1
        ELSE store the value '3' in register 1 [6]

35 External hardware devices

Specification coverage

3.7.4 External hardware devices

Digital camera

Exam tip

While you are not expected to remember how every piece of hardware works in every situation, you do need a good understanding of a selected range – you should be able to write a 4–6 mark passage on each one in the specification.

A **digital camera** is a device for recording still and moving images in digital form that can then be processed further using specialised software. In common with other devices, the camera takes analogue data, in this case light waves, and converts them into binary (0s and 1s). It does this in the following way:

- When a photograph is taken the shutter opens and lets light in through the lens.
- The light is focused onto a sensor, which is usually either a **charge coupled device (CCD)** or a **complementary metal oxide semiconductor (CMOS)**.
- The sensors are made up of millions of transistors, each of which stores the data for one or more pixels. (A pixel is a picture element or individual dot, and the whole image will be made up of millions of pixels.)
- As the light hits the sensor, it is converted into electrons and the amount of charge is recorded for each pixel in digital form.
- With light, all colours can be created from red, green and blue (RGB). Therefore to record colour, the camera will either have three different sensors, or use three different filters – one for red, one for green and one for blue.
- The data are typically stored on removable storage devices, usually referred to as flash memory, which use programmable ROM (see Solid state disks later in this chapter).
- Data are usually stored in compressed files; for example, TIFF, JPG or PNG.
- RAW files can also be generated, which are uncompressed and therefore contain all of the data from the original photograph.
- This digital data can now be decoded and manipulated using specialised software.

Figure 35.1 shows how light is let in through the shutter (1) and focused by the lens (2). It is directed through **RGB filters** (3) before being focused onto the CCD or CMOS sensor (4).

Figure 35.2 shows how the light is passed through the RGB filters to enable all possible colours to be created.

Digital camera: a device for creating digital images of photographs which can be printed or transferred onto a computer to be manipulated and stored.

Charge coupled device (CCD): in digital cameras it is a sensor that records the amount of light received and converts it into a digital value.

Complementary metal oxide semiconductor (CMOS): is an alternative technology that performs the same functions as a CCD.

RGB filter: red, green and blue filters that light passes through in order to create all other colours.

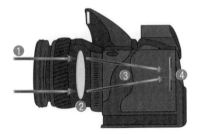

Figure 35.1 The workings of a digital camera

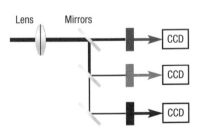

Figure 35.2 Red, green and blue (RGB) filters

Barcode reader

Barcode readers are one of a series of input devices that use scanner technology. These work in the following way:

- A light, usually an LED or laser, is passed over an image.
- Some form of light sensor is used to measure the intensity of light being reflected back. This is converted into a current, effectively generating a waveform. This could be achieved using a photodiode or a CCD sensor in the same way as a digital camera.
- White areas reflect most light and black areas the least, making it possible to use the waveform to distinguish the patterns of black and white bars.
- The waveform is analogue and therefore needs to be converted into digital form using an analogue to digital converter.
- The encoding will convert the black and white into binary codes; for example, black = 0 and white = 1.
- The signal is decoded into a form that can then be interpreted by software.

> **Barcode reader**: a device that uses lasers or LEDs to read the black and white lines of a barcode.

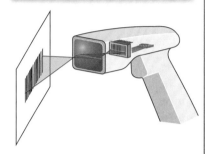

Figure 35.3 A barcode reader and barcode

RFID

Radio frequency identification (RFID) is a technique where small wireless tracking devices or tags are embedded onto or into other items. The tags, which are typically about the size of a grain of rice, can be attached to almost anything and will contain data about the item being tracked.

RFID works in the following way:

- The tag, which can be microscopically small, contains a chip which contains the data about the item and a modem to modulate and demodulate the radio signals.
- The tag also contains an antenna to send and receive signals.
- Tags can be either active, which means they have their own power source in the form of a small battery, or passive, which means that they will pick up electromagnetic power when they are in range of an RFID reader.
- Signals and therefore data can be transmitted in both directions using radio frequencies. This may be over a short or long distance depending on what the tags are being used for and how they are powered. The typical range of RFID tags is between 1 and 100 metres.
- Tags may be used simply to track the physical location of the tagged item or the item may transmit data back.

> **Radio frequency identification (RFID)**: a microscopic device that stores data and transmits it using radio waves – usually used in tags to track items.

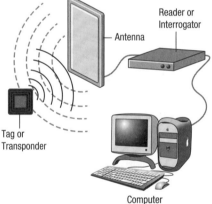

Figure 35.4 An RFID tag system

Laser printer

A **laser printer** works in the same way as a photocopier to produce high-quality black and white and/or colour images. They work in the following way:

- A rotating drum inside the printer is coated in a chemical which holds an electrical charge.

> **Laser printer**: a device that uses lasers and toner to create mono and colour prints.

- The laser beam is reflected onto the drum and where the light hits the drum the charge is discharged, effectively creating the image on the drum.
- As the drum rotates it picks up toner which is attracted to the charged part of the drum.
- Paper is passed over the drum and by charging the paper with the opposite charge to the toner, the toner is attracted to the paper and away from the drum.
- The paper is heat treated to fuse the toner onto the paper.

To achieve colour printing, four different coloured toners are used, and the process of transferring the toner to the drum is repeated for each colour. When printing, four colours are needed: cyan, magenta, yellow and black (CMYK).

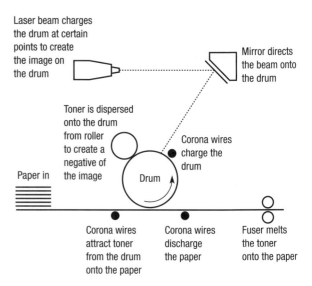

Figure 35.5 The workings of a laser printer

Magnetic hard disk

Hard disks are constructed of hard metallic material and are hermetically sealed. This is to protect them from being corrupted by dust or other debris. Most hard disks are in fact made up of a number of disks arranged in a stack. The disks are coated with a thin film of magnetic material. Changes in the direction of magnetism represent 0s and 1s.

Hard disks spin at speeds between 3600 and 12500 rpm as a series of heads read from and write to the disks. The heads do not actually touch the surface of the disk but float slightly above it by virtue of the speed at which the disk spins. There is an actuator arm which moves the head across the surface of the disk as it spins. The combination of the rotating of the disks with the lateral movement of the arm means that the heads can access every part of the disk surface.

The surface of the disk is organised into concentric tracks and each track is split into sectors, each of which can be individually addressed by the operating system. Because the head assembly can read any one of several disks, a cylinder reference is also used to identify which of the disks in the stack is being addressed.

> **Hard disk (HDD):** a secondary storage device made up of metallic disks that stores data magnetically.

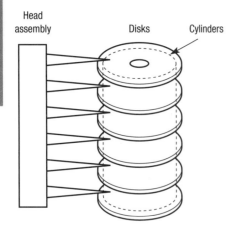

Figure 35.6 A magnetic hard disk array

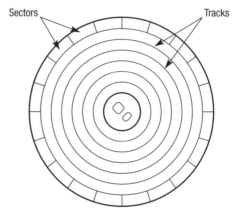

Figure 35.7 Tracks and sectors on a magnetic hard disk

Optical disk

Optical disk is a generic term for all variations of CD, DVD and Blu-Ray that use laser technology to read and write data. An optical disk is made up of one single spiral track that starts in the middle and works its way to the edge of the CD. The laser will read the data that are contained within this track by reading the pits and lands in combination with a sensor that measures how much light is reflected.

(a) Side view of a CD showing pits and lands

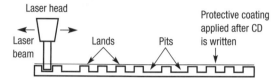

(b) Top view of a CD showing single spiral

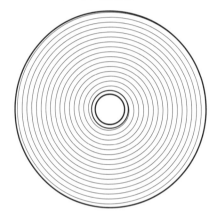

Figure 35.8 The workings of an optical disk

Figure 35.9 The workings of a writeable optical disk

For read-only optical disks, when data is written it is encoded as a series of bumps, or pits and lands within the track on the disk. A protective layer is then put over the surface to prevent any corruption of the data. The pattern of pits and lands is used to represent data. When the CD is read, the pits and lands are read by the laser which then interprets each as different electrical signals. In turn the electrical signals can be converted into binary codes.

For writeable optical disks, rather than using pits and lands the disk is coated with a photosensitive dye, which is translucent. When writing to the disk, the laser will alter the state of a dye spot that is coated onto the surface, making it opaque. The dye reflects a certain amount of light. A write laser alters the density of the dye and a read laser interprets the different densities to create binary patterns which in turn can represent data. Write lasers are higher powered than read lasers.

Solid state disk (SSD)

A solid state disk, also known as a solid state drive, is made up of semiconductors and is non-volatile, meaning that data is not lost when there is no power. A common implementation of this is the flash drive or memory stick, but this technology is also used to replace hard disks in computer systems.

They use programmable ROM chips stored inside a unit that looks like a hard disk and commonly uses a type of memory called NAND memory. This organises data into blocks in a similar way to a traditional hard disk as described earlier, with a **controller** being used to manage the blocks of data.

Blocks of a set physical size will be made up of binary data. Blocks are allocated to particular semiconductors. The advantage of this is that data can be added and deleted in blocks to different areas of the drive, so that only small parts of the drive have to be erased and written to. This enables very fast access times.

The semiconductors are able to retain their data due to the type of transistor used. It uses what is a called a **floating gate transistor**, which is able to trap and store charge. A floating gate transistor contains two gates: a floating gate and a control gate. A thin layer of oxide is placed between the two gates, effectively trapping the charge inside the floating gate even when the power is turned off.

Figure 35.10 Inside a solid state disk

Controller: in SSDs a controller is needed to organise data into blocks for storage purposes.

Block: in data storage it is the concept of storing data into set groups of bits and bytes of a fixed length.

Floating gate transistor: in SSDs it is a type of non-volatile transistor that stores data even without a power source.

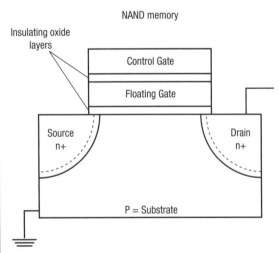

Figure 35.11 The workings of 'flash' memory

Storage devices compared

Table 35.1 shows a relative comparison of storage devices.

Table 35.1 Comparison of HDD, SSD, CD/DVD and Blu-ray

	Hard disk (HDD)	Solid state disk (SDD)	Optical disk (CD/DVD)	Optical disk (Blu-ray)
Typical capacity	High (500GB–4TB)	Medium (64–512GB)	Low (700 MB to 4.7 GB)	Low to medium (25–50 GB)
Relative cost	Low to medium	High	Low	Low
Easily portable	External disks are available	External disks are available	Yes	Yes
Relative power consumption	High	Low	High	High
Relative speed of access	Medium	High	Low	Low
Latency	High	Low	Very High	High
Fragmentation		None		
Reliability	Good	Very good	Fair	Fair
Relative physical size	Large	Small	Large	Large

Summary

- Digital cameras work by directing light into sensors made up of millions of cells and then converting this data into digital form.
- Digital cameras are often compared in terms of the number of pixels that they use to create an image.
- Three colours (red, green, blue) are needed to create all possible colours.
- Laser printers work by transferring toner off a drum and onto paper with electrical charge.
- Four print colours (cyan, magenta, yellow and black) are required to create all possible colours.
- RFID tags are tiny devices that can be attached to anything and transmit a signal containing data that can be picked up by a reader.
- Optical disks such as CDs and DVDs use lasers to read pits and lands on the surface of the disk that are encoded to represent data.
- Magnetic hard disks are made up of an array of metallic disks that are read by a reading head that floats across the surface.
- Solid state disks use programmable ROM chips.

Now test yourself

1 Describe the operation of an RFID reader and tag. [4]
2 Describe the operation of a laser printer. [4]
3 Describe the operation of a digital camera. [4]
4 Explain the similarities and differences in the operation of a magnetic hard disk and an SSD. [6]

36 Moral, ethical, legal and cultural issues

Specification coverage

3.8 Consequences of uses of computing

Moral and ethical issues

REVISED ☐

A moral issue is one that concerns our own individual behaviour and our own personal concept of right and wrong. We learn our moral values from other people such as our parents, teachers and peers, and we learn them for ourselves from experience. Ethics vary slightly from morals in that they are a way of trying to define a set of moral values or principles that people within society live by. **Ethical issues** are sometimes referred to therefore as social issues.

> **Ethical issues**: factors that define the set of moral values by which society functions.

The use and misuse of personal data

REVISED ☐

Most organisations collect data on an ongoing basis and much of these data are personal. At a basic level this might be name and address information, but may also include data about individuals' finances, health, relationship status, family, employment history and even their personal views.

> **Exam tip**
>
> Personal data is data which can be related to an identifiable living person.

This presents a number of issues:
- personal privacy
- data security
- misuse of data
- 'big brother'
- online profile
- profiling.

Other moral and social issues

REVISED ☐

> **Exam tip**
>
> Rather than being an expert in any one area, you should have a good broad understanding and the confidence to form your own thoughts.

There are a number of other moral and ethical issues relating to computer science:
- **unauthorised access**
- unauthorised use of software
- inappropriate behaviour
- inappropriate content
- freedom of speech
- unemployment
- access to the Internet.

> **Unauthorised access**: where computer systems or data are used by people who are not the intended users.

As is clear from the topics discussed above, ethical and **moral issues** become a matter of debate. When you are using your own computer at home, you make your own moral decisions about these issues. When you are using a computer in a school, college or any other organisation, you normally have to agree to a **code of conduct**.

The main principles of the British Computer Society (BCS) code of conduct are that members should:
- always operate in the public interest
- have a duty to the organisation that they work for, or the college they attend
- have a duty to the profession
- maintain professional competence and integrity.

> **Moral issues**: factors that define how an individual acts and behaves.
>
> **Code of conduct**: a voluntary set of rules that define the way in which individuals and organisations will behave.

Legal issues

Legal issues relate to those issues where a law has been passed by the Government. There are very few Acts of Parliament that are specific to the world of computing. The two main ones are the Data Protection Act and the Computer Misuse Act.

> **Legal issues**: factors that have been made into laws by the Government.

In addition, the Freedom of Information Act, the Regulation of Investigatory Powers Act and the Copyright, Designs and Patents Act are of particular relevance to computing.

Also, using a computer does not exempt you from all the other laws of the land. For example, someone who carries out an act of fraud on the Internet can be prosecuted under the Fraud Act. Someone who steals computer data can be prosecuted under the Theft Act. Someone who makes false allegations about someone else in an email can be prosecuted for libel.

Data Protection Act

The Data Protection Act places controls on organisations and individuals that store personal data electronically. The definition of personal data is any data on an individual where the person (known as the data subject) is alive and can be individually identified.

There are eight main principles behind the Data Protection Act. Anyone processing personal data must comply with the eight enforceable principles of good practice. They say that data must be:
- fairly and lawfully processed
- processed for limited purposes
- adequate, relevant and not excessive
- accurate
- not kept longer than necessary
- processed in accordance with the data subject's rights
- secure
- not transferred to countries without adequate data protection.

Another feature of the Act is that data subjects have the right to know what data are stored about them by any particular individual or organisation. These are known as subject access rights.

> **Exam tip**
>
> You are not expected to know every Act in the same detail as A-level ICT students, but an awareness of key concepts is a very good idea.

Freedom of Information Act

The Freedom of Information Act extends the subject access rights of the Data Protection Act and gives general rights of access to information held by public authorities such as hospitals, doctors, dentists, the police, schools and colleges.

The Act gives individuals access to both personal and non-personal data held by public authorities. The idea behind the Act was to provide more openness between the public and government agencies. Therefore, the agencies are obliged to give the public access to information and to respond to individual requests for information. Much of this is done through websites and email communications.

Computer Misuse Act

The Computer Misuse Act was introduced primarily to prevent hacking (**data misuse**) and contains three specific offences relating to computer usage:

- unauthorised access to computer programs or data
- unauthorised access with further criminal intent
- unauthorised modification of computer material.

> **Data misuse**: using data for purposes other than for which it was collected.

The Act was introduced before the widespread use of the Internet, which has led to problems with enforcement. Prior to the Internet, hacking did take place, but not on the scale that it does today. There are now millions of computers and networks connected to the Internet and the opportunities for hackers have increased enormously.

Regulation of Investigatory Powers (RIP) Act

The RIP Act was introduced to clarify the powers that government agencies have when investigating crime or suspected crime. It is not specific to the world of computing but was introduced partly to take account of changes in communication technology and the widespread use of the Internet.

There are five main parts to the Act. The most relevant to computing are Part 1 which relates to the interception of communications, including electronic data, and Part 3 which covers the investigation of electronic data protected by encryption. In simple terms, it gives the police and other law enforcement agencies the right to intercept communications where there is suspicion of criminal activity. They also have the right to decipher these data if they are encrypted, even if this means that the user must tell the police how to decrypt the data.

It also allows employers to monitor the computer activity of their employees; for example, by monitoring their email traffic or tracking which websites they visit during work time. This raises a number of issues relating to civil liberties.

Copyright, Designs and Patents Act

REVISED

This Act gives rights to the creators of certain kinds of material, allowing them control over the way in which the material is used. The law covers the copying, adapting and renting of materials.

The law covers all types of materials but of particular relevance to computing are:
- original works including instruction manuals, computer programs and some types of databases
- web content
- original musical works
- sound recordings
- films and videos.

Copyright applies to all works regardless of the format. Consequently, work produced on the Internet is also covered by copyright. It is illegal to produce pirate copies of software or run more versions on a network than have been paid for. It is an offence to adapt existing versions of software without permission. It is also an offence to download music or films without the permission of the copyright holder.

> **Copyright:** the legal ownership that applies to software, music, films and other content.

In computing, two techniques are used to protect copyright:
- Digital Rights Management (DRM)
- licensing.

Other acts relevant to computing

REVISED

Other acts that are particularly relevant to computing are:
- The Official Secrets Act prevents the disclosure of government data relating to national security.
- The Defamation Act prevents people from making untrue statements about others which will lead to their reputation being damaged.
- The Obscene Publications Act and the Protection of Children Act prevent people from disseminating pornographic or violent images.
- The Health and Safety (Display Screen Equipment) Regulations provides regulation on the correct use of screens and is a specific addition to the Health and Safety at Work Act, which contains more general regulations on keeping employees safe.
- The Equality Act makes it illegal to discriminate against anyone on the grounds of sex, sexual orientation, ethnicity, religion, disability or age. This includes the dissemination of derogatory material.
- The Digital Economy Act addresses media policy issues around digital media, especially copyright and use of domain names.

Cultural issues

REVISED

> **Exam tip**
>
> Questions from this section are likely to be discursive and include an element of QWC (Quality of Written Communication).

Cultural issues are all of the factors that influence the beliefs, attitudes and actions of people within society. Common cultural influences are family, the media, politics, economics and religion. There are cultural differences between different groups of people. For example, people from different countries often have a different culture.

> **Cultural issues:** factors that have an impact on the ways in which we function as a society.

There are elements of computer use that have a cultural impact in that they can change our attitudes, beliefs and actions:

- over-use of data
- invasive technologies
- over-reliance on computers
- over-reliance on technology companies
- 'big brother' culture
- globalisation.

Summary

- We are living through a technological revolution and as computer scientists we must consider the consequences of computing on individuals and society as a whole.
- Computing can bring about massive benefits but can also have a negative effect on individuals and society.
- There are a number of laws relating specifically to computing and other common laws also apply to actions that are undertaken on a computer.
- The Internet and World Wide Web have had a massive influence on our culture and will continue to do so.

Now test yourself

TESTED ☐

1 Some of your friends have been downloading MP3s from the Internet and sharing them. Discuss the moral, legal and ethical situation you might find yourself in should you engage in the same activity. [6]
2 Describe the difference between the law and a code of conduct. [4]
3 You have just found out your college is monitoring your emails and watching your computer screen in the common room. Discuss the moral, legal and ethical situation. [6]

Task

1 Spend some time researching the different acts on legislation.gov.uk – identify who might break them (deliberately or accidentally) and what measures you can take to protect yourself.
2 Investigate the Google Street View case and discuss the ethical conflicts.

37 Communication basics

Specification coverage

3.9.1 Communication methods

Serial and parallel transmission

Serial transmission sends and receives data one bit at a time in sequence. Serial connections are used to connect most of the peripherals to the computer such as the mouse and keyboard, and it is serial cables that connect computers together to form a network.

The speed of the transmission will depend on the type of cabling used so it is not necessarily the case that serial transmission is slow. For example, the Universal Serial Bus or USB is a high-speed serial connection that allows peripheral devices to be connected to your computer. Serial network cables are capable of transmissions rates of 1 Gbps (1000 million bits per second).

Parallel transmission uses a number of wires to send a number of bits simultaneously. The more wires there are, the more data can be sent at any one time. A 32-bit parallel connection, for example, may connect the processor and memory together.

> **Serial transmission**: data is transmitted one bit at a time down a single wire.
>
> **Parallel transmission**: data is transmitted several bits at a time using multiple wires.

> **Exam tip**
>
> While parallel wires may make sense, on anything over a very short distance the cost implications and difficulties in synchronising signals often make them prohibitive.

Serial: data transmitted one character at a time

Step 1	ANANA ———→	B
Step 2	NANA ———→	BA
Step 3	ANA ———→	BAN
Step 4	NA ———→	BANA
Step 5	A ———→	BANAN
Step 6	———→	BANANA

Parallel: data transmitted in one go

Step 1
B ———→	B
A ———→	A
N ———→	N
A ———→	A
N ———→	N
A ———→	A

Figure 37.1 Serial and parallel communication

Bandwidth

Bandwidth is the term used to describe the amount of data that can be transmitted along a communication channel. It relates to the range of frequencies that are available on the carrier wave that carries the data. The range in this case is the difference between the upper and lower frequencies. As the range of frequencies increases so does the amount of data that can be transmitted within the same time frame. We have already touched on the relative speed at which data can be transmitted. Speed is a vital factor in communications. Bandwidth is measured in hertz (Hz) and megahertz (mHz).

> **Bandwidth**: a measure of the capacity of the channel down which the data is being sent. Measured in hertz (Hz).

Bit rate

REVISED

Bit rate is the term used to describe the speed at which a particular transmission is taking place. It is closely linked to the bandwidth because the bit rate will be limited by how much bandwidth is available.

Bit rate is measured in bits per second (bps). Bandwidth represents the frequencies and therefore the capacity that is available and bit rate represents the actual speed of transfer. The bit rate that can be achieved is directly proportional to bandwidth.

> **Bit rate:** the rate at which data is actually being transmitted. Measured in bits per second.

> **Exam tip**
>
> Mbps or Gbps is **bits** per second, not bytes.

Baud rate

REVISED

Baud rate is another term used to describe the speed at which data can be transmitted. One baud represents one electronic state change per second. An electronic state change may be a change in frequency of the carrier wave, a change in voltage, a change in amplitude or a shift of a waveform. Traditionally, one bit is sent on each state change so one baud roughly equates to one bit per second. However, it is possible to send more than one bit per state change by using different voltage levels to represent the bits. In this case rather than sending bits, you are sending 'symbols', which may have any number of bits in them. The baud rate is determined by the transmission medium.

> **Exam tip**
>
> The link (and difference) between bit rate, baud rate and bandwidth is a regular question and commonly confused due to the similarity in the names.

Latency

REVISED

> **Exam tip**
>
> Do not confuse latency with the amount of time it takes for something to happen. Latency is often called lag but more detail than this may be needed.

Latency is the general term used to explain the time delay that occurs when any component within a computer system is responding to an instruction. This is because the instruction is being transmitted down cables, through buses and logic gates, all of which takes time. Therefore, latency can occur at any stage of the transmission process. These delays could be so short as to be unnoticeable.

> **Latency:** the time delay that occurs when transmitting data between devices.

There are three general causes of latency when communicating data:
- Propagation latency: The amount of time it takes for a logic gate within a circuit to transmit the data.
- Transmission latency: The amount of time it takes to pass through a particular communication medium; for example, fibre optic would have a lower latency than copper cable.
- Processing latency: The amount of time it takes data to pass around a network depending on how many servers or devices it has to pass through.

Synchronous and asynchronous data transmission

Synchronous means that the two devices which are communicating will synchronise their transmission signals. Using the system clock, the computer sending the data will control the transmission rate to be in time with the device or computer receiving the signal. If the two devices are not synchronised then data could be lost during transmission. Once they are synchronised the two devices can send and receive data without need for any further information.

> **Synchronous data transmission**: data is transmitted where the pulse of the clock of the sending and receiving device are in time with each other. The devices may share a common clock.

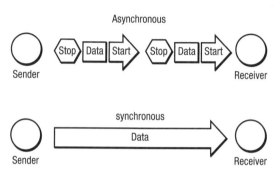

Figure 37.2 Asynchronous and synchronous data

Asynchronous transmission does not require the permanent synchronisation of the sender's and receiver's system clocks. Instead, it synchronises only for the duration of the transmission by sending additional bits of information called start and stop bits.

To send a character may require an 8-bit code to be transmitted. In addition to the eight bits, **asynchronous data transmission** requires at least two other bits. At the start of the eight bits there is a **start bit** and at the end, a **stop bit**. The character may also include a **parity bit**.

The process works as follows:
- The start bit causes the receiver to synchronise its clock to the same rate as the sender.
- Both devices must already have agreed on how many bits of data will follow (commonly 7 or 8 bits), whether a parity bit is being used, what type of parity it is, and how many stop bits there will be.
- The stop bit (or bits) indicate that the data has arrived so the processor on the receiver's device can now handle those bits, for example, by copying them into memory.
- If there is more data then another start bit will be sent and the cycle will continue.
- The sender's device sends data as soon as it is available rather than waiting for the clock pulse or a synchronisation signal from the receiving device.

> **Asynchronous data transmission**: data is transmitted between two devices that do not share a common clock signal.
>
> **Start bit**: a bit used to indicate the start of a unit of data in asynchronous data transmission.
>
> **Stop bit**: a bit used to indicate the end of a unit of data in asynchronous data transmission.
>
> **Parity bit**: a method of checking binary codes by counting the number of 0s and 1s in the code.

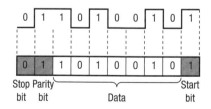

Figure 37.3 Start, stop and parity bits

Protocols

> **Exam tip**
>
> While the AS exam only requires you to be able to define a protocol, the A-level requires you to be familiar with a specific range of protocols.

Protocols are a method for ensuring that different computers can communicate with each other. A protocol is a set of rules. In the context of communications, there are a number of rules that have been established in relation to the transmission of data. **Protocols** cover aspects such as the format in which data should be transmitted and how items of data are identified.

From using the Internet, you will probably already have come across four common protocols:

- TCP/IP: Transmission Control Protocol/Internet Protocol is actually two protocols that are usually referred to as one and relate to the set of rules that govern the transmission of data around the Internet. Data sent around the Internet are split into packets. **TCP/IP** handles the routing and re-assembly of these data packets.
- HTTP: Hypertext Transfer Protocol. You may have seen http preceding Internet addresses, for example, http://www.aqa.org.uk, though you do not need to type it in yourself these days. **HTTP** is the set of rules governing the exchange of the different types of file that make up displayable web pages.
- FTP: File Transfer Protocol is similar to HTTP in that it provides the rules for the transfer of files on the Internet. **FTP** is commonly used when downloading program files or when you create a web page and upload to the ISP's server.

> **Protocols**: sets of rules.
>
> **TCP/IP:** a set of protocols (set of rules) for all TCP/IP network transmissions.
>
> **HTTP (Hypertext Transfer Protocol)**: the protocol (set of rules) to define the identification, request and transfer of multimedia content over the Internet.
>
> **FTP**: a protocol (set of rules) for handling file uploads and downloads.

Summary

- Serial transmission sends data one bit at a time.
- Parallel transmission sends data several bits at a time.
- Bandwidth is a measure of the physical capacity of a communication channel.
- Bit rate and baud rate are methods for quantifying how much data can actually be transmitted within a certain time frame.
- Latency is the delay that occurs when data is being transmitted.
- Synchronous data transmission takes place between devices that have synchronised their clocks.
- Asynchronous transmission does not require devices to be synchronised, instead it sends extra bits of data (start and stop bits).
- Protocols are the rules that define how transmission will take place.

Now test yourself

1 Describe the differences and links between baud rate, bit rate and bandwidth. [4]
2 Explain why parallel communication is not always more desirable than serial transmission. [2]
3 Define the term protocol. [1]

Tasks

1 Use the Internet to research a form of asynchronous communication.
2 Use the Internet to research a form of synchronous communication.

38 Networks

Specification coverage

3.9.2 Networking

Network basics

REVISED

Exam tip

In general, the level of detail required in definitions of things like networks will be higher in A-level exams than in AS exams.

A network is any number of computers connected together for communication, sharing processing power, storage capacity and other resources. In order to connect to a **network**, a computer must have a network adapter, more commonly known as a **Network Interface Card (NIC)**.

The NIC is a printed circuit board which is contained inside the computer like any other card (graphics and sound cards, for example). The NIC will be specifically designed to allow the computer to connect either via cable or wirelessly to the particular network topology being used. The type of card also dictates the speed of data transmissions that will be available between this device and the network. These are typically already integrated into modern mother boards.

Networks are usually described in terms of the geographical area that they cover and the way in which the connections are configured, known as **network topology**.

A **Local Area Network (LAN)** is a number of computers and peripherals connected over a small geographical distance, covering one building or site. Most LANs are made up of one or more servers and clients. A server is a high specification computer with sufficient processing power and storage capacity to service a number of users. A client is any computer attached to the network.

A **Wide Area Network (WAN)** is a number of computers and peripherals connected together over a large geographical distance. This could mean any network that extends beyond a single site right up to global networks such as the Internet. WANs make use of a wider variety of communication media including telephone wires, microwave links, satellite connections and fibre optic cables.

> **Network**: devices that are connected together to share data and resources.
>
> **Network adapter / Network Interface Card (NIC)**: a card that enables devices to connect to a network.
>
> **Network topology**: the layout of a network, usually in terms of its conceptual layout rather than physical layout.
>
> **Local Area Network (LAN)**: a network over a small geographical distance – usually on one site and typically used by one organisation.
>
> **Wide Area Network (WAN)**: a network spread over a large geographical distance.

Exam tip

LANs are normally owned and operated by a single organisation. WANs may be owned/operated by multiple organisations and will commonly use third-party communication technology.

In addition to the server and client the other critical device within a network is a router. Modern routers are actually a number of devices merged together into a single device. The typical router for a home network:

- receives every packet of data being transmitted, reads the header of the packet and then forwards it to its destination
- acts as a firewall, preventing certain packets from being forwarded
- acts as a switch, creating a connection between two devices on a network
- provides a wireless access point transmitting a WiFi signal
- acts as a modem to convert digital signals to analogue so that they can be transmitted down standard telephone cables.

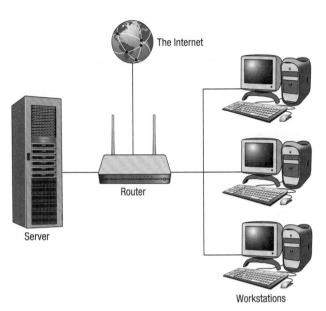

Figure 38.1 A LAN connected to the Internet

Star topology

A **star topology** takes its name from the simplified way in which it can be represented on paper as shown in Figure 38.2. This shows the way that the devices are conceptually connected together.

> **Star topology**: a way of connecting devices in a network where each workstation has a dedicated cable to a central computer or switch.

> **Exam tip**
>
> The specification expects you to understand star **physical** topologies and bus **logical** topologies. This is an excellent area to do some further reading on.

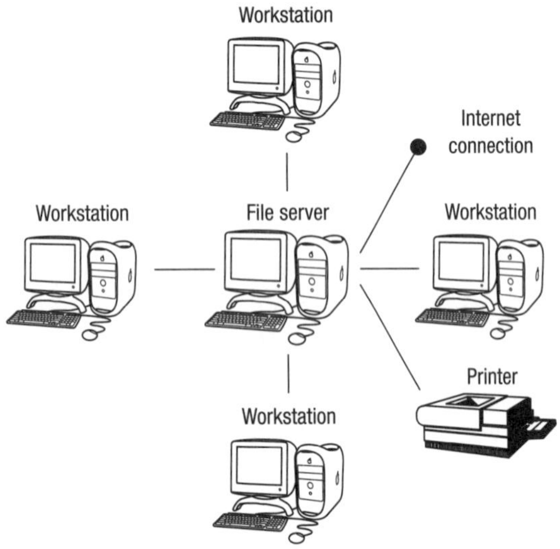

Figure 38.2 A star network

Figure 38.2 shows each client connected to a central server via an individual connection. The main feature is the dedicated connection between server and client. In reality it will be a switch in the centre with the server attached to one of the ports. The server will be a high specification machine with a large amount of processing power and storage capacity. The clients have access to the server through the cabling.

Table 38.1 Advantages and disadvantages of the star topology

Advantages of star topology	Disadvantages of star topology
Fast connection speed as each client has a dedicated cable.	Expensive to set up due to increased cabling costs.
Will not slow down as much as other network topologies when many users are online.	If the cable fails then that client may not be able to receive data.
Fault-finding is simpler as individual faults are easier to trace.	Difficult to install as multiple cables are needed. The problem is exaggerated where the LAN is split across a number of buildings.
Relatively secure as the connection from client to server is unique.	The server can get congested as all communications must pass through it.
New clients can be added without affecting the other clients.	
If one cable or client fails, then only that client is affected.	

Bus topology

REVISED

The other main network topology is the **bus topology**, where all of the nodes within the network are connected via one main cable. If there is a main server, all of the clients connect to it down this main cable. This cable carries data between the server and the clients with each client branching off the main bus cable.

> **Bus topology**: a network layout that uses one main data cable as a backbone to transmit data.

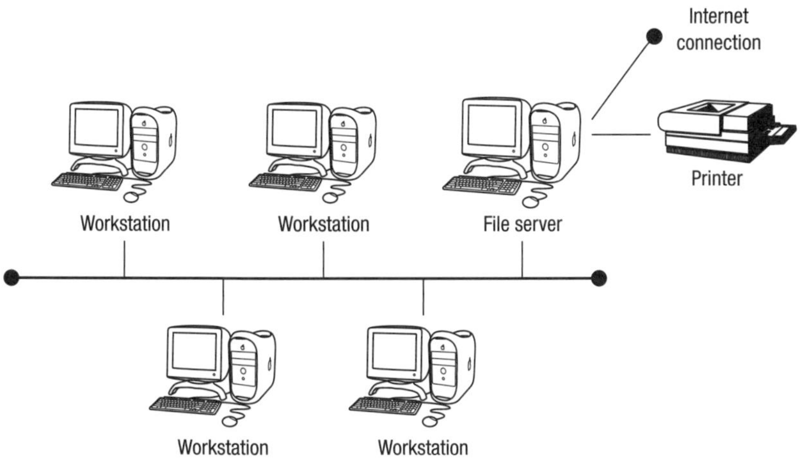

Figure 38.3 A bus network

The main cable or backbone must allow high-speed data transmission as all data must pass down this one channel. A common implementation of the bus system is an Ethernet network system.

Table 38.2 Advantages and disadvantages of a bus network

Advantages of bus topology	Disadvantages of bus topology
Cheaper to install than a star topology as only one main cable is required.	Less secure than a star network as all data are transmitted down one main cable.
Easier to install than a star topology.	Transmission times get slower when more users are on the network.
Easy to add new clients by branching them off the main cable.	If the main cable fails, then all clients are affected.
	Less reliable than a star network due to reliance on the main cable.
	More difficult to find faults.

There is a distinction to be made between the **physical topology** and **logical topology** of a network. Physical topology refers to the actual connection of cables. However, it is possible for networks that are connected in a particular physical topology to act in a different way with the addition of more hardware and software. For example, some Ethernet networks were physically laid out as a star, but used hubs to repeat signals, which effectively creating a bus network.

> **Physical topology:** the way in which devices in a network are physically connected.
>
> **Logical topology:** the conceptual way in, data is transmitted around a network (see Physical topology).

Client–server networks

REVISED

> **Exam tip**
>
> Don't fall into the trap of thinking that client–server and peer-to-peer networks are restricted to certain topologies.

In the star and bus topologies, the diagram shows a main server. Although the clients have local resources in terms of processing power and storage capacity, they are dependent upon the server. This is the most common way of constructing a LAN with a large number of users. The server will be a high-end computer with a large amount of processing power and storage capacity. It needs to be big enough and fast enough to cope with the demands placed upon it by the clients.

> **Client–server:** a network methodology where one computer has the main processing power and storage and the other computers act as clients requesting services from the server.

Peer-to-peer networks

REVISED

In a **peer-to-peer** network, no one computer is in overall control of the network. Instead the resources of each computer or workstation are available to all the computers in the network. Each workstation therefore can act either as a client or as the server, depending on the current task. This is more common among smaller networks or for certain applications such as file sharing.

> **Peer-to-peer:** a network methodology where all devices in a network share resources between them rather than having a server.

> **Exam tip**
>
> Peer-to-peer networks are often used at home where every computer and device has equal rights.

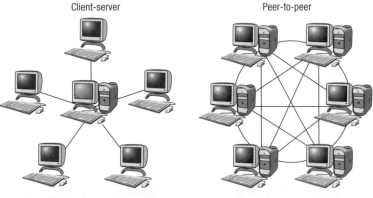

Key: Green = Server   Black = Client   Blue = Workstation

Figure 38.4 Client–server and peer-to-peer networks

Wireless networks

A wireless network varies from a wired network in that it does not use cables to make the physical connections between devices. Instead, the data is sent using radio waves. Wireless networks can be implemented over small or large geographical distances so it is possible to have wireless LANs (WLAN) and **wireless WANs (WWAN)**. Many business and home networks are set up wirelessly, doing away with the need for costly cabling and enabling easy access to the network from any device with a wireless network adapter (NIC).

All devices that are on a network have what is called a **Media Access Control (MAC)** address. This is a unique identifier encoded into the network interface card (NIC) in the format of six groups of two hex digits separated by colons, e.g. 02:32:45:77:89:ab. Any device that connects to a network using WiFi will connect through a wireless access point and must have its own unique MAC address. Every NIC ever manufactured has a unique address meaning that they can be used to identify every device uniquely. The first half of the MAC address is the manufacturer code and the second half is the unique device code allocated by that manufacturer.

WiFi is the generic term for a **Wireless Local Area Network (WLAN)** where devices can connect wirelessly to each other and where a connection can be made to the Internet providing one of the devices in the network is online. WiFi operates to a generic standard called IEEE 802.11, ensuring that all devices are compliant and can connect and transmit data around the network.

> **Wireless Wide Area Network (WWAN):** a WAN that does not use cables, but sends data using radio waves.
>
> **Media Access Control (MAC) address:** a unique code that identifies a particular device on a network.
>
> **WiFi:** a standard method for connecting devices wirelessly to a network and to the Internet.
>
> **Wireless Local Area Network (WLAN):** a LAN that does not use cables but connects using radio waves.

Protocols

There are sets of standards or **protocols** for wireless communications and WiFi to ensure that all devices are able to connect with each other and transmit and receive data. A protocol called Carrier Sense Multiple Access with Collision Avoidance (CSMA/CA) was developed to enable the various devices to transmit data at high speeds without interfering with each other.

> **Protocols:** sets of rules.

When data are sent around networks, they are sent in frames with all the frames being re-assembled at the receiving end. Any device on a wireless network may attempt to send frames. These data frames can be picked up by any nodes or devices within range. Before each frame is sent, the device uses the CSMA/CA protocol to see whether the transmission medium is idle or whether another device is using it. If the transmission media is idle, the data are sent. If it is busy, the device will wait and try again later. Each device will then wait a random amount of time before checking to see if the medium is free again so that it can send the data. This is known as a back-off mechanism and is random to reduce the chances of both devices trying to send simultaneously again.

If the transmission medium is free then the data can be sent. On receipt of the data, an acknowledgment is sent back to the sending device to confirm that the data have been received and not corrupted. If this is not received, again it will wait a random amount of time before resending.

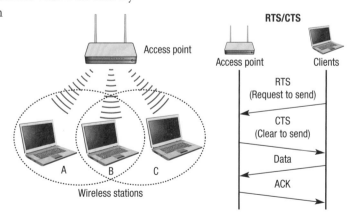

Figure 38.5 The CSMA/CA protocol using RTS/CTS

An optional extension to the protocol is a system called **Request to Send/ Clear to Send (RTS/CTS)**, which works between the nodes on a network. The RTS sends a message to the receiving node or access point and if a CTS message is received, it knows that the node is idle and that the data frame can be sent. If no CTS message is received, it will wait and send another RTS later.

> **Request to Send / Clear to Send (RTS/CTS)**: a protocol to ensure data does not collide when being transmitted on wireless networks.

SSID

The standard method of ensuring that wireless devices are connected to the correct network is by using a **Service Set Identifier (SSID)**, which is a 32-character code put into the header of each packet of data being sent. Each code is locally unique to the particular WLAN that is being used and therefore acts as an identifier allowing that frame of data to be transmitted around the WLAN. The network interface card must also be programmed with the same 32-character code so that the device can connect to the WLAN in the first place.

> **Service Set Identifier (SSID)**: a locally unique 32-character code that identifies a device on a wireless network.

Network security

There are a number of steps that can be taken to increase the level of security on a wireless network:
- Change the SSID from the default value and hide it from transmission.
- Ensure that all devices are **WiFi Protected Access (WPA/WPA2)** compliant.
- Use strong encryption (WPA/WPA2) (see Chapter 40).
- Create a 'white list' of MAC addresses from devices that you know to be trustworthy.

> **WiFi Protected Access (WPA/WPA2)**: a protocol for encrypting data and ensuring security on WiFi networks.

Summary

- A network is a collection of connected devices.
- Networks are either Local Area (LAN) or Wide Area (WAN) and may be wired or wireless.
- Networks can be constructed in a star or bus topology.
- Client–server networks have a server providing resources and services to clients.
- Peer-to-peer networks share resources between a number of workstations.

- All devices need a network interface card (NIC) and media access control (MAC) address in order to connect to a network.
- Various protocols and standards exist for wireless networks including the 802.11 WiFi standard and CSMA/CA collision protocol.
- There are particular issues with wireless networks in ensuring that wireless devices connect securely to the correct network.

Now test yourself

TESTED ☐

1 Describe the difference between a LAN and a WAN. [2]
2 Identify and justify a situation where you would use:
   (a) a peer-to-peer network [2]
   (b) a client–server network. [2]
3 Describe how the CSMA/CA protocol works. [3]
4 Identify three ways in which a wireless network may be secured. [3]

39 The Internet

The Internet and the World Wide Web

REVISED

The **Internet** started life as ARPANET in the late 1960s, set up by the American military as a secure way of transferring sensitive data during the Cold War with Russia. During the 1980s the network expanded and was used by a much wider community including universities and research centres. The Internet as we know it now started to take shape in the mid-1980s when Tim Berners-Lee, a British scientist working in Switzerland, created the World Wide Web (WWW), a service available on the Internet.

> **Internet**: a global network of networks.

Uniform Resource Locator (URL)

REVISED

A **URL** is the full address used to find files on the Internet. For example:

http://www.awebsite.co.uk/index.html

The contents of the file that a URL locates will vary depending on the Internet protocol being used. In this example, hypertext transfer protocol (HTTP) is being used. The file it points to is an html file called index.html which contains hyperlinks to further pages. HTTP indicates that the file can be accessed using a browser. Consequently, most URLs start with HTTP although it is not always necessary to type it in the address line.

> **Uniform resource locator (URL)**: a method for identifying the location of resources (e.g. websites) on the Internet.

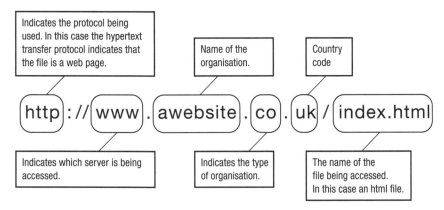

Figure 39.1 Uniform resource locator

The address is made up of several parts:
- the protocol being used, which could be http, https or ftp
- the filename to locate the specific file needed. If the file is located within a subdirectory on the server then a pathname, including the directory name and filename, will be given instead of a simple filename.

Domain name

The **domain name** identifies organisations or groups on the Internet. For example:

www.bbc.co.uk

- **www** indicates a fully qualified domain name (FQDN) as it relates to only one host.
- **bbc** is the name of the organisation.
- **.co** indicates that it is a company.
- **.uk** indicates that the website is registered in the UK.

> **Domain name**: the recognisable name of a domain on the Internet.

> **Exam tip**
>
> The host refers to a single computer – normally a server. In this case it is the server known as www in the bbc.co.uk domain. Although www is normally the web server, this is best practice rather than a requirement.

IP address

Internet Protocol (IP) address is a dotted quad number that identifies every computer that sends or receives data on a network and on the Internet. This was originally devised as a 32-bit or 4-byte code made up of four decimal numbers separated by dots, e.g. 234.233.32.123. As one byte is allocated to each of the four sets of numbers, the range of each is between 0 and 255.

> **Internet Protocol (IP) address**: a unique number that identifies devices on a network.

The numbers themselves make little sense to us as users, which is why we use the domain name. Domain names are designed to be easy to remember and relevant to the organisations.

However, the protocol used to transmit data (TCP/IP) can only work with numbers. Therefore, every domain name is mapped to a number. This number is the real Internet address and identifies the computer that is transmitting or receiving data. It is called an IP address because it uses the Internet Protocol.

> **Exam tip**
>
> The number of available IPv4 addresses has pretty much run out – IPv6 provides enough addresses to last for the foreseeable future.

Some IP addresses are classed as private or non-routable addresses. Typically, these are the IP addresses used by devices on a private network, perhaps in a home, school or business. The IP address is needed in order to route data around the network, however it does not need to be made public as that device is not directly connected to the Internet. It is hidden behind a router or firewall. Non-routable addresses only have to be unique within the LAN and therefore do not need to be allocated on a global basis.

> **Exam tip**
>
> Specific ranges of IP addresses are set aside for non-routable addresses and are reused over and over again.

Ports

A **port** is used to identify a particular process or application on a network. The port address is a 16-bit number attached to the IP address. By addressing that port, a process or application will be accessed on the client.

> **Port**: used to identify a particular process or application on a network.
>
> **POP3**: a protocol (set of rules) for receiving emails.

Port addresses are often used to run processes for common networking tasks and many have been assigned port numbers that are in widespread use. For example, port 25 is used for the SMTP application that checks for incoming email on an email server. Port 110 is used for the **POP3** application that fetches email from the email server.

Network Address Translation (NAT)

The system that is used to match up the private IP addresses with the public ones is called Network Address Translation (NAT). This has two main advantages. One is that a unique IP address is not needed for every single device on a network, only on the router or server that is physically connected. This means that only the public IP address needs to be registered with the **domain name server (DNS) system**. The second advantage is that there is an increased level of security as the private IP address is not being broadcast over the Internet, making that device more secure from unauthorised access.

Domain name server (DNS): a server that contains domain names and associated IP addresses.

The router will track connections and maintain a listing of the mappings between private IP addresses and port numbers and the corresponding public address. It does this by adding entries to a translation table which acts as a look-up between the internal IP address and the external IP address.

Port forwarding

Port forwarding is commonly used when a server inside a private network, with a non-routable IP address, is to be used to provide services to clients on the Internet. As the server has a non-routable IP address, it cannot be accessed directly from the Internet. Therefore, the client on the Internet must use the public IP address of the router that connects the private network with the server on it to initiate a connection. This router can be programmed so that requests sent to it on a particular port number are forwarded to a device with a specific IP address within the network.

Port forwarding: a method of routing data through additional ports.

Sockets

A **socket** is an endpoint of a communication flow across a computer network. Sockets are created in software not hardware. A TCP/IP socket is made up from the combination of an IP address and a port number. When a computer needs to communicate with a server it will send a request to the server using the server's IP address and port number for that type of request (e.g. HTTP is usually port 80). This is normally written as IP address:port, e.g. 123.45.67.89:300.

Socket: an endpoint of a communication flow across a computer network.

Subnet masking

IP addresses are split into a network identifier and a host identifier. Addresses are split up in this way to make networks easier to manage and to make it more efficient when routing data. Where a network is separated in this way, each part is known as a subnet or subnetwork.

Subnet masking: a method of dividing a network into multiple smaller networks.

When a computer on a network sends data to another computer, it needs to identify whether it is on the same subnet as the other computer. If it is, it can send data to it directly. If it is not, it will send data to the relevant router or gateway.

To identify whether the destination computer is on the same subnet, the sending computer needs to look at the network portion of the destination IP address to see if it is the same as its own. To do this a **subnet** mask is used.

IP address v4 and v6

IPv6 was created to increase the range of numbers available to assign to addresses as there are more digits in the number, and hex is being used rather than decimal, allowing for a greater range within each group of numbers.

IPv6 uses 128 bits represented as eight groups of four hex numbers separated by colons, for example:

`13E7:0000:0000:0000:51D5:9CC8:C0A8:6420`

The v6 IP addresses are slowly replacing the original v4 format.

Dynamic Host Configuration Protocol (DHCP)

IP addresses are defined as either static or dynamic. Static IP addresses are ones that are assigned and then never change. Dynamic IP addresses are allocated every time a device connects to a network and this is perhaps the most common approach. The allocation is done automatically by an application as you log on.

> **Dynamic Host Configuration Protocol (DHCP):** a set of rules for allocating locally unique IP addresses to devices as they connect to a network.

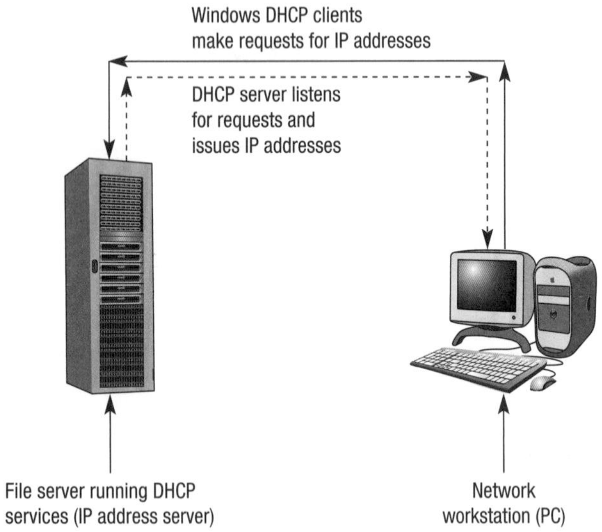

Windows DHCP clients make requests for IP addresses

DHCP server listens for requests and issues IP addresses

File server running DHCP services (IP address server)

Network workstation (PC)

Figure 39.2 The DCHP server

A dedicated DHCP server is used on the network and handles the requests by managing a pool of available IP addresses, usually within a defined range of numbers depending on how the network is physically configured.

Domain name server (DNS) system

Domain names are mapped to a unique IP address and this information is stored in databases on large servers called domain name servers (DNS). Humans use domain names as they are easier to remember than IP addresses. It is the DNS that maps the domain names to the IP addresses.

Figure 39.3 shows how this works. If a user on their laptop wants to connect to the BBC website, a request is sent to the DNS to establish the IP address. The DNS looks in its database and sends the IP address to the laptop. A connection can then be established between the laptop and the BBC server.

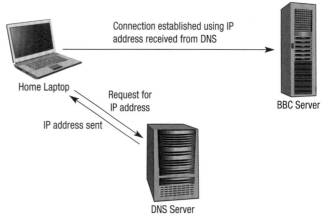

Figure 39.3 Process for connecting to the DNS server

Internet registries

The organisation that oversees the allocation of domain names and IP addresses is called ICANN – the Internet Corporation for Assigned Names and Numbers, which is based in the USA. They have a department called the Internet Assigned Numbers Authority (IANA), which, at the time of writing, manages a further five large organisations around the world called **Regional Internet Registries (RIR)**. Each of these has a defined region of the world and therefore a defined set of IP addresses that they are responsible for allocating.

In Europe, the RIR is called RIPE NCC. In turn, each RIR has several members called National Internet Registries (one per country) who in turn have members called Local Internet Registries, all of whom have responsibility for allocating the IP addresses in specific geographical areas.

> **Internet registries**: organisations who allocate and administer domain names and IP addresses.
>
> **Regional Internet Registry (RIR)**: one of five large organisations that allocate and administer domain names and IP addresses in different parts of the world.

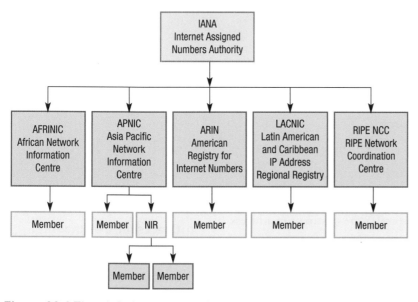

Figure 39.4 The global structure of Internet registries

Routing and gateways

REVISED

When you connect to the Internet, a connection is established between your computer and the website that you are visiting. This is not a direct link. In the first instance, you connect to your Internet Service Provider (ISP) which in turn connects to the ISP hosting the website. Data being transmitted around a WAN will be sent via a number of nodes. A node is one of the connections within the network. It knows where to send it as each piece of data is sent as a **packet**, and it will read the header information in each packet of data being sent.

Routing finds the optimum route between sender and receiver, which may be made up of many nodes. At each stage of the routing process, the data packets are sent to the next router in the path, often with reference to a routing table. The routing table stores information on the possible routes that each data packet may take between nodes on its path from sender to receiver. Routing algorithms are used to identify the next best step.

> **Gateway**: a node on a network that acts as a connection point to another network with different protocols.
>
> **Packet**: a block of data being transmitted.
>
> **Routing**: the process of directing packets of data between networks.

Packet switching

REVISED

One of the methods used to send data across networks is called **packet switching**. Each packet of data will also contain additional information including a packet sequence number, a source and destination address and a checksum. Packets of data are normally made up of a header, body and footer. For example, a 1 KB packet might contain information as shown in Figure 39.5.

> **Packet switching**: a method for transmitting packets of data via the quickest route on a network.

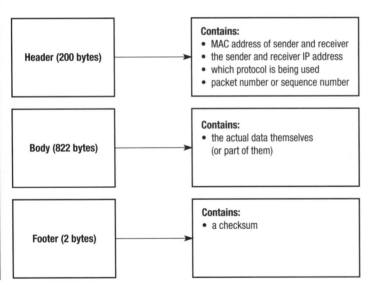

Header (200 bytes)

Contains:
- MAC address of sender and receiver
- the sender and receiver IP address
- which protocol is being used
- packet number or sequence number

Body (822 bytes)

Contains:
- the actual data themselves (or part of them)

Footer (2 bytes)

Contains:
- a checksum

Figure 39.5 The contents of a typical packet of data

The packets are sent to their destination using the destination address. They are re-assembled at the other end using the packet sequence number. The **checksum** will identify any errors. It works by adding together the values of all the data held in a packet and transmitting those data along with the packet.

> **Checksum**: a method of checking the integrity of data by calculating a sum based on the data being sent.

Each packet can take a different route to its destination as it can be re-assembled at the other end regardless of the sequence in which packets are received. Therefore, the packets are routed via the least congested and therefore the quickest route. Data are transferred quicker using this method and are more secure as the packets are taking different routes.

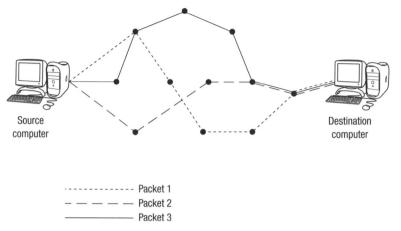

------------ Packet 1
— — — — — Packet 2
──────────── Packet 3

Figure 39.6 Packet switching showing three packets

Summary

- The Internet is a global network of networks.
- The WWW is a resource available on the Internet made up of millions of websites and web pages.
- A uniform resource locator (URL) is the unique address of a resource on the Internet.
- A domain name identifies a domain on the Internet and is usually registered to a particular organisation or individual.
- The IP address is a numeric identifier that maps to the domain name.
- IP addresses are allocated to devices on a network either statically or dynamically.

- A port identifies a specific application that can be accessed via a network. Common applications have dedicated port numbers which are called well-known ports.
- A socket is an endpoint of a communication flow across a computer network.
- Subnet masking is a method of identifying different subsets of a network.
- Internet domain names and IP addresses are administered by Internet Registries using the Database Name Server (DNS).
- Data is sent in packets and routed around using packet switching.

Now test yourself

TESTED ☐

1 Describe the difference between the Internet and the World Wide Web. [2]
2 Identify three parts of the URL https://www.coolcomputing.com/pages/index.html [3]
3 Identify two parts of the socket 43.123.32.5:23 [2]
4 A business cannot decide whether to purchase an IPv4 or IPv6 address. Discuss the differences. [6]

Tasks

1 Investigate subnet masking. What are its purposes?
2 Investigate Internet Registries and the role they play.
3 Investigate how packet switching works and how it evolved.
4 There are many videos available online describing the history of ARPANET. Have a look at some of them.

40 Internet security

Specification coverage

3.9.3.2 Internet security

Firewall

REVISED ☐

> **Exam tip**
>
> Many students become confused and think that firewalls stop viruses and anti-virus software stops hacking attempts. This is not the case.

A **firewall** describes the technique used to protect an organisation's network from unauthorised access by users outside the network. A firewall can be constructed using hardware, software or a combination of both. The most secure firewalls tend to be those constructed from both hardware and software.

One method, known as **packet filtering**, uses two network interface cards (NICs) – one for the LAN and one for the Internet. When data packets are received through the Internet NIC, they can be examined before being passed around internally via the LAN NIC.

The header information and/or the actual contents of each data packet can be examined. This is called **stateful inspection** and also involves the firewall examining where each data packet has come from. It keeps track of all open communication channels and therefore knows the context of each packet it receives.

> **Firewall**: hardware or software for protecting against unauthorised access to a network.
>
> **Packet filtering**: a technique for examining the contents of packets on a network and rejecting them if they do not conform to certain rules.
>
> **Stateful inspection**: a technique for examining the contents of packets on a network and rejecting them if they do not form part of a recognised communication.

Proxy server

REVISED ☐

One security measure that can be used at this stage is a proxy server. The word proxy means 'on behalf of' so in this context it is a server that acts on behalf of another computer. By routing through a proxy server there is no direct connection between the computer on the LAN and the Internet. Instead, all requests get passed through the proxy server and can be evaluated to ensure that they come from a legitimate source or to filter users so that they only have access to specific websites.

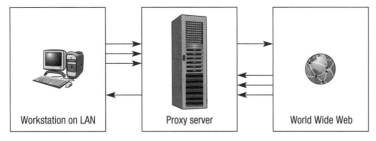

Workstation on LAN   Proxy server   World Wide Web

Figure 40.1 A proxy server

In Figure 40.1, the arrows represent requests which are then filtered through the proxy server, with only certain data being allowed through in each direction, depending on how the proxy server has been set up.

Private/public key encryption

Encryption techniques make use of a key, which is a string of numbers or characters that are used as a code to encrypt and then decrypt the message. Typically, the key may be 128-bit or 256-bit enabling billions of permutations for the way in which data can be encrypted. Without the key, the message cannot be understood.

One method is **symmetric encryption** where one key is shared between the sender and the recipient as shown in Figure 40.2.

> **Symmetric encryption**: where the sender and receiver both use the same key to encrypt and decrypt data.

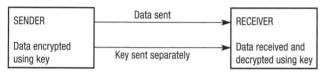

Figure 40.2 Symmetric encryption

In addition to the data, at some point the sender has to send the receiver the key. This is known as key exchange. It is possible but not advisable to send the key with the data.

There is an inherent weakness with this system in that if the key is intercepted then it would be possible to work out what it is, therefore making all further communications vulnerable to unauthorised access.

One way of getting round this is to use **asymmetric encryption**, which makes use of two related keys in combination, a private one and a public one. The algorithm used to create the two keys results in so many permutations that it is almost impossible to work out the combined key. Both sender and receiver have their own pair of public and private keys.

> **Asymmetric encryption**: where a public and private key are used to encrypt and decrypt data.
>
> **Private key**: a code used to encrypt/decrypt data that is only known by one user but is mathematically linked to a corresponding public key.
>
> **Public key**: a code used to encrypt/decrypt data that can be made public and is linked to a corresponding private key.

For example, with two computers A and B:
- A will have a **private key** known only to A.
- A will also have a **public key**, which is mathematically related to the private key. It is called a public key as anyone can access it.
- B will also have a private key and a related public key.
- For A to send a secure message to B, A will first encrypt the message using B's public key.
- As the private and public keys are related, the message can only be decrypted by B using B's private key.
- As no one else knows B's private key, even if the message were intercepted, it could not be decrypted.

Figure 40.3 Public and private key encryption

Digital certificates and signatures

REVISED

A **digital certificate** is a means of proving who you are when dealing with people and organisations on the Internet. It is usually used by businesses to authenticate that they are genuine and is important in the use of asymmetric encryption as a secure way of sharing public keys.

The certificate typically contains the name of the organisation, their domain and server name and a serial number which is registered with a **certification authority** who issues the certificates.

A **digital signature** is another method of ensuring the authenticity of the sender. In the same way that a signature helps to prove someone's identity in real life, a digital signature does the same thing on the computer. However, rather than being an actual signature, a digital signature uses mathematical functions and the public/private key method.

Digital certificate: a method of ensuring that an encrypted message is from a trusted source as they have a certificate from a certification authority.

Certification authority: a trusted organisation that provides digital certificates and signatures.

Digital signature: a method of ensuring that an encrypted message is from a trusted source as they have a unique, encrypted signature verified by a certification authority.

Trojans

REVISED

Exam tip

Trojans get their name from the legend of the Trojan horse.

A **Trojan** is a computer program designed to cause harm to a computer system or to allow a hacker unauthorised access. It is one of a group of malware programs, which is short for malicious software. The distinguishing feature of a Trojan is that it is hidden away inside another file and it is not always obvious that a computer is infected. The Trojan does not replicate itself in the same way as other malware and therefore it can remain undetected for a long time. It is activated when the program containing the trojan is executed.

Trojan: malware that is hidden within another file on your computer.

Viruses

REVISED

A **virus** is a small malware program that is designed to cause damage to a computer system or the data stored on it. A computer gets infected when the malware installs itself on the computer from a number of sources including pop-ups, email attachments or file downloads.

The virus itself will be attached to another file but once installed on the host machine, it will activate. The defining feature of a virus is that it replicates itself and can therefore cause extensive damage to individual computers and networks as, like a human virus, it can spread anywhere.

Virus: a generic term for malware where the program attaches itself to another file in order to infect a computer.

Worms

REVISED

Exam tip

Worms, like their living counterparts, dig and tunnel through defences.

Worms replicate themselves and are designed to spread, exploiting any weaknesses in a computer's defences. The defining feature of a worm is that it does not need to be attached to another file to infect the computer.

Worm: malware or a type of virus that replicates itself and spreads around a computer system. It does not need to be attached to another file in order to infect a computer.

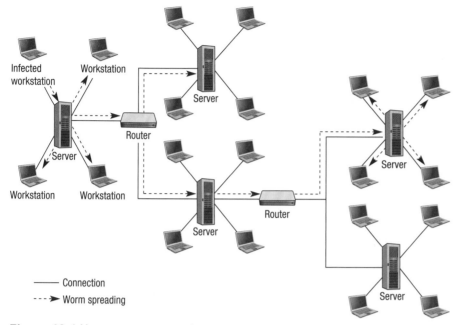

Connection
- - -> Worm spreading

Figure 40.4 How worms spread

Protecting against Trojans, viruses and worms

As users there are many things we can do as individuals to protect our computers:

- use anti-virus software and other anti-malware software and keep it up to date
- keep operating system software up to date
- use a firewall
- do not open attachments or click on pop-ups from unknown senders
- operate a white list of trusted sites
- ensure sites use HTTPS, digital signatures and certificates
- use passwords on programs and files
- encrypt data files.

As programmers we can:

- select a programming language with in-built security features including tools that check for common security errors
- use recognised encryption techniques for all data stored within the program
- set administrative rights as part of the program and carefully control access and permission rights for different users
- don't load up lots of Internet services as part of your code unless they are needed
- thoroughly test your code as errors can be exploited, specifically testing for known security issues
- keep code up to date in light of new security threats
- never trust the user! Many threats are internal to an organisation and might not be malicious. Major problems can be caused through accidental misuse by a user.

> **Exam tip**
>
> Make sure you know the difference between anti-virus software and firewalls.

As a system administrator we can:

- ensure that requests are coming from recognised sources
- use a network firewall and use the packet filtering and stateful inspection techniques as described earlier in this chapter
- use encryption techniques as described earlier and ensure digital certificates and signatures are used and are up to date
- keep anti-virus software up to date
- update the network operating system regularly
- keep accurate logs of all activity.

Summary

- A firewall can be implemented using software and hardware and protects networks from unauthorised access.
- Data can be routed through a proxy server so that a network's server is not connected directly to the Internet.
- Symmetric encryption is where the sender and receiver both use the same key to encrypt and decrypt data.

- Private/public key encryption or asymmetric encryption uses two related keys, a public key to encrypt data and a private key to decrypt data.
- Digital certificates and signatures are verified by trustworthy organisations and ensure that data is coming from a trusted source.
- Viruses, Trojans and worms are all examples of malicious programs that can cause damage to your data or systems.

Now test yourself

TESTED ☐

1 Describe the difference between a firewall and a proxy server. [2]
2 Explain how asymmetrical encryption works. [5]
3 Describe how a digital certificate can be used to ensure a message or web page comes from a trusted source. [2]
4 Identify the differences between a virus, a worm and a Trojan. [6]
5 Identify three ways that:
   (a) a user and [3]
   (b) a programmer [3]
   can protect against Trojans, viruses and other threats.

Task

1 Investigate the numbers of threats and how they have changed over time.

Now test yourself answers at www.therevisionbutton.co.uk/myrevisionnotes

41 Transmission Control Protocol / Internet Protocol (TCP/IP)

A-level only

Specification coverage

3.9.4.1 TCIP/IP
3.9.4.2 Standard application layer protocols

TCP/IP

REVISED

The TCP/IP stack defines the rules relating to transmission of data packets. IP controls the delivery of the packets and TCP keeps track of the packets and re-assembles them on receipt. **TCP/IP** is made up of a number of layers which are collectively referred to as a protocol stack. Within each layer there are a number of other **protocols**.

TCP/IP is made up of four main layers, as shown in Figure 41.1:

- **Layer 4 – Application layer**: The application layer handles the Domain Name System and a series of other protocols such as FTP, HTTP, HTTPS, POP3, SMTP and SSH.
- **Layer 3 – Transport layer**: This contains most of the configuration and coordination associated with the transmission that ensures that all the packets have arrived and that there are no errors in the packets. It also handles the way in which connections are made to create a path for data to travel between nodes. The sender and receiver are identified and authenticated and the communication is set up, coordinated and terminated. Network resources are identified to ensure that they are sufficient for the communication to take place.
- **Layer 2 – Network or Internet layer**: Defines the IP addresses of devices that send and receive data and handles the creation and routing of packets being sent and received.
- **Layer 1 – Link layer**: This layer provides synchronisation of devices so that the receiving device can manage the flow of data being received. It identifies what network topology is being used and controls the physical signals that transmit the strings of bits around the network, that is, the actual transmission of the 0s and 1s. It also controls physical characteristics such as data transmission rates and the physical connections in a network. On wireless networks it handles the CSMA/CA protocol.

> **TCP/IP**: a set of protocols (set of rules) for all TCP/IP network transmissions.
>
> **Protocols**: sets of rules.

TCP/IP

Application layer
Transport layer
Internet layer
Link layer

Figure 41.1 The layers of the TCP/IP stack

Hypertext Transfer Protocol (HTTP) and Secure HTTP (HTTPS)

REVISED

Hypertext Transfer Protocol (HTTP) is the set of rules that govern how multimedia files are transmitted around the Internet. The content of the WWW is such that text, graphics, video and sound can all be transferred as part of a web page. **HTTP** ensures that the files are transferred and received in a common format. HTTP handles the transmission of this data. The formatting and display of web pages is handled separately, typically by HTML.

> **HTTP**: a protocol (set of rules) for transmitting and displaying web pages.

Hypertext refers to the fact that the web pages will have hyperlinks to other files. When you select a URL, either by typing it in or by clicking on a hyperlink, the HTTP protocol on your computer sends a request to the IP address of the computer that contains the web page. The HTTP protocol on this computer then handles the request and sends back the web page in the appropriate format.

HTTPS is an extension of the protocol with added security. This is commonly used on websites where personal information is used, such as banking websites. Additional security includes authenticating the web server and encrypting data that is being transmitted. It works by using either the Secure Socket Layer (SSL) protocol or the Transport Layer Security (TLS) protocol, both of which use data encryption.

HTTPS: as above but with encrypted transmission.

Figure 41.2 HTTP and HTTPS

File Transfer Protocol (FTP)

REVISED

FTP is another set of rules relating to the transfer of files around the Internet. It is commonly used when a web page is uploaded from the computer of the person who created the site to the web hosting server. It is also used when software is downloaded from websites. When FTP is being used for this purpose, it will be shown as the prefix in the URL.

FTP: a protocol (set of rules) for handling file uploads and downloads.

It is similar to HTTP in that it works using the standard layers of TCP/IP. However, HTTP tends to be used to transfer viewable content (web pages) whereas FTP is commonly used to transfer program and data files.

Secure Shell (SSH) Protocol

REVISED

> **Exam tip**
>
> SSH was preceded by Telnet. The best way of envisioning SSH is to think of using Remote Desktop or Team Viewer, but only on the command line. However, what is shown on the screen of the client is not shown on the screen of the server.

The Internet is often used to enable a user to connect to a remote computer and execute programs and access resources on that computer. This uses the **client–server model** whereby the computer that you use acts as the client and the computer that you control is the server. The server computer is more commonly referred to as the host.

Client–server model: a way of implementing a connection between computers where one computer (the client) makes use of resources of another computer (the server).

In these situations, **SSH** is used to improve the security of the connection. It does this partially by creating a secure network of nodes through which the access is made available. Encryption is used on the data being transmitted using public key encryption. In addition, password and username login details would normally be required.

Secure Shell (SSH) Protocol: a protocol (set of rules) for remote access to computers.

SSH commands are usually input using a command line interface. This means that you have to know specific command words and the syntax (or format) in which you need to type the words in.

Simple Mail Transfer Protocol (SMTP) and Post Office Protocol (POP3)

REVISED

> **Exam tip**
>
> Most webmail services work with an alternative to POP3 called IMAP that views rather than downloads messages.

SMTP and **POP3** are protocols used for sending and receiving emails. SMTP is a specific protocol for sending emails and works through a series of SMTP servers which store the email addresses of senders and recipients. By linking with DNS servers, the IP address of the recipient is identified and a connection can be established between sender and receiver. The data in the email can then be transmitted. SMTP uses ports 25 and 587.

> **SMTP**: a protocol (set of rules) for sending emails.
>
> **POP3**: a protocol (set of rules) for receiving emails.

Where the data cannot be sent for any reason, SMTP uses a queuing system to hold on to the email and then attempts to send it at a later time. It will continue to do this for a set number of times. If it still fails to send, it will send a message back to the sender indicating that delivery has failed. You also get a message if the SMTP or DNS server fails to identify the email address or IP address.

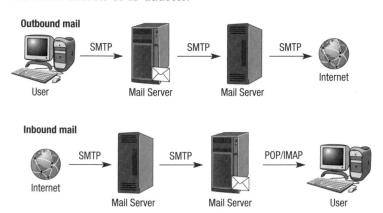

Figure 41.3 The SMTP and POP protocols

In order to receive mail, the client must first connect to the email server. POP3 is a protocol which checks for incoming mail using port 110. It works by creating a text file of any incoming messages associated with your email address. If a message is received, it will append it to your text file and the next time you log on, you will be able to access it in the form of an email message using an email client, which is the chosen email application being used on the network, such as MS Outlook.

Email and web servers

REVISED

Within a network, there may be one or more servers providing access to applications, storage space and other resources. Often servers are set up to perform specific functions on the network. Two examples of this are **email servers** and **web servers.**

> **Email server**: a dedicated computer on a network for handling email.
>
> **Web server**: a dedicated computer on a network for handling web content.

● Email servers are typically high specification machines with large storage capacity that store a database of all the network users and their email addresses. They also store all outgoing and incoming mail. Specific software on the server is used to handle the storage and transmission of emails, allowing users to access their emails regardless of what other services are available.

- The web server hosts a website and handles traffic from users to the site. Data stored on a web server may be in various formats including text, scripts, and multimedia content. Web servers will make use of various protocols including HTTP to ensure that all of these data are correctly handled and formatted so that they appear correctly when viewed over the Internet regardless of the hardware and software being used by the user.

Web browsers

A **web browser** is an application that allows users to view web pages and other resources and is critical in ensuring that websites appear exactly how they were designed. In simple terms a browser needs to retrieve resources via the URL, format them so that they display correctly on the screen and allow some form of navigation and other user features such as bookmarking and searching. This process may require several requests being made to the server in order to load the various resources that make up a web page including scripts, images, and style sheets.

Web browser: an application for viewing web pages.

When a web page is loaded, a request is made to the domain name server (DNS), which translates the URL into an IP address. This IP address is then used to access the web page host. The host then serves the web page to the browser on the client computer.

Summary

- Protocols are sets of rules. There are several protocols that related to the transmission of data around networks.
- The TCP/IP stack is a four-layered set of protocols for computer networks, including the Internet.
- A socket is an endpoint of a communication flow on a computer network that uniquely identifies an application and device.
- Hypertext Transfer Protocol (HTTP) is the set of rules that govern how multimedia files are transmitted around the Internet.
- FTP is a set of rules relating to the transfer of files around the Internet.
- SSH is a set of rules relating to the remote access of computers on a network.
- SMTP, POP3 and IMAP are protocols relating to email.

Now test yourself

1 Describe how a web page is requested and received through the TCP/IP stack. [8]
2 How does HTTPS differ from HTTP? [1]
3 Define the term protocol. [1]
4 If a web page contains three images, a movie and an external file script, plus three links to other web pages, how many HTTP requests will need to be made? [1]

Tasks

1 Experiment using both Lynx and Telnet to browse web pages.
2 Investigate sending and reading emails through a Telnet client. You may need to do this from home.

42 The client–server model

Specification coverage

3.9.4.10 Client–server model
3.9.4.11 Thin- versus thick-client computing

The client-server model

REVISED

The client–server model is a methodology for connecting computers together, usually over a network where one computer provides access to resources for other computers that are connected to it. Typically this might involve having a main server with large amounts of processing power and storage capacity with any number of other computers (clients) attached to it that then use the resources of the server.

The client may have few resources of its own and therefore has to request the services of the server. In a typical star topology like the one shown in Figure 42.1, each client has its own physical cable connection to the server.

Servers and clients can take on different roles depending on what tasks are completed by the users. Examples of different servers include:

- File server: In a traditional network, the file server contains any type of computer file, which could be programs or data.
- Web server: A server is used to serve up web pages for an Intranet.
- Proxy server: Each client computer is provided with a gateway to the Internet through the server.
- Print server: All client print requests are sent to the same server where they are prioritised, buffered and then printed.
- Database server: The server will store the contents of the databases and requests for access to the data will come from the individual clients.
- Application server: The server executes all of the procedures needed to run applications.

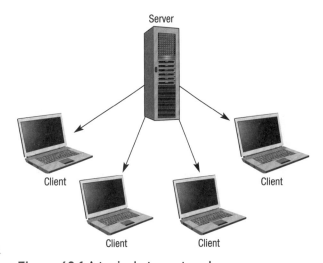

Figure 42.1 A typical star network

The client–server model works on the basic principle of sender and receiver. To initiate any communication and sharing of resources, the client must make a request to the server. In turn the server responds to that request and then provides the service that is being requested.

The client–server model is also used on the Internet. For example, email is built on this model with each user being the client, sending requests to their email provider, who responds to each request as it is received. FTP services also use the model with the client making a request to upload a file, which is then handled by the FTP server.

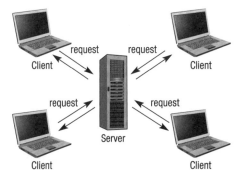

Figure 42.2 The client–server model

Application Program Interface (API)

An **application program interface (API)** defines the way in which programs can work together. They are usually made up of standardised subroutines that can be customised to provide an interface between one program and another. When using web services, an API can also define the protocols that will be used.

One of these is the **websocket protocol**, which creates a connection between a client and a server. The client first sends a handshaking request to the server in order to establish the connection. In response, the server creates a full duplex connection on a single socket. This allows simultaneous exchange of data in both directions, enabling the client and server to communicate on an ongoing basis without the need to constantly refresh a full web page. Effectively, the websocket has created a dedicated link between the two computers. This is routed through port 80, the dedicated HTTP port, meaning that it will work in situations where non-web Internet connections have been blocked using a firewall.

> **Application program interface (API):** a set of subroutines that enable one program to interface with another program.
>
> **Websocket protocol:** a set of rules that creates a persistent connection between two computers on a network to enable real-time collaboration.

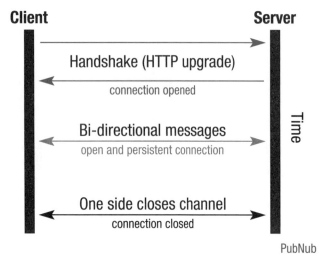

Figure 42.3 A websocket handling data passing between client and server

CRUD

There are conventions and styles that are used to ensure that data is stored, managed and represented correctly on databases that are accessed via the Internet. The four main processes required with databases can be defined by the acronym **CRUD**:
- C: Create
- R: Retrieve
- U: Update
- D: Delete

As well as representing the main database functions, it also refers to the way in which data is actually displayed and reported on via the user interface. Without these four functions it is not possible to have a complete database. All databases will conform to the CRUD principle regardless of how they are built. Relational databases conform to the CRUD standard. In fact there is a one-to-one relationship between CRUD and **SQL** commands as shown in the table on the right.

> **CRUD:** an acronym that explains the main functions of a database: Create, Retrieve, Update, Delete.
>
> **SQL (Structured query language):** a programming language used to manage data within a relational database.

CRUD	SQL
Create	INSERT
Retrieve	SELECT
Update	UPDATE
Delete	DELETE

Now test yourself answers at www.therevisionbutton.co.uk/myrevisionnotes

REST

REST stands for REpresentational State Transfer and is a design methodology for networked database applications. It uses the hypertext transfer protocol (HTTP) to carry out each of the four CRUD operations on a networked database.

HTTP uses request methods which define the way in which data will be handled. In the same way that CRUD can be mapped to SQL statements, it can also be mapped to the HTTP request methods, as shown in the table.

REST is an efficient way of implementing database applications over a network as it makes use of existing protocols within **HTTP**, which has already been adopted as the standard way of transferring data. This means that it will work on any type of local machine architecture, with any operating system and can be run through a firewall for added security. The basic process is shown in Figure 42.4.

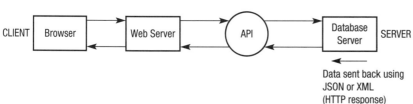

Figure 42.4 The REST model

- The client makes a request to the server from the browser of the local machine.
- The service requested is the database identified by its Uniform Resource Locator (URL), which uniquely identifies the resource on the server and contains the database query.
- The API is run from the server and accessed by the browser to coordinate processes between client and server applications.
- HTML files are used to ensure data is displayed in the correct format on the client side.
- Requests and data are transferred using HTTP.
- JSON (JavaScript Online Notation) or XML (Extensible Markup Language) are used to return the results of the query.

JSON (JavaScript Online Notation) and XML (Extensible Markup Language)

JSON and **XML** are two alternative methods for formatting data objects that are being transferred across servers and web applications. Both have become standard methods.

JSON is a data format originally created as part of the JavaScript programming language, but now available as a standalone format that can be implemented using most programming languages. It is defined as human-readable and is made up of an object and values.

REST (REpresentational State Transfer): a methodology for implementing a networked database.

CRUD	HTTP
Create	POST
Retrieve	GET
Update	PUT
Delete	DELETE

HTTP (Hypertext transfer protocol): the protocol (set of rules) to define the identification, request and transfer of multimedia content over the Internet.

Exam tip

CRUD, XML and JSON are new to the specification, but there is lots of information about them online as they are in regular active use. Be careful when reading around the subject – don't get bogged down in areas which are off-specification.

JSON (JavaScript object notation): a standard format for transmitting data.

XML (Extensible Markup Language): a method of defining data formats for data that will be transmitted around a network.

XML is a markup language that defines how data is encoded. Formatting data in XML is similar to writing code in a programming language and therefore requires more knowledge than producing a JSON file.

Exam tip

XHTML is a subset of XML so if you are confident in HTML, XML can be much easier to understand.

JSON vs XML

REVISED

JSON and XML have developed as the two main methods of sharing data on networked **client–server databases**. They have many things in common but there are also differences. Table 42.1 summarises the main similarities and differences.

Client–server database: a way of implementing a database where the database is put into a server and various users can access it from their workstations. The processing, for example, running a query, will take place on the server.

Table 42.1 Comparison of JSON and XML

	JSON	XML
Human readable	Very easy to read as it is based on defining objects and values.	Slightly less easy to read as data is contained within markup tags.
Compact code	Less code is created than XML.	Requires more code than JSON.
Speed of parsing	Quicker than XML as data is clearly defined as object and value.	Slower than JSON as the data has to be extracted from the tags.
Ease of creation	Easier to create as the syntax of the coding is easier.	Similar to programming so therefore more knowledge is required.
Flexibility and extendibility	Works with a limited range of data types, which may not be sufficient for all applications.	Provides complete freedom over what data types are created and therefore allows greater flexibility.

Thin- vs thick-client computing

REVISED

Exam tip

You need to be able to make an argument for either thick- or thin-client architecture in a particular case, and justify your decisions. Comments such as 'it is cheaper' do not generally receive marks, while 'the cost of each workstation will be less for thin clients than thick' would.

A **thin client** is a computer that depends heavily on a more powerful server to fulfil most of its requirements and processing. The server would be a large powerful computer with lots of processing power and storage capacity that stores the main programs and datasets. The client then taps into these resources, which are not available on the local machine, using a much lower specification computer. In this scenario the server actually runs the software with the client machine simply acting as a '**terminal**' with very little processing power and no hard disk.

A **thick client** is a fully specified computer like the ones most people have at home. They do not need servers to carry out their processing most of the time. In thick-client computing the resources are allocated between client and server in a different way giving the client greater processing power, more local storage and access to software that is installed and

Thin client: in a network where one computer contains the majority of resources, processing power and storage capacity, which it distributes to other clients.

Terminal: a computer that has little or no processing power or storage capacity used as a client in a thin-client network

Thick client: in a network where resources, processing power and storage capacity are distributed between the server and the client computers.

Now test yourself answers at www.therevisionbutton.co.uk/myrevisionnotes

run from the client machine. In this scenario more of the hardware and software resources are at the client end.

There are advantages and disadvantages with each system as shown in Tables 42.2 and 42.3.

Table 42.2 Advantages and disadvantages of the thin-client model

Advantages	Disadvantages
Easy and cheaper to set up new clients as fewer resources are needed.	Clients are dependent on the server so if it goes down, all clients are affected.
The server can be configured to distribute all the hardware and software resources needed.	Can slow down with heavy use.
Hardware and software changes only need to be implemented on the server.	May require greater bandwidth to cope with client request.
Easier for the network manager to control clients.	High-specification servers are expensive.
Greater security as clients have fewer access rights.	

Table 42.3 Advantages and disadvantages of the thick-client model

Advantages	Disadvantages
Reduced pressure on the server leading to more uptime.	Reduced security if clients can download software or access the Internet remotely.
Clients can store programs and data locally giving them more control.	More difficult to manage and update as new hardware and software need installing on each client machine.
Fewer servers and lower bandwidth can be used.	Data is more likely to be lost or deleted on the client side.
Suitable for tablets and mobile phones that require more of the processing and storage to be done on the server side.	Can be difficult to ensure data integrity where many clients are working on local data.

Summary

- The client–server model is a methodology for connecting computers together, usually over a network where one computer provides access to resources for other computers that are connected to it.
- An application program interface (API) defines the way in which programs can work together.
- CRUD stands for Create, Retrieve, Update, Delete.
- Representational State Transfer is a design methodology for networked database applications.
- JSON and XML are two alternative methods for formatting data objects that are being transferred across servers and web applications.
- A thin client is a computer that depends heavily on a more powerful server to fulfil most of its requirements and processing.
- A thick client is a fully specified computer like the ones most people have at home.

Now test yourself

TESTED

1 Describe how the client–server model works. [3]
2 Explain the term CRUD in terms of computerised databases. [5]
3 Explain the term API. [2]
4 A company has a small office consisting of eight members of staff. They carry out surveys and analyse the results. Decide whether you would recommend a thin- or thick-client based system and justify your decision. [6]

Tasks

1 Investigate and review a real-world example of the use of:
   (a) JSON
   (b) XML.
2 Ask your network technician to show you the servers in your school or college network and explain their purposes.

43 Relational databases

Relational databases

REVISED

A **relational database** models data as mathematical relations, with each relation being composed of tuples of data, and the data within each tuple being related in some way. When a relational database model is implemented by software, a relational database program will represent each relation as a table, and each tuple will be a record within a table. The data in different tables can be linked together to express relationships that exist between the data in the tables.

> **Relational database**: a method of creating a database using tables of related data, with relationships between the tables.

Relationships

REVISED

If you were to set up a database for a movie download site, you might create one **table** to store customer data, one to store data about the movies and one to store download details:

- The **CUSTOMER** table contains data all of which are related to the customer; for example, their name and address.
- The **MOVIE** table contains data related to the movie; for example, the title and genre.
- The **DOWNLOAD** table contains data related to the actual download itself; for example, when it was downloaded, how much the customer paid, what file type was downloaded.

> **Table**: a method for implementing an entity and attributes as a group of related data.

There are some real-world relationships between these three tables. For example:

- one-to-many: one customer may have many downloads
- many-to-many: one customer could download many movies and one movie could be downloaded by many customers.

It is also possible, albeit less common, to have a one-to-one relationship although there are none in this particular example.

> **Exam tip**
>
> Logical terminology (e.g. relation) and physical terminology (e.g. table) can be used interchangeably but you need to be aware of both.

Entities

REVISED

In a relational database, a relation stores information about an **entity** and its attributes. An entity is an object about which data will be stored. In our movie example, a customer may be an entity that has attributes such as name and address. These relations are described and stored within tables. In this example, we have already identified three tables: **CUSTOMER, MOVIE** and **DOWNLOAD**.

> **Entity**: an object about which data will be stored.

Attributes

REVISED

An **attribute** is a piece of information about an entity, which is implemented as a field in a relational database. With the movie download database example, we will store different items of data relating to each entity in a table. Possible attributes, only some of which we will use, include:

> **Attribute**: a characteristic or piece of information about an entity, which would be stored as a field in a relational database.

```
CUSTOMER: Customer Name, Address, Phone Number, Date of Birth
MOVIE: Movie Title, Age Classification, Genre
DOWNLOAD: Date of Download, Price, Method of Payment
MOVIEFORMAT: File type
```

Entity relationship diagrams

REVISED

A relationship is the link created between two entities. Each entity is likely to be related to at least one of the other entities. There are three types, or degrees, of relationship:

- One-to-many: One customer will have many downloads.
- Many-to-many: Many customers could have many downloads.
- One-to-one: One customer may have one download.

Entity relationship diagrams are used to show these relationships as shown in Figure 43.1.

> **Exam tip**
>
> Relationships can sometimes be easier to identify if you say it in English, e.g. *one movie can have many downloads.*

> **Entity relationship diagram**: a visual method of describing relationships between entities.

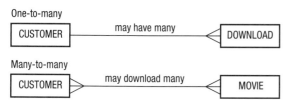

Figure 43.1 Entity relationship diagram

The nature of relationships is sometimes hard to define. You should choose the one that best describes the relationship in logical terms. You should replace any many-to-many relationships with one-to-many relationships. In the example, we replace the many customers to many movies relationship setting up the **DOWNLOAD** entity as a link as shown:

Figure 43.2 Resolving a many-to-many relationship

Primary and foreign keys and entity identifier

REVISED

The **primary key** is the attribute in each table that uniquely identifies each record. It is related to the concept of an **entity identifier**, which is an attribute that can be used to uniquely identify each instance of an entity at the conceptual level. There must be a way of ensuring that every record in an entity table can be identified individually, otherwise the relationships between the tables cannot be made. The options are: use a unique attribute; create a unique attribute; use a composite key.

> **Primary key**: an attribute that can be used to uniquely identify every record within a table.
>
> **Entity identifier**: an attribute which can uniquely identify each instance of an entity.

Exam tip

In some questions, identifying an attribute as the primary key 'because it is the unique identifier' is not sufficient; sometimes more information (such as that it is the foreign key in another table) is needed.

A **foreign key** is an attribute that appears in more than one table and is used to create the link between tables. The foreign key in a table must be a primary key from another table.

In this case the `CustomerID` in the `DOWNLOAD` table is a foreign key. The relationships in our movie download case study could be shown as in Figure 43.3.

Foreign key: an attribute in a table that is a primary key in another table and is used to link tables together.

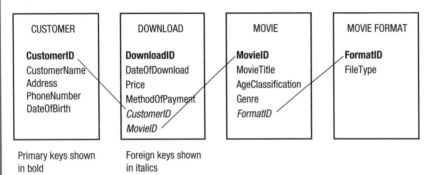

Primary keys shown in bold

Foreign keys shown in italics

Figure 43.3 Links between tables

- Primary keys have been added for each entity in the form of unique IDs.
- `CustomerID` appears on the `CUSTOMER` table as the primary key and on the `DOWNLOAD` table as a foreign key.
- `MovieID` appears on the `MOVIE` table as the primary key and on the `DOWNLOAD` table as a foreign key.
- `FormatID` appears on the `MOVIEFORMAT` table as the primary key and on the `MOVIE` table as a foreign key.

Now that the relationships have been created, the four tables become one database. Users of the database will be unaware of the structure in the background. As far as they are concerned they are dealing with one database that contains all the information they need. It is common practice to write out the details of relational databases in standard database notation as shown:

```
CUSTOMER (CustomerID, CustomerName, Address, PhoneNumber, DateOfBirth)
MOVIE (MovieID, MovieTitle, AgeClassification, Genre, FormatID)
DOWNLOAD (DownloadID, DateOfDownload, Price, MethodOfPayment, CustomerID, MovieID)
MOVIEFORMAT (FormatID, FileType)
```

Note:
- the name of the table is shown in capitals
- all the attributes are placed between brackets
- primary keys are underlined.

Exam tip

Standard notation questions come up quite regularly, either needing to be written out from a description or needing to be interpreted.

Exam tip

Note that composite keys have all of their contributing parts underlined.

Normalisation

Normalisation is the process of ensuring that a relational database conforms to certain rules that ensure that the data within it is stored in the most efficient way. In simple terms a database is normalised when there is no redundant data and when each item of data is stored in the correct table and at an atomic level.

- Redundant data occurs when the same field is unnecessarily duplicated in two or more tables.
- Storing the same data multiple times can also lead to the problem of data inconsistency.
- Storing data at an atomic level means that they cannot be further decomposed.

When a database is constructed according to these rules it is said to be in normal form.

There are various levels of normal form and the level that a programmer needs to go to depends on the complexity of the database. For A level, you should be able to develop a database to 'third normal form' (3NF).

- To satisfy first normal form (1NF), repeating groups should be replaced.
- To satisfy second normal form (2NF), the database must be in 1NF and then remove attributes that depend upon part but not all of the primary key by creating additional tables.
- To satisfy third normal form (3NF), the database must be in 2NF and then remove non-key attributes that depend upon other non-key attributes by creating additional tables.

The final, fully normalised design of the database is as follows:

> **Normalisation**: the process of ensuring that a relational database is structured efficiently.

> **Exam tip**
>
> Normalising databases is a frequent A-level question.

CUSTOMER

CustomerID	CustomerName	Address
1	John Smith	1 High Street
2	Mary Jones	14 Acacia Avenue
3	John Smith	23 Maple Drive

MOVIE

MovieID	MovieTitle	Genre	Format
1	The Hangover	Comedy	LowRes
2	22 Jump Street	Comedy	LowRes
3	The Hunger Games	Sci-Fi	HiRes
4	Robocop	Sci-Fi	HiRes
5	How to Train Your Dragon	Children	HiRes

MOVIEFORMAT

Format	FileType
LowRes	MPEG-2
HiRes	MPEG-4

DOWNLOAD

CustomerID	MovieID	DateOfDownload
1	1	19/03/15
1	2	19/03/15
2	3	19/03/15
2	4	19/03/15
2	2	19/03/15
3	5	19/03/15
3	4	19/03/15

In summary, the characteristics that a relational database design must have to be fully normalised are:

● All of the data must be atomic / there must be no repeating groups / no repeating attributes.
● There should be no partial dependencies, where a non-key attribute depends upon part but not all of the primary key.
● There should be no non-key dependencies, where a non-key attribute depends upon another non-key attribute.

Summary

● Relational databases are made up of related data stored within a series of linked tables.
● Entity relationship diagrams can be used to show the relationships that exist between tables.
● The main relationships are: one-to-one, one-to-many and many-to-many.

● Primary keys uniquely identify each record within a table.
● A foreign key in one table is the primary key in another table and is used to link the tables together.
● Normalisation is the process of ensuring that data is stored efficiently to eliminate data redundancy and ensure data consistency.

Now test yourself

TESTED ☐

1 The notation below describes a database used by a kitchen unit supplier that is in third normal form:

```
Unit (UnitID, UnitName, UnitType, UnitColour, UnitSize, Price)
CustomerOrder (OrderID, CustomerID, Date, Paid)
CustomerOrderLine (OrderID, UnitID, Quantity, Discounted)
Customer (CustomerID, CustomerName, EmailAddress)
```

(a) What does it mean to be in third normal form? [2]
(b) Why is it important for databases to be in third normal form? [2]
(c) Show any four relationships between the tables. [4]

CustomerOrderLine		Unit

CustomerOrder		Customer

2 A company sells shirts of three different types (T-shirt, polo, sweatshirt), of multiple colours (red, blue, yellow, black). The shirts cost either £15 or £20 and attract 10% and 20% tax respectively. Complete the 3NF relations below with appropriate identifiers and primary keys. [3]

```
Items    (                    )
Prices   (                    )
Taxes    (                    )
```

44 Structured query language (SQL)

3.10.4 Structured query language (SQL)
3.10.5 Client–server databases

Structured Query Language (SQL) is a specialised programming language that is used for managing relational databases. Its functions allow users to define tables, insert, update and delete data and to carry out queries on data to produce and output subsets of the main data. In common with other programming languages, SQL works by typing in lines of code.

> **Structured query language (SQL):** a specialised programming language for manipulating databases.

Defining a table

REVISED

To create a **table** the user needs to define the name of the table and each of the attributes including the data type and length. If you have used MS Access or any other proprietary database package, you will notice that this is a very similar process, but is achieved through typing code in the correct **syntax** rather than using a graphical user interface.

```
CREATE TABLE Customer
(
CustomerID varchar (5),
CustomerName varchar (255),
CustomerAddress varchar (255),
PRIMARY KEY (CustomerID)
);
```

There are a number of supported data types, with examples shown in Table 44.1.

> **Table:** a method for implementing an entity and attributes as a group of related data.
>
> **Syntax:** the rules of how words are used within a given language.

Exam tip

It is customary, although not required, to write keywords in capitals.

Exam tip

Remember that the pattern for a field is field name, data type, size.

Table 44.1 Examples of supported data types in SQL

Character (n)	character string with fixed length (n)
Varchar (n)	character string variable length with maximum field length (n)
Boolean	true or false
Int	short for integer and is a whole number
Decimal (p,s)	decimal number with number of digits before and after the decimal point
Real	any number up to 7 decimal places
Date	in the format day, month, year
Time	in the format hour, minutes, seconds

Exam tip

PRIMARY KEY can be put on a separate line like in this example, or combined on the same line as the field, e.g. `CustomerID varchar(5) PRIMARY KEY`

Exam tip

One of the most common mistakes is to use a **string** data type instead of a **varchar**.

Entering and updating data

To enter data into a table, you need to specify the name of the table and the column where you want to enter it:

```
INSERT INTO Customer (CustomerID, Name, Address)
VALUES ("1", "John Smith", "1 High Street");
```

To update data, you need to specify the table and column and identify the item of data that needs updating. For example, to update John Smith's address:

```
UPDATE Customer
SET Address = "29 Wellington Street"
WHERE CustomerID = "1";
```

Notice that the **WHERE** command is being used to make a selection using the **CustomerID** rather than the name to ensure the correct record is updated.

> **Exam tip**
>
> The order of key words, brackets etc. is important for SQL and may cost marks if incorrect. Like most programming, you will learn best by using SQL.

> **Exam tip**
>
> Remember that multiple records can be updated using this method.

Deleting data

Deleting data is a similar process to updating data as you have to define the table and then use a selection statement to identify the data that you want to delete. To delete John Smith from the database:

```
DELETE FROM Customer
WHERE CustomerID = "1";
```

You can use wildcards within a selection statement. For example, to delete all records:

```
DELETE * FROM Customer;
```

Querying data

In simple terms a **query** is a search and/or sort. An extract of code is shown below relating to a query that extracts the name and address of all customers called John Smith in the database:

```
SELECT CustomerName, CustomerAddress
FROM Customer
WHERE CustomerName = "John Smith"
ORDER BY CustomerName DESC;
```

> **Query**: a search or sort carried out on data that retrieves the answer to a question.

Where the columns are from more than one table and if the field name is used in more than one table, it is necessary to include the name of the table followed by a full stop and then the name of the column. For example, **Customer.CustomerName** indicates that we wish to extract the **CustomerName** column from the **Customer** table.

More complex statements can be used within the **WHERE** structure including AND and OR statements. For example, the condition could be **CustomerName = "John Smith" OR CustomerName = "Mary Jones"**. To extract all the data for such records, the following SQL would be written:

```
SELECT *
FROM Customer
WHERE CustomerName = "John Smith" OR CustomerName = "Mary Jones";
```

> **Exam tip**
>
> While it is not necessary to include table names in dot-notation where no duplication is found, some students prefer to 'play it safe'.

Now test yourself answers at www.therevisionbutton.co.uk/myrevisionnotes

Note that the ★ is used as a wildcard which means that all attributes are extracted when the query is run.

Client–server databases

Where databases are being used in a network environment it is likely that there will be a dedicated database server, particularly where the organisation has a large and complex database. The database server holds and manages the database itself so that all amendments, searches and so on are carried out at the server.

This would normally be done through a **database management system** or DBMS, which is a program that controls the data that is kept on the database. This will help to maintain the integrity of the data as it ensures that there is only ever one version of the data.

The DBMS controls the data that are kept on the database. It also manages how the data are stored, whereabouts in the system they are kept, and it can control access rights as well. The diagram shows how the four departments in a company all access the data files via the DBMS – none of them have direct access to the data.

Client–server database: a way of implementing a database where the database is put into a server and various users can access it from their workstations. The processing, for example, running a query, will take place on the server.

Database management system: software that enables the management of all aspects of a database including adding, updating and querying data.

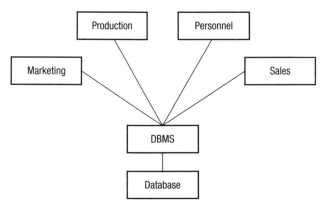

Figure 44.1 Database management system

Issues with concurrent access on shared databases

One common problem with a database that is accessible to a number of users is what to do if a number of users are trying to access the same data at the same time. Solutions to this problem are:

● **Record locks**: As soon as a user with write access takes an item of data, a lock is put on that data item so that no other user can save to that location, and the second person will not be able to save their version of the data without acknowledging that the data may have been altered by another user.
● **Serialisation**: Only allows transactions on a particular database to take place one at a time, that is, in serial format.

Record locks: a technique to temporarily prevent access to certain records held on a database.

Serialisation: a technique to ensure that only one transaction at a time is executed from multiple users on a database.

- **Timestamp ordering**: Every transaction that takes place on the database will have a read and write timestamp that indicates the last time the record was written to or read from.
- **Commitment ordering**: This system looks at each command it has been asked to execute on the database in terms of when it was made but also in terms of whether it should take precedence over other commands.

> **Timestamp ordering**: a technique to ensure multiple users can execute commands on a shared database based on the timestamp of when the data was last written to or read from.
>
> **Commitment ordering**: a technique to ensure concurrent transactions on a shared database are executed based on the timestamp of when the request is made and also the precedence the request takes over another simultaneous request.

Summary

- SQL is a query language usually used with relational databases, which works in a similar way to a programming language in that you need to type in lines of code.
- SQL can be used to define tables and add, update and remove data.
- SQL can be used to search and sort data held within one or more tables.
- A database management system (DBMS) is used to control and administrate databases.
- Databases can be made available to users using the client–server model where the database is stored on a database server.
- Problems can arise where several users are accessing the data at the same time.
- There are various techniques for dealing with these problems including record locking, serialisation, timestamp ordering and commitment ordering.

Now test yourself

TESTED ☐

1 AJ Bike Loans loan out BMX bikes at the local super-BMX track. Look at the following database they use to keep track of their loan bikes.

```
Bike (BikeID, Make, Model, Year)
Borrower (MemberID, Surname, Forename, HouseNumber, StreetName, Town,
County, Postcode, DateOfBirth)
Loan(MemberID, BikeID, LoanTime, LoanHours, ReturnedOk)
```

(a) AJ Bike Loans want a list of all borrowers that have borrowed a bike made by 'Heffmann'. Write the SQL they will have to use. [5]

SELECT
_____
_____

FROM
_____
_____

WHERE
_____
_____

(b) AJ Bike Loans have bought a new 2015 'Animal' made by MuddyGoat and have given it the BikeID MG0013. Write the SQL to insert the bike into the database. [2]

INSERT INTO
_____
_____

VALUES
_____
_____

(c) Compare and contrast two different methodologies that can be used to deal with issues caused by concurrent access of the database. [4]

45 Big data

Specification coverage

3.11 Big data

Big data

REVISED

Big data is a generic term given to datasets that are so large or complicated that they are difficult to store, manipulate and analyse. The three main features of big data are:

- volume: the sheer amount of data is on a very large scale
- variety: the type of data being collected is wide-ranging, varied and may be difficult to classify
- velocity: the data changes quickly and may include constantly changing data sources.

Big data is used for different purposes. In some cases, it is used to record factual data such as banking transactions. However, it is increasingly being used to analyse trends and try to make predictions based on relationships and correlations within the data. Big data is being created all the time in many different areas of life. Examples include:

- scientific research
- retail
- banking
- government
- mobile networks
- security
- real-time applications
- the Internet.

Latency is critical here and could be described as the time delay between a user making a request for data and those data being received, or the amount of time it takes to turn the raw data into meaningful information. With big data there may be a large degree of latency due to the amount of time taken to access and manipulate the sheer number of records.

> **Big data**: a generic term for large or complex datasets that are difficult to store and analyse.

> **Exam tip**
>
> Exact definitions of 'big data' sizes differ, so try and discuss principles and generalities rather than focusing on minutiae in an exam question.

> **Latency**: the time delay that occurs when transmitting data between devices.

Structured and unstructured data

REVISED

Most databases work on the model that the data will fall into columns and rows, otherwise referred to as fields and records. This makes data easy to organise and store as they can be entered into the appropriate fields. When data are analysed, it is relatively easy to carry out searches and sorts to query the data as we saw in the previous chapter. Some data do not fit into this model. Data can be defined as either structured or unstructured.

- **Structured data**: These are data that can be defined using traditional database techniques using fields and records.
- **Unstructured data**: These are data that cannot be defined in columns and rows. These might include multimedia data, web pages and the contents of emails, documents, presentations. This type of data is much harder to analyse.

> **Structured data**: data that fit into a standard database structure of columns and rows (fields and records).
>
> **Unstructured data**: data that do not fit into a standard database structure of columns and rows (fields and records).

Machine learning techniques

Where **quantitative** data are stored in standard relational database format it makes it relatively simple to query data to produce results. For example, if an online retailer wanted to know how many of a particular product they sold this week, they can do a simple query to find this information. Even on a large dataset, this could be produced relatively quickly and accurately.

However, **qualitative** data are much harder to analyse and it is this type of data that is most likely to be unstructured. For example, if the online retailer asks for feedback from their website in the form of customer comments, they could receive millions of items of data, all written in free text. It would take a long time for someone to read all of these, so techniques collectively known as machine learning can be used to automate the process.

Machine learning covers everything from pattern recognition to artificial intelligence systems. In this context, at a simple level, the machine could learn to look for patterns of words within a text in determining the nature of the feedback.

A more advanced form of machine learning is where the computer is able to develop its own knowledge based on the data it is manipulating. This is particularly valuable with big data as there may be patterns and correlations that exist within the data that are not immediately obvious. One technique, called predictive analytics, is widely used in the financial and insurance sectors to predict risk.

> **Quantitative**: can be measured, normally numeric.
>
> **Qualitative**: hard to measure, normally text of some kind.

Issues with big data

There are a number of issues with big data:
- Datasets are so large that they are difficult to store and analyse.
- Unstructured data can be very difficult to analyse in an automated way.
- Specialised software is needed to manage and then extract meaningful information from the data.
- Massive storage and processing power is needed, meaning that many big data applications may only be carried out on supercomputers or large dedicated networks.
- Data are constantly changing so it is difficult to keep track of every change.
- Finding a correlation in a dataset does not necessarily mean you have found the answer to a problem. In other words, it is possible to infer the wrong conclusion from the data.
- There is an issue with concurrency where several users are working on the data at the same time.

Modelling big data

One method for understanding big data is to use fact-based **modelling** which attempts to identify fundamental facts within the data that in turn identify all of the entities within the data. These are represented as diagrams or expressed in natural language.

To represent this in graphical form, **graph schema** can be created based on the graph data type made up of **nodes**, **properties** and **edges**. A graph schema for a dataset for an online retailer might look like that shown in Figure 45.1.

> **Modelling**: recreating a real-life situation on a computer.
>
> **Graph schema (database)**: a method of defining a database in terms of nodes, edges and properties.
>
> **Node**: in database modelling, it is an entity.
>
> **Properties**: in database modelling, they are items of information stored within each entity.
>
> **Edge**: in a database graph schema, it refers to the link and relationship between two nodes.

Now test yourself answers at www.therevisionbutton.co.uk/myrevisionnotes

- A node is an entity such as a customer, product or picker.
- A property is relevant data relating to the node, such as the customer or product name.
- An edge shows the link and describes the relationship between the two nodes; for example, it shows which customer bought which product, or which picker has been assigned to collect and post the items.

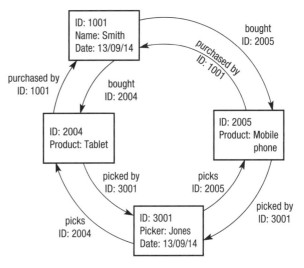

Figure 45.1 Graph schema for big data

Distributed processing

For big data, often a dedicated network is set up to work on the same main task. Typically, one computer will be allocated as the master computer within the network and will control the others through the operating system and specialist software. Each computer on the network is allocated its own subtask and messages are then passed between the computers in order to meet the overall goal. The network can be implemented on a client–server or peer-to-peer basis.

This is known as **distributed processing** or **distributed computing**. This can be implemented as a distributed network with each of the main computers being a server and then further workstations being attached to the server. Similarly, the network can be extended to include Internet services, such as the use of online data storage. This is an example of cloud computing where the Internet is used to provide a service that you would normally get from the LAN.

> **Exam tip**
>
> Distributed processing is not a new principle and examples dating back 15–20 years are available; for example, the server farms used for rendering animated movies such as *Toy Story*.

> **Distributed processing / computing**: the principle of spreading large and complex tasks over a number of computers or servers.

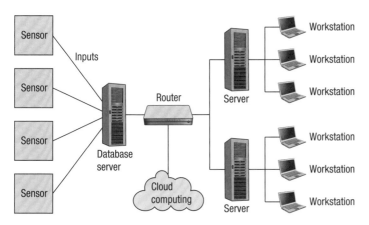

Figure 45.2 Distributed processing

Where specialist software is used to tackle a task using distributed computing, it is referred to as a **distributed program**. There are implications for programmers writing distributed programs in terms of dealing with multiple users and ensuring the integrity of large datasets. One resolution to this is to use **functional programming** techniques.

> **Distributed program**: a program specifically written to be used in a distributed processing environment.
>
> **Functional programming**: a programming paradigm that uses functions to create programs.

Functional programming for distributed programs

Functional programs use expressions that are similar to normal mathematical expressions in order to evaluate data. There are no **variables** as such, as every item of data is treated as a function. A feature of a variable in an imperative language is that it is **mutable**, which means it will change as the program runs. This means that it will have a **state**, which is the current value of the variable at any given point when the program is being run.

This is said to have **side effects**, which means that the programmer has changed the state of a variable and this may impact on how the program runs. This is a normal consequence of using **imperative** or **object-oriented** languages. Where the side effect is known it is then possible to write future lines of code in the knowledge of what has gone before.

This presents a problem where many computers might be working on the same data at the same time, as each computer will need to know the state of the variable at any point. With functions, the values and the expressions are all that is needed to make up the lines of programming code. This means that the value produced by any one line of code is entirely the result of the **function** and is not dependent on the state of any of the variables.

This makes this type of coding particularly suited to analysing big data using distributed processing, as there will be multiple users all accessing the data at the same time from different computers. This is known as **concurrence** and it is problematic because it can cause data locking as we saw in the previous chapter. Also, where there are several users, the side effects of any previous coding may not be apparent.

Because functional programming does not use variables as such and as the value of the variable is not changing, there will be few or no side effects. This means that the user always gets the original value of the variable to put into their own functions and the output of the function will be local to their machine.

Variable: a data item whose value will change as the program is run.

Mutable: changeable.

State: in programming it refers to the state that the variables are in, i.e. the value that is currently stored.

Side effects: in programming it refers to the fact that the value contained within a variable will change as the program is run, which has implications for other parts of the program.

Imperative language: a language based on giving the computer commands or procedures to follow.

Object-oriented language: a programming paradigm that encapsulates instructions and data together into objects.

Function: a subroutine that returns a single value.

Concurrence: the concept of two users trying to access the same data item at the same time.

Summary

- Big data is data that are either too large or too complex to be handled using traditional database techniques.
- Big data is becoming more common, particularly with the volumes of data being generated via the Internet.
- Some data cannot be structured into the columns and rows of a traditional database.
- Unstructured data are more difficult to query and techniques such as machine learning are used to interrogate unstructured data.
- Data models can be produced to try and understand how big data is structured.
- Big data is often spread across a number of servers in order to cope with its size. Where this is the case there is an added complication of working on data split across two or more servers.

Now test yourself

TESTED

1 What is big data? [3]
2 A research company uses brain scans captured in millisecond intervals to study dementia. Each patient's file may be 2–4 Tb of data.
   (a) Describe three big-data-related problems the company may face. [3]
   (b) Describe three methodologies the company may choose to employ to deal with big-data-related problems. [3]

Now test yourself answers at www.therevisionbutton.co.uk/myrevisionnotes

46 Basics of functional programming

Specification coverage

3.12.1 Functional programming paradigm

The functional programming paradigm

Exam tip

Functional programming is completely new to the 2015 A-level specification so be very careful when reading around the subject – don't get bogged down in detail which is at a deeper level than you need.

A programming paradigm is a method of programming. The **functional programming paradigm** is an example of a **declarative programming language** where all the algorithms call functions. This means that the lines of code look and behave like mathematical functions, requiring an input and producing an output. A value is produced for each function call. The idea is that there is one main function, which in turn calls further functions in order to achieve a specific task. Each function may call another function, or call itself recursively in order to generate a result.

The concept is that where a function is being used, it will always return the same value if it is given the same input so there can be no unforeseen side effects. One of the problems with **procedural programming languages** is that the value of a variable can change throughout the program and that changes made to the value in one subroutine may have an impact within another subroutine.

The motivations behind using the functional programming paradigm include:
- Program requirements may be better defined as a series of abstractions based on functions rather than a more complex series of steps.
- Broader abstractions can lead to fewer errors during implementation.
- Functions can be applied at any level of data abstraction making them highly reusable within a program.
- Functional code is easier to test and debug as each function cannot have any side effects, so only needs testing once.
- There are no concurrency issues as no data is modified by two threads at the same time.
- In multi-processor environments the sequence that functions are evaluated in is not critical.

As functional programs use mathematical expressions they lend themselves to writing applications that require lots of calculations. There are some languages that specifically use the functional programming paradigm such as Lisp, Haskell, Standard ML, Scheme and Erlang. Other languages provide support for functional programming including Python, Perl, C#, D, F#, Java 8 and Delphi XE.

Functional programming paradigm: a language where each line of code is made up of calls to a function, which in turn may be made up of other functions, or result in a value.

Declarative programming languages: languages that declare or specify what properties a result should have, e.g. results will be based on functions.

Procedural programming languages: languages where the programmer specifies the steps that must be carried out in order to achieve a result.

Function types

A **function type** refers to the way in which the expression is created. All functions are of the type A → B where it is defined with an argument type (A) and a result type (B). In our example, A is the set that contains {1, 2, 3, 4, 5} and B is the set that contains {1, 4, 9, 16, 25}.

A is also called the **domain** and contains objects within a particular data type, in this case integers. B is called the **codomain** and is the set from which the output values are chosen.

In functional programming, a value that is passed to a function is known as an argument. For example, in the expressions $a = f(x)$ and $b = f(2, 4)$, x, 2 and 4 are arguments.

> **Function type**: refers to the way in which the expression is created; for example, integer of the domain and codomain, where f: A → B is the type of function.
>
> **Domain**: a set of data of the same type which are the inputs of a function.
>
> **Codomain**: the set of values from which the outputs of a function must be drawn.

First-class objects and higher order functions

Within a functional programming environment, a function is a **first-class object**. A broad definition of a first-class object is any object that can be passed as an argument to or can be returned by a function. In functional programming, this means that a function can be passed as an argument to another function or can be returned from a function as the result. Other objects, such as integer values which can be passed as arguments to a function, are also first-class objects.

A function which can accept another function as an argument is known as a **higher order function**, the three most common of which are `map`, `fold` and `filter`. As an example of a first-class object, in Haskell you might write the function:

```
map (*2) [1,2,3,4,5]
```

`map` is a function, which takes in another function and applies it to every element in a list. `*2` (multiply by two) is the function that `map` is taking in. `[1,2,3,4,5]` is the list on which the function is applied.

The result of this higher order function would be `[2,4,6,8,10]`

In this example, `map` is a higher order function and `*2, 1, 2, 3, 4` and `5` are all first-class objects.

> **First-class object**: any object that can be used as an argument or result of a function call.
>
> **Higher order function**: a function that takes a function as its inputs or creates a function as its output.

Function application

The process of providing the function with its inputs is known as **function application**. With our earlier example we had the function $f(x) = x^2$ and two sets – the domain and codomain. Set A (the domain) contained the inputs, which were all integers and set B (the codomain) contained the outputs, also integers.

We input a single value from A, which can be described as the function taking its argument, or the argument being passed to the function. The function is then applied to the argument, which in this case means it squares it, to produce an output in B.

> **Function application**: the process of calculating the result of a function by passing it some data to produce a result.

Partial function application

It is possible to pass any number of arguments into a function. Where this is the case, partial function application can be used to fix the number of arguments that will be passed. The idea of this is that when you have one function that takes lots of arguments, by partially applying the function you effectively create a new function that performs just part of the calculation. The **partial application of a function** can produce results that are useful in their own right in addition to the full application of the function.

> **Partial application (of a function)**: the process of applying a function by creating an intermediate function by fixing some of the arguments to the function.

For example, consider the two notations for a function that adds two integers together by taking two arguments:

```
add: int x int → int        add: int → int → int
```

- The first is a full application of the function which takes two integers as arguments and adds them together to create a result that is also an integer. Both values are passed as arguments at the same time.
- The second is a partial application that shows a new function being created, which always adds the first argument value onto a number. This new function is then applied to the second argument to produce the overall result.

Function composition

Function composition is the process of creating a new function by combining two existing functions together. This is one of the key principles of functional programming as the concept is to have complex functions that in turn are made up of simpler functions. As each component function produces its result, this is passed as an argument result to the calling function. This process continues for each of the component functions until a result is produced for the complex function as a whole.

> **Function composition**: combining two or more functions together to create more complex functions.

Summary

- A mathematical function is an expression or rule that takes an input value from a set and returns an output value from another set.
- A programming paradigm defines a methodology for programming.
- Functions can be of different types defined by the way they are constructed.
- A function is an example of a first-class object.
- A broad definition of a first-class object is any object that can be passed as an argument or can be returned from a function.
- Functions can be applied partially or fully.
- Functions can be combined together to create new functions.

Now test yourself

1 What is a functional programming language? [2]
2 Describe the difference between a first-class object and a higher-order function. [2]

Task

1 Visit the Haskell website (https://www.haskell.org/) and follow the tutorials.

47 Writing functional programs

Specification coverage

3.12.2 Writing functional programs
3.12.3 Lists in functional programming

The map function

REVISED

Exam tip

Functional programming is new to the A-level specification. The Haskell website is a good starting point for learning the basics.

> **Map function**: a function that generates an output list from an input list by applying a function to each element in the input list.

The **map function** applies a given function to every element within a list and returns a corresponding list of results. In this chapter we will look at code that can carry out the function on every element of the list in one pass.

For example, for $f(x) = x^2$, our data might look like this when represented as a list:

It is called a map function because it maps one element of the input list (List1) to the corresponding element in the output list (List2). The function it performs could be anything.

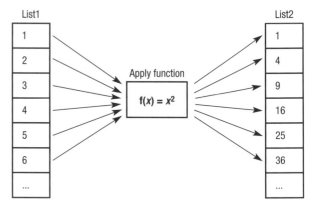

Figure 47.1 A function applied to a list that generates a new list

The filter function

REVISED

The **filter function** processes a list and then creates a new list that contains elements that match certain criteria. The operation is very similar to a search.

> **Filter function**: a method of creating a subset based on specified criteria.

In order to create the filtered list, some kind of selection criteria needs to be applied to the list. This is sometimes called a predicate function and returns a Boolean value of either TRUE or FALSE. For example, a list could be filtered to include all values over 50, or all odd numbers. The way in which the statement is actually written depends on the programming language being used. Typical examples would be **If**, **Select**, **Remove_if**, **list.filter** and **where** statements.

For example, we might use the function **odd** to filter the odd numbers in a list (List1) into a new list (List2).

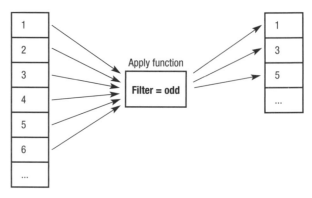

Figure 47.2 A function to filter odd values from a list

The reduce or fold function

The **reduce or fold function** takes a list of values and reduces it to a single value. This is a recursive process as the function keeps processing until the list is empty. For example, if you took a simple example where you wanted to add the items of a list together, you could reduce the list until you ended up with just one item in it. Let's assume the numbers 1–5 are in the list.

> **Reduce/fold function**: a method of reducing a list to a single element by combining the elements using a function.

Table 47.1 The process of reducing/folding a list

Instructions	Original list	Apply function (add)	Result
Start with a list	[1, 2, 3, 4, 5]		
Take the first item out of the original list and apply the function	[2, 3, 4, 5]	1	1
Recurse	[3, 4, 5]	2 + 1	3
Recurse	[4, 5]	3 + 3	6
Recurse	[5]	4 + 6	10
Recurse	[empty]	5 + 10	15
List is now empty so the function will not recurse			

List processing

A **list** is a set of data items of the same type stored using a single **identifier**. It is made up of any number of elements and can contain any type of numeric or text strings. The only rule is that you cannot mix data types within a list. You can carry out operations on lists of data, which is much more efficient than trying to carry out operations on individual data items.

> **List**: a collection of data items of the same type.
>
> **Identifier**: the name of a list.

Lists have a few components as shown in Table 47.2.

Table 47.2 Components of lists

List components	Explanation
Identifier	The name given to the list.
Data type	Identifies the data type being stored, e.g. text strings, integers, reals. In this case, it is text strings.
Elements	These are the individual values stored in the list. These are identified by their position in the list.
Head	The first element in a list.
Tail	All the other elements in the list apart from the head.
Length	The number of elements in the list. In this case there are eight.

The **tail** of the list is not just the last item, but all of the items apart from the **head**. A list can be empty. This may be when it is set up and no data has been entered or it may be after a list has been processed and there is no data left to process. The **empty list** is often represented as brackets with nothing between them, e.g. [ ].

> **Tail**: every element in a list apart from the head.
>
> **Head**: the first element in a list.
>
> **Empty list**: a list with no elements in it.

There are various standard processes that can be carried out on lists, as shown in Table 47.3.

Table 47.3 Standard processes that can be carried out on lists

Process	Description	Haskell code
Return the head of a list	Identifies the first element in the list.	head [1,2,3,4,5] 1
Return the tail of a list	Identifies all of the other elements apart from the head.	tail [1,2,3,4,5] [2,3,4,5]
Test for an empty list	Checks whether there are any elements in the list.	let MyList = [4,8,15,16,23,42] MyList [4,8,15,16,23,42] null MyList False let MyList = [] MyList [] null MyList True
Return the length of a list	Identifies how many elements there are in a list.	length [1,2,3,4,5] 5
Construct an empty list	Creates a list that has no elements in it.	let emptylist = [] emptylist []
Prepend an item to a list	Adds an item to the beginning of a list.	let SetA = [1,2,3,4] SetA [1,2,3,4] let SetB = [0] ++ SetA SetB [0,1,2,3,4]
Append an item to a list	Adds an item to the end of a list.	let SetC = SetA ++ [0] SetC [1,2,3,4,0]

Summary

- A higher order function takes a function or functions as its argument and/or produces a function as the result of a function.
- The map function applies a given function to every element within a list and returns a corresponding list of results.
- The filter function processes a list and then creates a new list that contains elements that match certain criteria.
- The reduce or fold function takes a list of values and reduces it to a single value by applying a function.
- Functional programming uses lists of values. The functions can be applied to each element in the list.

Now test yourself

TESTED ☐

1 Given a list of the first four prime numbers and the map function $f(x) = 2(x)$, write out the output list. [1]
2 What do you think the output list will be for the Haskell command filter (>5) [32, 32, 1, 3, 5, 31, 3, 5, 212]? [2]
3 What would be the result if you were to perform fold (*) 1 [2,3,4] in Haskell? [1]

48 Aspects of software development

Specification coverage

3.3.1 Aspects of software development
3.13.1 Aspects of software development

Software development

REVISED

Software development is the process of creating and maintaining programs or applications. The process comprises a number of stages that a developer will work through to solve computer-based problems, typically: analysis, design, implementation, testing and evaluation.

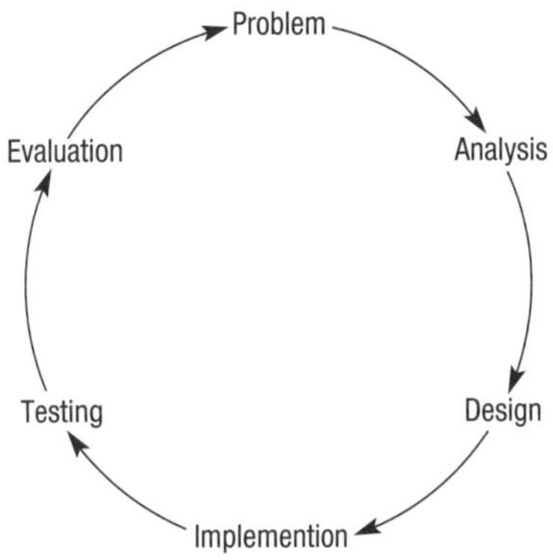

Figure 48.1 Stages of system development

Exam tip

There is no one set methodology of development that is always right, and there is much disagreement as to what discrete elements make up the systems development life cycle. As long as you cover the five core sections discussed here you will be ready for the exam.

Analysis

REVISED

The first stage is to identify and fully analyse the nature of the problem. **Analysis** includes:

- understanding what has prompted the need for a new system
- gathering information
- carrying out a feasibility study.

Analysis: the first stage of system development where the problem is identified, researched and alternative solutions proposed.

Defining the problem

The developer should keep an open mind and concentrate on getting to grips with what the problem involves rather than looking for possible solutions. This involves identifying the scope of a problem and being realistic about how much of the problem a new system can solve. Any constraining factors may be identified here.

If you are creating a solution for someone else, it is important that you agree the specification and scope of the work before you start. In general, the more you can involve the end users, the less likely you are to do something they do not want.

Prompts for a new system

There are many reasons for creating a new computer system:

- Some existing systems simply cannot cope with the increased volume of data they are being asked to handle.
- New technology has meant that existing systems soon become outdated.
- The current system may be inflexible or inefficient.
- New technology has created new opportunities.

- Commercial reasons. Many new systems are created in order to generate demand from customers.
- New platforms and operating systems.
- Increased processing power.
- Increased network power.

Methods of gathering information

There are several ways in which you can gather data about an existing system:

- Interview people who are involved with the current system.
- Use a questionnaire or survey.
- Observe current practices.
- Examine the current system.

Feasibility study

A **feasibility study** is a preliminary report to the person who asked for the new system in the first place. It will identify possible solutions and suggest the best way forward. The report will indicate how practical a solution is in terms of time and other resources, such as the availability of suitable software and hardware and the abilities of the end user to cope with the proposed method of solution.

Feasibility study: an analysis of whether it is possible or desirable to create a system.

Design

REVISED

Design: the second stage of system development where the algorithms, data and interface are designed.

The process of looking at a big problem and breaking it down into smaller problems and then breaking each of the smaller problems down, and so on until each problem is manageable, is known as the **'top-down' design** approach. The benefits of this approach are similar to the **modular design** system mentioned above, though there is the potential problem of getting too engrossed in small details such as the fine-tuning of the human–computer interface. It makes more sense to solve the overall problem first before you get too involved in screen layouts.

Data flow diagram (DFD)

There are a number of ways of representing a problem and its possible solution. **A data flow diagram** is concerned purely with how data are moved round a system and as such it only needs four symbols.

Top-down design: related to the modular approach, this starts with the main system at the top and breaks it down into smaller and smaller units a bit like a family tree.

Modular design: a method of system design that breaks a whole system down into smaller units, or modules.

Data flow diagram (DFD): a visual method of showing how data passes around a system.

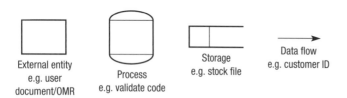

External entity
e.g. user
document/OMR

Process
e.g. validate code

Storage
e.g. stock file

Data flow
e.g. customer ID

Figure 48.2 Data flow diagram symbols

The next diagram shows how a DFD might be used. It shows what happens after the electricity meter at a house has been read.

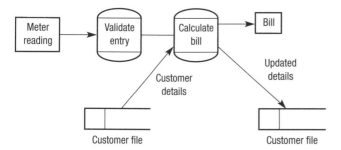

Figure 48.3 A DFD showing data flows for reading an electricity meter

Describing algorithms

It may be appropriate to work the algorithms into pseudo-code that reflects the programming language being used. For example, if a functional programming language is being used, the main functions should be identified at the design stage. If a relational database is being used, the main SQL statements should be identified.

Data dictionary

Where relevant, a **data dictionary** should be produced to show what data will be used and how it will be stored. Details of the data to be stored, including the data type, length, title and any validation checks, will be stored in a data dictionary. This can be seen as a database about the database – it holds background details but not the data itself. Figure 48.4 shows part of the definition of a table in Microsoft Access. This forms part of the data dictionary that defines the whole solution.

Field Name	Data Type	Description
CustomerID	AutoNumber	
Surname	Text	max length 30
Forname	Text	max length 20
Date of Birth	Date/Time	dd/mm/yy
Height (cm)	Number	between 150 and 210

Figure 48.4 Data dictionary definition of a table from MS Access

Variables table and data structures

Declaring variables at the start of the program allows the programmer much tighter control of their program. The programmer will need to decide about certain characteristics of each variable – type, length, name and whether the variable is local or global.

The overall program may be broken up into blocks or modules to make a project more manageable. Allocating names to these procedures and defining local variables used within them is also best carried out at this stage.

> **Exam tip**
>
> Skills from this section may be examined in paper 1, but they really come into play in the A-level NEA where you will be expected to perform these tasks.

> **Data dictionary**: a list of all the data being used in the system including name, length, data type and validation.

> **Variables table**: a list of all the variables that a program will use, including names and data types.

Volumetrics

Consider the throughput of data – how many transactions the system will need to cope with in a given time span – and also how much data the system will need to store at any one time. This will affect the storage media that is used, and it will also be a consideration when back-up strategies are being decided. The programmer will also need to consider how many users will be allowed to access the files and programs at one time.

The human–computer interface (HCI)

The human–computer interface is the term given to any form of communication between a computer and its user. For the majority of us this might seem limited to the computer screen with its familiar graphical user interface (GUI), but it can also include the layout of buttons on a mobile phone or house alarm system and the way information is presented on a tablet or smart phone or the flight controls of an aircraft.

There are a number of aspects that need to be considered when designing an effective HCI. These include:
- ease of use
- target audience
- technology
- ergonomics.

> **Exam tip**
>
> The HCI is a fundamental weak point of many systems – it doesn't matter how well a system performs if real-life users find it too hard to utilise.

Prototypes

A **prototype** is often developed to help ensure that the HCI is exactly what the user wants.

The functionality of a prototype may vary depending on the nature of the project. For example, the human–computer interface may be very well developed in the prototype and quite closely reflect the finished system. However, the functionality behind it may be incomplete. At this stage the end user is asked to comment on the product so far, and they will check to make sure all the major functions work as expected.

> **Prototype**: a stripped down version of a whole system built at the design stage to test whether the concept works.

Test plan

The **test plan** should be written at the design phase to ensure that it is based on the required functionality of the system and not influenced by the implementation.

Implementation

REVISED

The process of implementing a system is based on the design, and the programmer(s) will need to be fully aware of the requirements set out in the design. It is important to note that many systems are modular and that the different modules do not all have to be written at the same time. In some cases, one module is dependent on another one. In other cases, the design of one part of the system may change as a result of the implementation of another part. Systems development has to be a responsive process and the developer may need to respond to issues as they arise throughout the development process.

> **Implementation**: the third stage of system development where the actual code and data structures are created.

Testing

There are a number of test strategies that can be used and it is important to understand that any testing plan must include tests that are carried out as the code is written and not just at the end.

Test data are data that generate a known result, and test data will need to be devised that test every aspect of the solution from the expected responses to the extremes that humans can subject a computer program to.

Test data are data that will generate a known response. Typically three types of test data are used:

- **Normal**: Data that the system is expected to handle as they are within an acceptable range. For example, an age field could be tested with values between 0 and 110.
- **Boundary**: Data that are on the extremes of the acceptable range. This means testing the minimum and maximum values and those that are just inside and just outside the range. For example, with age, you might use 0, 1, 109 and 110.
- **Erroneous**: Data that are clearly incorrect and therefore you would expect the program to catch the error. For example, test data for age could be 1000 or an item of text instead of a value.

Development testing

Black box testing involves entering test data into a routine or procedure and checking the resulting output against the expected outcome.

White box testing involves testing every aspect of a routine or procedure. White box testing checks all pathways through the code, looking inside it and potentially adding extra commands to check what is happening.

Unit testing makes sure each unit carries out the function it has been designed for. It incorporates both black box and white box testing.

Once all units have been tested, they are put together to form bigger sections. Integration testing is the process of making sure that the different modules that have been tested as individual units will work together.

System testing

System testing involves testing the system as a complete unit rather than as individual modules and making sure that it satisfies the specification agreed with the user.

Alpha testing is carried out on the finished system. This involves creating test data in-house.

Beta testing involves passing your software to a number of people that have not been involved with the development. The testers will all use the system in slightly different ways and so highlight faults that might not have been found by normal means.

Although the developers will test the system they have developed as thoroughly as possible, it is the end users that need to be satisfied that the solution does what they wanted it to.

Testing: the fourth stage of system development that includes a range of tests using a variety of data.

Normal test data: test data that is within the expected range for the system and should therefore produce the correct result.

Boundary test data: test data on or close to the boundary of the acceptable range.

Erroneous test data: test data that is clearly incorrect and should produce an error.

Development testing: testing that takes place during the development of the program.

Black box testing: using test data to test for an expected outcome.

White box testing: checks all pathways through the code, looking inside it and potentially adding extra commands to check what is happening.

Unit testing: testing carried out on just one module or component of the whole system.

System testing: a range of tests carried out on the system once it has been completed.

Acceptance testing is carried out by the intended user. They enter their own live data and make sure the system matches the specification that was agreed with the program writers.

Some problems may only come to light some time after the system has been implemented by the user. These might include issues involving the volume of data the system is asked to cope with. Problems such as these will be resolved as part of the systems maintenance.

Evaluation

The final stage of the system development is **evaluation**, which compares the actual outcome with the specification. It should also contain suggestions for future improvements. Several criteria may be used to evaluate a system. For example:

- Functionality: Does it do what it is supposed to?
- Ease of use: This is not the same as 'easy to use' but it means that the level of complexity is appropriate to the user.
- Ease of implementation: How easy was it to transfer from the old system to the new system?
- Reliability: A measure of how much the system is 'up' or 'down'.
- Performance: Does the system meet its performance criteria, which might relate, for example, to the speed of operation or the amount of data it can handle?
- Cost effectiveness: Refers to how much it costs to implement the solution and whether the cost is justified.
- Ease of maintenance and adaptability: How easy is it to fix faults or add new modules?
- Longevity: How future-proof is the system?
- Maintenance: Ensuring that the system continues to function as required.

> **Evaluation**: the final stage of system development where the system is judged according to certain criteria.

> **Exam tip**
>
> Remember that this is a cycle and the evaluation should form the backbone of the next cycle of systems development.

Summary

- Software development is the process of creating and maintaining programs or applications. The first stage is analysis to identify and fully analyse the nature of the problem.
- The second stage is design, where suitable algorithms, data structures and user interfaces are identified.
- The third stage is implementation, when the program is written.
- The fourth stage is testing, where various methods are used to ensure the system works and does what it was designed to do.
- The final stage is evaluation, where the system is assessed.

Now test yourself

1 Describe the fundamental aspects of what happens in each of the following stages:
   (a) analysis [3]
   (b) design [3]
   (c) implementation [3]
   (d) testing [3]
   (e) evaluation. [3]
2 What are the differences between white box, black box, and unit testing? [3]
3 How do the three core types of test data differ? [3]
4 What is a data flow diagram? [2]